PENGUIN BOOKS

CANNIBAL JACK

Trevor Bentley was educated at The University of Auckland and The University of Waikato, and has a special interest in researching, teaching and writing about the interaction of Māori and Pākehā in pre-Treaty New Zealand. He is the author of two previous books, both published by Penguin: *Pakeha Maori* (1999) and *Captured by Maori* (2004). Bentley is an adult education manager for four colleges in the South Waikato, and an inveterate surfer and traveler in his spare time. He lives in Tauranga with his wife Helen.

For Dave and Suzanne

TREVOR BENTLEY

CANNIBAL JACK

The Life & Times
of Jacky Marmon,
a Pākehā-Māori

PENGUIN BOOKS

PENGUIN BOOKS
Published by the Penguin Group
Penguin Group (NZ), 67 Apollo Drive, Rosedale,
North Shore 0632, New Zealand (a division of Pearson New Zealand Ltd)
Penguin Group (USA) Inc., 375 Hudson Street,
New York, New York 10014, USA
Penguin Group (Canada), 90 Eglinton Avenue East, Suite 700, Toronto,
Ontario, M4P 2Y3, Canada (a division of Pearson Penguin Canada Inc.)
Penguin Books Ltd, 80 Strand, London, WC2R 0RL, England
Penguin Ireland, 25 St Stephen's Green,
Dublin 2, Ireland (a division of Penguin Books Ltd)
Penguin Group (Australia), 250 Camberwell Road, Camberwell,
Victoria 3124, Australia (a division of Pearson Australia Group Pty Ltd)
Penguin Books India Pvt Ltd, 11, Community Centre,
Panchsheel Park, New Delhi – 110 017, India
Penguin Books (South Africa) (Pty) Ltd, 24 Sturdee Avenue,
Rosebank, Johannesburg 2196, South Africa

Penguin Books Ltd, Registered Offices: 80 Strand, London, WC2R 0RL, England

First published by Penguin Group (NZ), 2010
1 3 5 7 9 10 8 6 4 2

Copyright © Trevor Bentley, 2010

The right of Trevor Bentley to be identified as the author of this work in terms of
section 96 of the Copyright Act 1994 is hereby asserted.

Designed and typeset by Pindar (NZ)
Printed in Australia by McPherson's Printing Group

ISBN 9780143203827

A catalogue record for this book is available
from the National Library of New Zealand.

www.penguin.co.nz

OBITUARIES

J. Marmon, aged 81 years, died at Hokianga on Friday 3rd. inst. He was the only white man living in New Zealand when Capt. Herd's settlers arrived in 1826, at which time Marmon was living with the Maoris, and had the reputation of having lived on human flesh in company with the natives. When first seen, he was travelling along the beach, with a war party, and a full kit of human flesh upon his back.

— Northern Luminary, 4 September 1880.

John Marmon who died at Hokianga a few weeks ago, and who first saw the shores of New Zealand in 1811, has left behind him, a full account of his life and adventures. The narrative is exceedingly interesting and valuable. Though not an educated man, he possessed keen powers of observation, and a splendid memory for dates and names. His experiences in the early days of whaling and flax trading were absolutely unrivalled.

— New Zealand Herald, Saturday, 9 October 1880.

On 3 September 1880 John Marmon, born Sydney, father Patrick Marmon, died at Rawhia, Hokianga.

— Office of Registrar-General, Wellington.

CONTENTS

PREFACE

My interest in Europeans 'gone native' was born out my own boundary crossings between New Zealand, where I live and work, and my ancestral villages of Saleilua and Poutasi in the Falealili district of Western Samoa. My interest in Pākehā-Māori was ignited during the 1980s and 1990s, through the beachcomber stories I heard during sojourns in these villages. Among the stories of colourful characters and bizarre happenings was the tale of one of my European ancestors, a castaway Portuguese sailor who, armed with a fabled sword of steel, distinguished himself in the wars against the Tongans. I subsequently developed an ongoing interest in culture-crossing Europeans in Polynesia and this third book on Pākehā-Māori is a continuation of that interest.

At a time when many Pākehā and Māori New Zealanders are exploring their bicultural ancestries, a re-evaluation of the life of Jacky Marmon the Pākehā-Māori is long overdue. Combining parts of his *New Zealand Herald* and *Auckland Star* memoirs with modern historical research, this biographical study focuses mainly on his life among Māori at the Bay of Islands and the Hokianga between 1817 and 1845. It describes and expands on his participation in some of the key events and trends that helped shape early race relations and New Zealand history. It details the places he knew, the observations he made and his interactions with many well known and influential Māori and Pākehā in northern New Zealand.

One of the most significant recent developments in New Zealand history has been the remarkable expansion of writing about culture-crossing Pākehā. This is part of the trend to 'history from below', where writers and readers are less concerned with political, economic and social elites and more interested in the lives of ordinary men and women. Today, books about respectable culture-crossing Europeans such as Augustus Earle, John Boultbee, Jock McGregor and Marianne Williams are being published alongside non-fiction works about Pākehā-Māori like Frederick Maning, Richard Barrett and Jacky Marmon, and fictional stories about Kimball Bent, Charlotte Badger and Elizabeth Guard. Recognising the merits of acknowledging an intercultural past, these accounts of Pākehā–Māori co-existence signal the possibilities for cross-cultural co-operation and accommodation in modern New Zealand.

Cannibal Jack has relevance as Pākehā-Māori now stand in a very special position in our history. Their children were the portents of the mixed race that historian Keith Sinclair believed would characterise New Zealand's population by the mid twenty-first century. Pākehā-Māori can also be considered prototypes for modern bicultural Pākehā and this book is part of the current effort by some modern writers to use Pākehā-Māori to help us understand who we are in New Zealand and where many New Zealanders come from.

ACKNOWLEDGEMENTS

I have been encouraged and assisted by many people and institutions during my researches on Jacky Marmon. I wish to thank Peter Gibbons at the University of Waikato who first raised the possibility of a Marmon biography, and Creative New Zealand for providing the funds necessary to travel and carry out the research. To my good friends Dave and Suzanne Davis to whom this book is dedicated, my heartfelt gratitude for their ongoing support and encouragement.

I am particularly beholden to my son Daniel for his proofreading and valuable suggestions. My brother Michael Bentley of Taipa provided access to his many contacts at the Bay of Islands and Hokianga. Special thanks to Queenie Puru, Anna Farrelly and Edith Anderson (née Shears) for guidance and information regarding their Pākehā-Māori tīpuna, and to Bob Simeon, Trevor Blundell, Faye Leaf and Peter Kipa for their co-operation and input.

Cannibal Jack follows numerous abbreviated Marmon biographies in books about the history of northern New Zealand. Two of the more competent are found in Ormond Wilson's *From Hongi Hika to Hone Heke* and Jack Lee's *An Unholy Trinity*.[1] There is, in addition, a scholarly critique of the Marmon memoirs by Roger Wigglesworth in his meticulously researched 1974 BA thesis 'The Myth and the Reality' and a concise profile by the same author in *The Dictionary of New Zealand Biography, Volume 1*. Their research and writings have informed and enhanced many of the perspectives contained in this book.[2]

I wish to acknowledge the assistance of archivists and illustrations specialists at the Alexander Turnbull Library, Wellington, the Hocken Library, Dunedin, the National Library of Australia, Canberra, and the State Library of New South Wales, Sydney. My thanks, as always, to the ever-cheerful staff of the New Zealand room at Tauranga Public Library for their knowledge and expertise. Finally, my thanks to both Geoff Walker of Penguin Books and my incomparable wife Helen who showed heroic reserves of patience during this project.

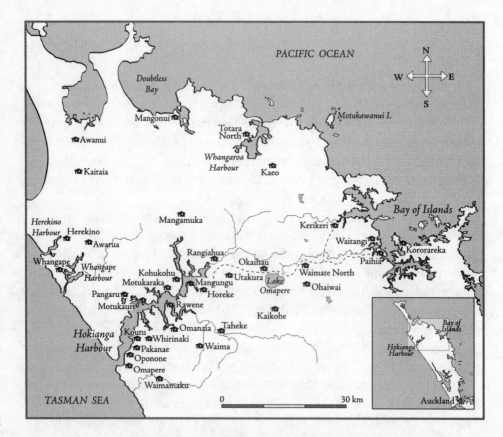

Map of the Northland region showing the main Bay of Islands and Hokianga Māori settlements before 1840.

The *New Zealand Herald* and *Auckland Star* 'autobiographies'

John (Jacky) Marmon was New Zealand's most infamous Pākehā-Māori. Described in the writings of early missionaries and temporary visitors who encountered him as a 'dangerous', 'vile' and 'lawless animal', some settlers and colonial officials added the epithets 'notorious', 'murderer', 'cannibal' and 'white savage'. Colonial historians subsequently attached the labels 'illiterate', 'brutal' and 'unscrupulous'. Modern historians have added 'convict' and 'braggart, liar and knave'.[1]

Marmon's first biographer, Ormond Wilson, was more complimentary and considered his subject 'not innocent' but generally good-natured.[2] The historians Laurie Barber and James Belich acknowledge the extraordinary depth of Marmon's assimilation, describing him respectively as 'the Ngapuhi white cannibal' and 'tohunga'.[3] The anthropologist Anne Salmond considered him an astute and reliable observer.[4]

Who, then, was the real Jacky Marmon? Where does the fictional Marmon end and the true Marmon begin? Aimed at readers interested in the history of pre-Treaty New Zealand and New Zealanders, *Cannibal Jack* attempts to cut through many of the biased contemporary reports, apocryphal stories and legends surrounding the most 'notorious' of all Pākehā-Māori. It endeavours to cast new light on Marmon the man,

John (Jacky) Marmon
This sketch of Marmon appeared in the *Auckland Weekly News* in April 1892.

and his life and times.

Born in Sydney in 1798, the son of Irish convict parents, Jacky first became familiar with New Zealand as a cabin boy and sailor on Pacific sealing, whaling and trading vessels. Disillusioned with life in a colonial society and drawn to the Māori way of life, he fled his ship to settle temporarily among the Hokianga colonist settlement of Hikutu people on the Kerikeri River, Bay of Islands between 1817 and 1820, and again from 1820 to 1822. Returning to Sydney where he was arrested and convicted for petty theft, Marmon was sentenced to two years' hard labour aboard colonial government ships before again deserting to settle permanently among the Popoto and Ngāti Hao people at Hokianga from 1823 until his death in 1880.

Physically tough, quick-witted and capable, Marmon adapted to a variety of changing frontier situations, using his linguistic and practical skills to make himself indispensable to both races. Shrewd and calculating in his dealings with Māori, he amassed material possessions, land and personal mana by readily manipulating their social conventions. Nevertheless, he loyally served his chiefs and their hapū as advisor, mediator, gun-trader, tohunga and fighting man.

Marmon's notoriety was founded primarily on the depth of his assimilation, particularly his predilection for intertribal combat, human flesh and mākutu (magic). Between 1820 and 1826 he lived a completely separate Māori existence at the Bay of Islands and Hokianga where he was known by the transliterated names Hake Mamene, Tiaki Mahamai or his tohunga title Te Manene (The Stranger). Ingratiating himself with leading chiefs including Hongi Hika, and later, Muriwai, Patuone and Tamati Waka Nene, Marmon made strategic marriages to chiefly women, acquiring status, extensive landholdings and slaves. Esteemed by Māori for his loyalty, belligerence and the respect he paid to customs of peace and war, he was protected from ships' captains and colonial officials who sought to arrest and return him to prison in Sydney.

Ormond Wilson has asserted that in nineteenth-century Aotearoa, there were two main categories of New Zealander, Māori and Pākehā, and a third type, Pākehā-Māori.[5] We are not certain how nineteenth-century Māori and Pākehā recognised this third type of New Zealander, but they certainly recognised a Pākehā-Māori when they encountered one. Many missionaries, colonial officials, travelling artists, scientists, soldiers and ethnologists lived in Māori communities for extended periods. Becoming fluent in the language of their hosts, they honoured selected Māori customs in the pursuit of souls, profit or 'scientific' knowledge. Few, however, crossed cultures sexually or socially and they were never labelled 'Pākehā-Māori' by contemporary Māori or Pākehā.

The consensus among modern writers is that to become a Pākehā-Māori, or to be recognised as one, involved an accretion of elements, not all of equal weight, which identified them as having 'gone native': Māori language, a Māori spouse and kinsfolk, empathy with and observance of Māori custom, the subordination of their own interests to the tribe, and for some like Marmon in the pre-annexation period, polygamy, tattooing, participation in intertribal battles and cannibalism.

While many modern New Zealanders are familiar with the role Pākehā-Māori played as trading intermediaries on the early coastal and inland frontiers, the term 'Pākehā-Māori' was always an ambiguous and contested one. During the nineteenth century, the term was a condition or class marker, and could be used as a term of opprobrium or disapproval by settlers, often in the same era.

Applied to trader Pākehā-Māori such as Frederick Maning at Hokianga, Dicky Barrett at Taranaki and Hans Tapsell in the Bay of Plenty during the pre-Treaty era, the term was a respectful epithet. In mediating contact and trade between the races, these men took Māori wives, honoured Māori customs and participated in the defence of their tribes, but they generally retained their European clothing, values and commercial goals, and never wholly capitulated to Māori.

The term 'Pākehā-Māori' as applied to the 'white savages' such as Jacky Marmon of Ngāpuhi, James Caddell of Ngāi Tahu and Smith of Ngāti Toa, was a derogatory label. It was used with a measure of contempt and anxiety in fragile frontier communities that were trying to practise 'civilised' behaviour. Permanently identifying with their tribes, these Pākehā-Māori not only participated in intertribal warfare, but in cannibalism and acts of resistance against their former countrymen. Viewed by contemporary settlers as lawless renegades, who had betrayed their parent culture by capitulating to Māori and becoming 'naturalised', they were considered untrustworthy and a disgrace.

Jacky Marmon first entered New Zealand folklore when a 15,000-word, serialised version of his memoirs appeared in *The New Zealand Herald* and the *Weekly News* during 1880. A 75,000-word serial soon followed in the *Auckland Star*, with a similar but shorter version in the *Otago Witness* in 1881 and 1882. The poet and literary archaeologist Kendrick Smithyman speculated that Marmon may have dictated two separate memoirs.[6] The *Herald* and *Star* versions, however, seem to be based on the account Marmon dictated during the 1870s. They contain similar material and have chapter breaks and paragraphs in the same order. The scribe was Mrs Alice Bennett, former governess of the Clendon and Von Sturmer children at Hokianga. She was commissioned by Chief Justice Thomas Gillies of Auckland, a keen amateur ethnographer, to 'write up' Marmon's life.[7]

Written by two authors with different agendas, the *Star* and *Herald* 'autobiographies' depict two different personalities. The *Herald* memoir has Marmon settling in New Zealand in 1827, but living apart from, and critical of Māori; a respectable old settler with a 'splendid memory'. The

Herald's editorial note promises a full account of Marmon's adventures, but delivers the briefest sketches. His Pākehā-Māori and soldiering reminiscences are omitted and the memoir concludes abruptly in 1837. Unlike the *Star*, and perhaps catering for the sensibilities of its late-Victorian New Zealand audience, there are no references by the *Herald* writer to Marmon's self-confessed and well-documented enthusiasm for Māori customs, women, warfare, human flesh and alcohol.

The *Star* reproduced most of the original Bennett manuscript which was entitled 'The Life and Adventures of John Marmon, The Hokianga Pakeha Maori or Seventy-Five Years in New Zealand'. It ran to 19 instalments, with Jacky describing his early life in Sydney and seafaring years (30,000 words), his Pākehā-Māori years (30,000 words) and events preceding and during the Northern War of 1845 (15,000 words). The *Star* first places Marmon among Māori in 1817 and concludes in 1877.

Many New Zealand historians have accepted the *Herald* account as a reliable, 'honest' autobiography for much of it can be verified against contemporary records. The *Herald* narrative is certainly distinctive or its direct, laconic economy of words, much like the notes taken in a lecture, while the *Star* account is written prose. However, several late-nineteenth and early-twentieth century historians and document collectors including R. A. A. Sherrin, Robert McNab, T. Lindsay Buick and James Cowan also considered the *Star* a largely credible memoir.[8] From the late twentieth century, however, concerned about its sensationalism and chronological and factual inconsistencies, some historians began to dismiss the *Star* account as an unreliable source of biography and history.[9] It is important, therefore, to provide a brief background to the *Star* memoir and outline to the reader the advantages and disadvantages of any Marmon biography that draws heavily on this source.

The *Herald* memoir is the work of a hack writer (or writers) who ruthlessly edited the manuscript, suppressing Marmon's assimilations and excluding his use of Māori terms and phrases. The *Star* memoir is the work of a gifted writer, a master of hyperbole, irony, and melodrama who, in embellishing Marmon's memoirs, pushed journalistic licence to its limits. This writer was unusual among late-Victorian Pakeha New Zealanders, as he, like Marmon, was bilingual and possessed a comprehensive knowledge of early Pākehā, Māori and Pākehā-Māori personalities in northern New Zealand. A devious character, the *Star* writer used his considerable literary skills to subtly manipulate his readers into sharing his own prejudices about Marmon and Māori.

Wigglesworth speculates that Frederick Maning (the Hokianga Pākehā-Māori who later became a Native Land Court judge) may have colluded with Chief Justice Gillies in Auckland to rework the original Bennett manuscript and titillate readers of the *Star*.[10] This fits with Maning's residence in Auckland between 1880 and 1882, the delight he took as an embittered old man in goading and misleading new settlers, and the malice and contempt for Cannibal Jack that Maning later shared with his coterie of respectable friends at Hokianga. It also fits Maning's eagerness in his book *Old New Zealand* to debase savage Pākehā-Māori and Māori by manufacturing or embellishing violent, criminal, unattractive and ridiculous events relating to them.

Frederick Maning was indeed the author of the *Star* serial and his treatment of Marmon reflects a time when social hierarchies of race and class characterised the thoughts and attitudes of 'educated' Europeans. As a trader Pākehā-Māori at Hokianga during the 1830s and 40s, Maning's own position had been ambivalent. Although considered the property of his chiefs, he was permitted to live with his Māori wife and mixed-race children in a European-style house beyond the kāinga. Maning raised his children as Māori, but considered himself a gentleman, kept Māori servants and corresponded regularly with literate European residents and colonial officials.

Published in 1863, Maning's own Pākehā-Māori narrative, *Old New Zealand*, was a best-seller in its own day. It subsequently became a colonial classic and one of New Zealand's most reprinted and studied books. Here, Maning casts his less respectable Pākehā-Māori peers: a Pākehā enslaved by Māori on the West Coast, the white fugitives and mercenaries at the Bay of Islands and a Hokianga Pākehā-Māori (very likely Marmon), who believed in the powers of the Māori tohunga, as pathetic, degenerate men and 'greater savages by far than the natives themselves'.[11]

Marmon freely admitted to polygamous and monogamous marriages and Maning's antipathy towards him may also have been motivated by guilt about his own marriage to Moengaroa, the sister of the Ngāpuhi chief Hauraki, which he suppressed in *Old New Zealand*. Maning's dislike was additionally founded on his resolve to preserve his own reputation as 'the Pākehā-Māori', a widely recognised expert on all things Māori. *Old New Zealand* was the first self-representation by a Pākehā-Māori to be read widely, both in New Zealand and abroad. By 1880, and the publication of the *Herald* memoir, Maning's courageous, uncompromising Hokianga trader had became the master-type for representations of Pākehā-Māori in many subsequent history books. Although Maning had already become an indelible image, a blueprint, creating an enduring model for Pākehā-Māori, public interest in Jacky Marmon, the white savage, threatened his dominant narrative and status.[12]

In *Old New Zealand*, Maning is an eloquent and witty commentator and his attractive prose style permeates the *Star* account. In extending Marmon's reminiscences to 22 chapters, Maning added much fallacious and superfluous material as padding. These insertions indicate that, as with *Old New Zealand*, Maning had an eye to a very wide audience and was fully aware of the content and literary conventions the market demanded. Seeking a wide audience, increased circulation and profit from his columns, he was all too willing to exploit racial and social stereotypes and the popular taste for the exotic.

For more than 40 years, Marmon and Maning lived as neighbours on the Hokianga River and both fought on the British side, in the same loyalist Māori contingents, during the battles of Hone Heke's Northern War of 1845. Maning lived mainly in Auckland between 1880 and 1882 and was a regular contributor to *Free Lance*. He drew on his own intimate knowledge of Marmon's adventures garnered over the years and while both men were living in Auckland during 1880 to help extend the *Star* account. Following Marmon's death, however, Maning went to extreme lengths to bastardise and undermine its veracity. He diminished Marmon's adaptations and actions by frequently attributing false motives to them. He and/or Justice Gillies then inserted extraneous material on Māori customs and waiata and events plagiarised from other published sources, including Richard Taylor's *Te Ika a Maui* and H. Carleton's *The Life of Henry Williams*.[13]

The Pākehā-Māori 'autobiographies' of Maning and Marmon were published as narrated commentaries on their life and times. Maning's *Old New Zealand* is highly digressive and the *Star* account is also

Frederick Maning

Frederick Maning, himself a former Pākehā-Māori, distorted Marmon's memoirs for
his *Auckland Star* serialisation in 1881–82.
R. A. A. Sherrin and J. H. Wallace, Early History of New Zealand: From Earliest Times to 1840,
Auckland, 1890, p. 97.

distinguished by lengthy sensationalist episodes unsupported by contemporary records. These fictionalised digressions, characterised by
Maning's animated prose, depicted Marmon variously as a serial seducer
of Māori women, a murderous shipwrecked sailor, captain of the King
of Tahiti's 15-ton cutter, convict paramour of a Sydney prostitute, jolly
Tasmanian bushranger and a likeable character in old age.

In *Old New Zealand*, Maning assumed the persona of a semi-literate
Pākehā-Māori who seems unable to control the order of his narrative, but
his protagonist is a decisive, forceful and daring frontier trader. In the
Star, Maning depicts Marmon as his antithesis, an indolent, irresolute,
shiftless runaway who is unable to control his destiny. Maning signals
his agenda in the *Star*'s opening lines where he casts Marmon as 'the
favourite football of fate'. Maning received a good, basic education

which he supplemented with copious reading. Jacky received a limited education and admitted having little interest in reading. Maning, however, could not resist suggesting that Marmon's enthusiasm for seafaring life was inspired by the latter's reading of *Robinson Crusoe* and *The Voyage of the Nancy*.[14]

Furthermore, both *Old New Zealand* and the *Star* account advise and lecture their audiences and seek to involve them in the story by appealing to the understanding and sympathy of 'the dear reader', 'the gentle reader' or 'the patient reader', as one might in a conversation. Finally, several passages in the *Star* are brief, thinly disguised borrowings from *Old New Zealand*. These include Marmon's first encounter with the law of tapu, his welcome by Māori on the Kerikeri River in 1817, and his lament in 1840 for the passing of old New Zealand, 'when a man could act according to the freedom of his own sweet will'.

The *Herald* writer/s acknowledged Marmon's excellent memory and powers of observation and most ships, people and events described are verifiable in the contemporary literature. Maning, however, connived to fill much of the *Star* serialisation with untraceable people, ships and events which the historian Jack Lee suggested 'may well be evidence of the extent to which a bitter man may go to debase another, using his talents to indulge his sour prejudices'.[15] Wigglesworth suggests that Maning and Gillies' machinations were motivated by 'a combination of jest and malice towards Marmon'.[16]

Jacky's own narrative style did not help his cause. Long years among Māori left permanent traces upon his psyche and several passages in the *Star* are distinguished by a chronologically disordered narrative. Unlike European narrators, Marmon did not adhere to strict chronological sequence. As 'a well conducted and conditioned Pakeha-Maori' he recalled, as did the old Māori narrators, people, places and events from his past as he remembered them, a convention regarded as tika or perfectly correct by Māori. As a 'told to' account the memoir also evolved through a process involving Marmon the narrator and Alice Bennett, the first editor to select and restructure his report. Maning, no doubt pleased to find several of these disordered narrations in the original Bennett manuscript, reproduced them verbatim for the *Star*.

Marmon is responsible for further irregularities in the *Herald* and *Star* accounts which are part throwback to the Pākehā-Māori narratives of the fugitive convicts George Bruce and John Rutherford.[17] All three were experts at covering their tracks and selective about what they disclosed to their interviewers. Never placing themselves among the many lawless sealing and whaling crews known to have attacked and plundered coastal Māori during the contact period, they were also reluctant to admit combatant roles in intertribal battles where victories were invariably followed by the slaughter of civilian populations and cannibal feasts.

Nevertheless, recognising that many portions of the narrative had the value of actual experience, the late nineteenth-century ethnologists S. Percy Smith and John White plagiarised Marmon's *Star* account.[18] Rather than acknowledge 'the notorious Jacky Marmon' as their source, however, they preferred to manufacture fictitious Māori informants. Meanwhile their contemporaries, the compilers R. A. A. Sherrin and T. W. Leys, acknowledged Marmon as a credible 'inside' source and quoted passages from the *Star* memoir in their 1890 published collection of historical records, *Early History of New Zealand*.[19] As other colonial writers began to plunder the *Star* account to give credibility to their own books, and these borrowings were recycled by later writers, much of Marmon's *Star* memoir has become inextricably woven into New Zealand history.

For this book, the *Star*'s chronologically scrambled sections have been resequenced to recreate a more coherent narrative. Most Maning asides, plagiarisms and sensationalised digressions have been omitted, though several examples of his delightfully exuberant prose have been retained and attention is drawn to these. For late nineteenth-century *Star* readers Maning was a necessary and effective editor. His pace and humour invigorated Marmon's original narrative, transforming a lengthy, grindingly factual memoir into an entertaining and exceedingly readable one.

Marmon's correspondence with colonial officials from the 1830s reveals a semi-literate, plain-speaking man. The *Herald* retains Marmon's original and distinctive vernacular: simple, stark and graphic and a few of his distinctive turns of phrase and dropped aitches have slipped past Maning into the *Star* account.[20] Some *Star* passages on Marmon's life as a sailor and soldier are similar in style to the *Herald* version, and many of these are cited verbatim. Shifts in the spelling of Māori names and the *Star*'s use of Māori terms with and without italics have been retained.

While it is impossible to mitigate all Maning's attempts to devalue Marmon, the essential integrity of Jacky's Pākehā-Māori narrative remains. His descriptions of Māori customs and way of life, and his own adaptations, can be confirmed by the reports of Pākehā-Māori and other culture-crossing Europeans who had similar experiences among Māori and made comparable observations.

In this book, key passages from the *Herald* are juxtaposed with those from the *Star* in an endeavour to retain as much of Marmon's original voice as possible, but, unless otherwise indicated, quotations are mainly drawn from the latter. Having expunged much of the *Star*'s sensationalist and manifestly fictitious material relating to Jacky's years as Pacific sailor and Pākehā-Māori, we are still left with a generally credible 50,000-word account which recaptures something of the variety, colour and excitement of his life and times.

Alice Bennett, herself part Māori, must have found Marmon an enthusiastic and fascinating narrator, a Western Other, psychologically altered by his culture-crossing experiences. When she recorded Marmon's memoir, during the 1870s, he was living in rum-soaked obscurity in his house at Rawhia on the northern bank of the Hokianga River. Though the daily demands that traditional Māori culture imposed were receding, Marmon nevertheless retained strong emotional and spiritual links with areas where his children were born and where his wives and his chiefs Hōne Raumati, Muriwai and Waka Nene were buried. Marmon also continued to participate in traditional rituals on local marae as he had done for 60 years and these rituals of encounter constituted his roots, origins and identity.

While the *Herald* and *Star* editors perpetuate colonial stereotypes about Māori by emphasising warfare, cannibalism and native 'superstitions', Marmon's core *Star* narrative contains an underlying story about belonging and describes the many ways he belonged to the Māori world. Marmon's personality and reminiscences were shaped by his life among Māori and the *Star* reveals the extent to which he retained the psychology and faculty of a semi-autonomous Pākehā-Māori. Despite Maning's racist agenda, Marmon comes close to telling a completely different story about Māori as a people possessed of a culture with an integrity of its own.

Marmon's welfare is inextricably linked with the fortunes of his tribes:

plundering raids, battles, scandals, disease, the death of his wives and his chiefs; and at many points the *Star* memoir illuminates many little-known aspects of Ngāpuhi tribal history. Words and phrases relating to identity, status, friendship, kinship and belonging recur throughout the *Star* narrative: 'my wife', 'my chief', 'our tribe', 'our dead'. Despite Frederick Maning's contrivances, the memoir still retains alternative images of Māori, revealing them as human and undercutting a covertly racist account. By 1880, Maning had rejected Māori culture, his former kinsfolk and his own mixed-race children, but when Marmon dictated his reminiscences, he still retained close links with his whānau and tribe, and retained many fond memories of his life among them.

The re-emergence of Jacky Marmon, a 'savage' Pākehā-Māori, in the literature of the late nineteenth century is intriguing. During the pre-annexation era, missionaries, visitors and colonial officials had frequently represented Pākehā-Māori in their reports as unsalvageable white savages. During the 1840s and 1850s, however, a period largely characterised by peace and co-operation between the races, visitors and writers like Edward Jerningham Wakefield, George Angas, Ernst Dieffenbach and Arthur Thomson helped rehabilitate perceptions of Pākehā-Māori. Their published texts emphasised the roles of these culture-crossing Europeans as frontier traders, hosts, guides, translators, ships' pilots and agents of progress who had assisted in 'civilising' and assimilating Māori.[21]

During the New Zealand Wars of the 1860s and 1870s and in their aftermath, the boundaries between the cultures became more rigid and 'Pākehā-Māori' again became a pejorative term. Books by or about trader Pākehā-Māori such as Maning, Charles Marshall and Richard Barrett published in this era normalised or 'Europeanised' these culture-crossers, distancing them from 'savage' Māori and the 12 British and colonial military deserters who became renegade Pākehā-Māori during the 1860s and 1870s.[22]

By the 1880s the trauma of the New Zealand Wars was fading. It became safe for publishers to reintroduce naturalised or 'savage' Pākehā-Māori into the literature. Consequently, the narratives of the tattooed men James Caddell, John Rutherford and Barnet Burns were quoted or reprinted alongside Maning's *Old New Zealand*. Marmon's *Star* memoir became another means by which a colonial population that disapproved of white savages could satisfy its curiosity about them. Meanwhile, the 140,000 immigrants attracted to New Zealand in the Vogel era had no memory of the New Zealand Wars and no reason to fear Māori and Pākehā-Māori. For this new readership Marmon's *Star* serialisation served as a frontier adventure story, and an opportunity to cross cultures vicariously.

Until the publication of his newspaper reminiscences, Jacky Marmon was an obscure bit player in New Zealand's colourful pre-annexation past. At a time when the extinction of Māori seemed inevitable, the memoir of a naturalised or savage Pākehā-Māori attracted enormous attention. Despite Maning's machinations or partly because of them, Marmon gained national notoriety. He also won a place, albeit a minor one, in published histories of New Zealand from George Rusden and Frederick Moss in the nineteenth century to Anne Salmond and James Belich in modern times. Unlike most of his more respectable Pākehā-Māori peers, from the 1880s it was Jacky Marmon who more often entered history each time the story of New Zealand was told and retold in print. Today he lives on through these published histories and the stories that continue to be told about him by his descendants at the Bay of Islands and Hokianga.

CHAPTER ONE

Sailor, 1805–17

Since my birth in Sydney, N.S.W; on the 5th of June, 1798, I have been the favourite football of fate. To-and-fro have I been tossed – now high in the air and speeding on the wings of fortune – now licking the dust in the depths of deprivation. My life, therefore, has been an eventful one, and it may interest some readers to learn the history of a fellow creature who has looked at the world from many points of view.

Born in a convict settlement – the son of a convict – nay by Satan's devices a convict myself, – I have experienced all the horrors and brutality of those early days when a man's will was not his own, but any arbitrary tyrant's whom luck gave him as master. I have been a sailor, too, have traversed many seas and seen many lands, from Tahiti, the Pearl of the Pacific, to distant Tristan D'Achuna. I have tacked with many a wind and weathered many a gale. Many a queer scene ashore and aboard have I beheld; have got into many a scrape from rum-broaching to mutiny; have tipped many a grog-can, and chucked many a pretty girl under the chin; have knocked many men down, and have been knocked down by as many more; have fought with Tongans, and taken leg-bail from ferociously hospitable Tahitians, who came to ask me to dinner on myself; have lived for many years with the Maoris, adopting their customs, and was initiated into their great tribal secrets as one of themselves; mingling in their rites, nay, after a war-raid, partaking of their human banquet.

This is a sketch of my history, and an insight into the life and mysteries of the unknown that I have gained through these long years, I promise you, if you will sit down and do a pipe with me over Cannibal New Zealand. Only reader be not critical. I am not much of a scholar, for the education in a convict settlement was of the lowest class – lower than even the instruction vouchsafed by the hedge-schoolmaster in the Green Isle, whence my father came.

The name Marmon was an Anglicised version of the old Irish, Limerick surname rendered variously as Mawne, Mawme and by Jacky himself as Mawmon. Having opposed political union with Great Britain, Marmon's father was transported to Port Jackson (Sydney) with the first fleet of convict ships in 1789. At Port Jackson, he worked briefly as a stonemason, sailor and storehand and was a servant in the Dawes' expedition which crossed the Blue Mountains later that year.[1] 'The unfortunate result is well known. After penetrating but ten miles into the interior, they were forced to return in a most exhausted and emaciated condition.'

From this he reverted to stonemasonry again. The charms of a Killarney maiden recently arrived in a convict vessel proving too much for him, he married her in 1797, from which union I was the happy consequence. This I have related minutely, that I might establish a plea of hereditary instability. If there be any element more unstable than that to which I have likened my parent it would apply to me, since if he were fickle, much more so was I.

Early Port Jackson was a convict colony with a military government whose governors, until 1824, had absolute power and alone formulated policy. The officers of the New South Wales Corps quickly gained a monopoly over trade, particularly rum imports. Known locally as 'the Rum Corps', it was notoriously corrupt and insubordinate. Rum soon became the currency and combined with a convict population and the general lack of respect for authority, its effects on the infant colony were devastating.[2]

We were a motley mixture of soldiers, sailors, convicts (male and female), a missionary or two, a few merchants. . . . Grog shops, gaming houses and [brothels] were the chief buildings. . . . Governor King was lord and master of everything, including the lives of the people, many ending them very suddenly by the then very popular mode of hanging to a rope for one hour . . . without even the pretence of a trial, a convict would receive his dozen lashes. True, it was necessary to maintain order, but the basis of order is justice, even in such a pandemonium as a convict settlement . . . but all efforts to restrain vice, crime, and disorder were unavailing. . . . The regular order of life in or about Sydney was interspersed at frequent intervals by cases of murder and robbery, fires, suicides, hanging, fights with the natives, and revolts between the prisoners and guards &c.

I was but six years of age when . . . impressed upon my memory [was] the rebellion of the convicts stationed at Castle Hill. . . . I can well collect the terror. . . . The nightly patrols were increased, the guards over the convicts were strengthened; aid was asked and obtained from some vessels lately come into Port Jackson, and arms distributed to all considered trustworthy. Even at my tender years I was initiated into the use of the musket. The rebel convicts, believing that they could reach China overland . . . armed themselves with pikes, choppers, knives, stones, sticks and every lethal weapon proceeded on their way.

The Castle Hill Rebellion was a revolt of some 300 Irish convicts, many of whom were political prisoners. Led by William Johnson who had been transported for participating in the 1798 Irish Rebellion, the rebel force was intercepted and defeated near Parramatta by troops under Major Johnstone. Nine convicts were killed in the clash, nine ringleaders hanged, and many others cruelly flogged.[3]

Sydney, as I have said, was at this period essentially a convict settlement; therefore, the tenor of its existence was necessarily shaped by convict discipline. Thus all Sydney rose with the peal of the big bell of the prison at 6 a.m; went to breakfast on its brazen order at 8, and at 9 to work, when the prisoners trooped to stone-breaking and road forming, to building and brick-making, the merchants repaired to their stores, the scholars to school. At three its heavy toll announced all work for the day to be over, then came the watchman at 9 p.m. and at 10 all Sydney was supposed to be asleep.

Such was our life, dreary and monotonous enough you will say. So it would have been had not ways and means been found of evading even law and discipline. The only occasion other than termination of sentence for any pleasurable change was amongst the female prisoners when a settler was escorted through the factories to interrupt the ceaseless spinning of blankets by his presence, as all knew he was in search of a wife and would thereby obtain her partial freedom after selection and marriage.

By 1800, Sydney Cove had become the centre for the profitable South Pacific whaling and sealing trade. Most Pacific whalers were American vessels from the New England ports but colonial Australian and British whalers monopolised New Zealand waters until 1835. The Bay of Islands became a favoured refitting and reprovisioning port for whaling skippers who began recruiting Māori as sailors, translators and mediators.[4] Marmon recalled first visiting the Bay aboard an Australian whaler under Captain Mallory at the age of seven. While building a chimney for the skipper, Marmon senior agreed to allow Jacky to join the voyage as ship's mascot.

In the superstitious world of seafarers, ships' mascots were popular. With his dark hair and bright blue eyes, Jacky, a precocious and spirited scamp, was viewed by the Irishman Captain Mallory as a 'lucky' person, who would consistently escape misfortune. His presence aboard also pleased the officers and crew who, perceiving his good luck as advantageous to them all, afforded their talisman special treatment and protection to help retain his 'luck'. The crew gradually assimilated Jacky into a seafaring culture with its own language, customs and beliefs. On deck he observed how the crew left a little rum from their daily ration in their mugs to tip into the sea as an offering for Neptune. He learned that a shark following astern was a sure sign that someone would die, and that pet animals were bad luck with the exception of the ship's cat or cats which controlled the rat population. Jacky was cautioned never to whistle, lest he 'whistle up a storm' by angering Neptune. Yet,

Convict transportees
Marmon's parents were among the first of many thousands of Irish convicts
transported to New South Wales from 1789.
'*A Fleet of Transports under Convoy*', 1871. PIC U3909 NK1225 LOC 3842,
National Library of Australia.

when the ship was becalmed, as the youngest member of the crew and
the least offensive to the sea god, he was sent aft to whistle softly and
hopefully raise a breeze.[5]

Marmon recalled his first contact with Māori.

We called in at the Bay of Islands. Some chiefs came aboard and had
potatoes to their dinner. They liked them so much that the captain gave
them some to plant. This was in 1805. After I went home my father sent
me to school, but I was too fond of play and the street to get any good.[6]

By 1805, North Island Māori were already growing the introduced *Solanum tuberosum* or white potato in such abundance that it had become their staple, and visiting ships were being amply provisioned with this vegetable. Unlike the kūmara, white potatoes were a highly productive, long-life non-tapu crop. They were planted and harvested twice a year in northern New Zealand by women and slaves, without the participation of men who were freed to engage in interseasonal musket raids. Captain Mallory may have provided the chiefs who were often enthusiastic and knowledgeable agriculturalists with a specific variety of potato.

The voyage instilled in Jacky an enduring desire for the seafarers' life, with its adventure and exotic locations. In Sydney, he reluctantly joined the town's Catholic children who received a basic education under Jerry Cavanagh, a schoolmaster based in the district known today as The Rocks. The area was noted for Gallows Hill, where crowds gathered to watch the hanging of prisoners from George Street Jail, and for its plentiful grog shops, the haunt of visiting sailors.[7] During his three years at school the young Jacky recalled 'being, pleasantly flogged by the redoubtable Jerry through the mysteries of the alphabet, through strokes and pothooks, through the mazy twistings of the multiplication table. . . . I was never a boy much addicted to reading and study, the charms of amusement were too dear to me.'

Using his connections in the building trade, Marmon senior next secured his restless son a place as 'supernumarary cabin boy' aboard the sealing and whaling brig *Commerce*. Jacky recalled, 'to my delight I found myself an incipient sailor'. Struck by the detail of Marmon's observations, Robert McNab incorporated excerpts from Marmon's recollections into his 1907 history of early southern New Zealand, *Murihiku and the Southern Islands*.

On 6 February 1808 the Commerce was sent from Sydney to visit the southern islands. She returned on 10 July of the same year with about 3,000 skins. For an account of the voyage we are indebted to the records of a pakeha Maori named John Marmon. . . . Some of his dates according to the records do not, when compared with the Historical records of New South Wales, appear quite correct, but there is no reason to doubt the substantial accuracy of the narrative.[8]

Skippered by Captain 'Sirone' (Ceroni), 'a careful, trustworthy sailor', and a hand-picked crew of 30, the *Commerce* weighed anchor and worked slowly out of Port Jackson bound for the Auckland Islands; 'Some of the Sydney merchants having heard of the vast number of seals that that congregated there' had fitted out the ship for the voyage. Ostensibly hired as a cabin boy to serve the ship's officers, Jacky was also permitted to work on deck where his fantasies of a romantic sailor's life were soon dispelled by the cold, wet and windy realities of life topside a southern sealing ship.

Ere long we were in the open sea, and my visions of the romance of navigation were dimmed by a most persistent seasickness. . . . How bitterly I hated that brute of a mate, Bouncing Bill, who dragged me from my hammock, telling me to go to work for a lubberly son of a land-shark, little thinking that it was rough sailorly kindness that prompted him to do it, so that my mind be taken off my misery. With returning health my thoughts became brighter, and I was able to look about me.

Bouncing Bill and the crew of the *Commerce* may also have perceived Jacky as a lucky mascot for many first mates were tyrannical overseers, prone to chivvying along sluggish sailors with a knotted rope's end. Learning a bewildering array of terms relating to the ship and the sealing trade, Marmon soon acquired the distinctive vernacular of the deep-sea mariner, a language completely unintelligible to 'land lubbers'. 'Learning the ropes' meant learning the name, location and purpose of each of the hundreds of lines and pieces of rigging used in every part of the ship's operation, which entailed considerable rote memorisation. As sailors were generally illiterate and manuals therefore useless, the crew assisted their novice shipmate's understanding by teaching him a host of useful rhymes and shanties.[9]

Soon I became familiarised with the working of a vessel, learned to distinguish between the starboard and port sides and their respective watches, to know each yard and halyard, each sail and rope, to strike the bells with tolerable regularity, to recognise the mood of each man on board, and keep out of the way when he was in a bad temper. How I longed to go aloft and reef the sails, when I saw the 'boys' swarming up the shrouds like cats, and singing 'Yo ho!' as they did their work. But to my request Captain Sirone returned a negative, stating it would be time enough when I had *cut* my mother's apron-strings.

As an apprentice seaman, Jacky was initiated into a semi-mythical world of ghost ships, sea monsters, mermaids, cannibal isles, island paradises, freak storms, water spouts and rogue whales. Below deck he listened in awe to tales of 'Timor Jack', the bull sperm whale that continued to smash every boat sent against him, and 'New Zealand Tom', the humpback that destroyed nine whaleboats 'before breakfast' one day in 1804.[10] Marmon inhabited a world where nautical beliefs and traditions went against reason and logic. Like his shipmates, he came to believe that the *Commerce* was a living thing, a person, always a 'she' with her own thoughts, feelings, moods and eccentricities. Treated well by the crew, she would keep them safe. If they neglected or slighted her, she would abandon them to the mercies of a pitiless ocean.[11]

Following a voyage of 12 days, the North Cape of New Zealand was sighted and the *Commerce* continued south to visit the Chatham and

Early Sydney
Born and raised on the turbulent convict settlement of Sydney Cove, Marmon initially led a life of adventure aboard colonial sealing and whaling vessels.
R. A. A. Sherrin and J. H. Wallace, Early History of New Zealand: From Earliest Times to 1840, Auckland, 1890, p. 107.

Bounty Islands. For two months the crew successfully slaughtered and skinned seals alongside two rival gangs on the Auckland Islands. Jacky, already a keen and insightful observer, appears to have remained aboard for he provides no description of the sealing gangs' bloody operations ashore. The *Commerce* then sailed by way of the Trapp Islands to the Chathams to trade for more seal skins.

Besides several sealing gangs stationed here, we found a considerable number of the natives, called in their own tongue Moriori, who seemed in dialect, colour and customs to resemble the Maoris as I afterwards found him. One extraordinary thing I observed here, was that in many places the island (Chatham) was on fire; not a mere surface conflageration, but a steady underground combustion. There are large formations of peat, one of the sealers told me, and these having become ignited, have burned steadily for years and may be yet burning for all I know.

However, we did not remain here long enough for me to see more; but after the purchase of some 300 seal skins, ran up the East Coast of New Zealand, and brought up in Mercury Bay. There I had the honour of going ashore with the captain, and stood upon the spot which Captain Cook, 28 years previously, had selected as his point of observation during the transit of Mercury. As the Maoris of Mercury Bay bore far from a good name, and had on many previous occasions evinced a marked predilection for cooked pakeha, we were only permitted to go ashore in large parties and heavily armed. To us, however, they exhibited themselves in a very friendly light, seeming only to wish to establish a trade for their kumaras (sweet potato), taro, figs, and mats for muskets and iron.

The sight of their hideously tattooed faces and bodies steeped in red ochre was sufficiently terrifying to many of us, especially as they bore in their hands most suspicious looking spears and clubs. We had a Chatham Islander on board, Horareka, who having resided some little time at the Bay Of Islands, was familiar with their customs and language. He, although their dialect differed from theirs, was able to act as our interpreter, and conduct our trade.

Had it not been for this man, when ashore one day, I should have been robbed of my musket in a most summary manner, but yet a manner, I afterwards came to know was one of the leading laws in Maoridom.

Moments of encounter on the beaches of New Zealand were fraught with tension and ambiguity. Simple words, gestures or actions could be easily misconstrued with fatal consequences for one or both sides. Marmon recalled one of these encounters, at which point the *Star*'s formal narrative style gives way to Maning's animated prose. In *Old New Zealand*, Maning illustrated the laws of tapu and muru for his readers by an entertaining account of how his own tribe reacted when he picked up a Māori skull from a beach.[12] In the *Star* account Maning masterfully tailored Marmon's description of a similar event to again elucidate the laws of tapu and muru for his readers.

I had picked up a Maori skull upon the beach, which I was anxious to carry back to the vessel as a curiosity. Having wrapped it in my handkerchief I carried it along bravely for a considerable distance, until, when a brisk barter was going on between my comrades, I felt it slipping out. Not wishing to offend the feelings of, for all I knew, the defunct's relatives, by an unseasonal display of his remains, I laid my musket on the ground beside me, whilst I made the bundle more secure. In an instant a gentleman highly tattooed and of a very diabolical countenance indeed stepped forward, and placing his foot upon the weapon said emphatically 'Ko taku iwi Tuararoa tenei.'

'Thank ye kindly, mister, very well,' said I, supposing he was asking for my health, and feeling grateful for the compliment.

'He says your musket is his backbone,' said Horareka, 'and the law of tapu will give it to him.'

'The devil it is. Tell the gentleman he must have had an extra allowance of grog this morning. It's no more like a backbone than his head's like a flying jib – here mister, that's my gun, clear out.'

But the amiable savage was immovable. It was clear that if he never had a backbone before he meant to have one now, and my musket was to do service for it. Horareka explained the law to me, telling me by the same process I may claim whatever I chose from him.

How it might have ended I know not, as my mates were preparing to fight when Horareka's wit came to our aid. Snatching the skull from my grasp, and displaying it to the eyes of his sorrowing relatives he cried 'Pakeha tapu' (the white man is defiled). In two minutes not a Maori was in range, the dread of contamination exceeded the desire for gain. For my part, shouldering my musket, I made for the shore, followed at no great distance by my comrades.

But we could not even get on board without falling foul of another of these confounded Maori customs. As we were slipping and tumbling over the rocks towards the vessel with all the haste we could, Jack Smith must fall and bleed his nose. These fiends of perdition, who had followed us slowly beyond range of contamination, when they saw the accident cried 'Muru! Muru!' and rushed off in a body for the bush.

'What, in the name of Moses, is wrong now?' said the mate, who was with us.

Horareka explained that in Maori code to injure one self or another, unwittingly, was a mark of the great Deity's displeasure: and that they would probably come back in great force to mark their approval of the Divine Visitation by plundering all he had. Such was the law of muru.

As Horareka predicted, they came down to the shore in great numbers, and seemed anxious to board us. But the skipper, desirous to avoid bloodshed . . . ordered the anchor to be weighed and the sails set. Just as the foremost canoe touched the water, the Commerce swung round towards the North, and stood out to sea. The scene that ensued defies description. Yells and shrieks proceeded from the shore, as the savages saw their mine of wealth slowly slipping from their grasp, and as we disappeared beyond an adjoining headland, we beheld them, one and all, relieving their feelings by a furious war-dance upon the shore.

The *Commerce* sailed north to Tokarau or the Bay of Islands and anchored off the village of Te Puna in the territory of the Ngapuhi chief Te Pahi. Having visited Sydney and been welcomed by Governor King, this leading rangatira was noted for protecting visiting Europeans and his enthusiasm for their knowledge, skills, technology and crops. Captain Ceroni found Te Pahi deeply distressed by the depredations of lawless ships' crews at the Bay. Seamen from ships such as the *Venus*, *Parramatta*, *Elizabeth* and the *Seringapam* had variously kidnapped Māori women, sailed off without paying for provisions, shot and wounded Māori provisioners and raided potato plantations and storehouses. Māori had also been lured below decks before being stripped of their clothing and possessions.[13]

Having supplied Captain Ceroni with logs suitable for flooring boards and masts, perhaps to pay for his passage, Te Pahi stated that he wished to visit William Bligh, the new Governor of New South Wales. He was distraught at the loss of his daughter Atahoe and his son-in-law, the Pākehā-Māori George Bruce, whom he believed had been kidnapped by Captain Dalrymple of the *General Wellesley*. Marmon's close description of Te Pahi was founded on his direct association with the chief who, with his three sons and several attendants, joined the *Commerce* for the return voyage to Sydney.[14]

Ti Pihi was a fine specimen of a savage. His countenance was expressive of much intelligence, his manners were affable, and in every way he seemed anxious to evince regard and esteem for the pakeha. His desire to acquire a knowledge of anything that would raise the condition of his tribe was evident. . . . He was one of the finest natives it ever was my fortune to meet. . . . Of course, as a boy, I could not pick up much regarding the customs of the Maori. That must be reserved for a later period of my life, yet I could not, even at this stage, but be struck with the rigid distinctions of rank existing amongst them. Mates who have been to Calcutta have told me how exclusive is Hindoo caste. Not less so is Maori, with this addition, that in the chiefs of the latter, there was supposed to rest the mysterious tapu, rendering sacred everything he touched or to which he addressed himself. . . . Having taken in supplies of wood, water and sundry vegetables, we set sail for Sydney.

J. S. Cumpston in his *Shipping Arrivals and Departures, Sydney, 1788–1825* noted: 'On 10 July [1808], the brig Commerce, Capt. Ceroni, returned to Port Jackson from the Sealing Islands with about 3000 skins and the chief Tipahee.'[15]

I was back once more to the old rough life of Sydney. A person of some importance I was now amongst my companions, one whom it was an honour to imitate, and a still greater honour to walk with. There was a vast increase in their consumption of tobacco, through each one of them at the earliest opportunity investing in the necessaries for smoking, and a spreading mania seized them for hitching their inexpressibles [trousers] as they had seen me do. Nor did true love run smoothly with any of them since my experiences upon deep waters having constituted me a hero

Hunters and prey

A sealing gang's hunting camp and elephant seals on one of the many southern sealing islands.

Pillement, Victoire, 'Nouvelle-Hollande, Ile King, L'Elephant-Marin Ou Phooque A Trompe (Phoca Proboscidea, N), Vue De La Baie des Elephants'. PIC-AN7570306, National Library of Australia.

of the highest order, the soft eyes of beauty in pinafores were directed to me alone. A happy time of it I had smoking, spinning travellers' yarns, and even at times doing my toothful of grog with the nonchalance of hardened habit.

[At] this time several vessels were in Port Jackson landing convicts and emigrant settlers, and it was rare fun to watch the vacant stare of the strangers at our customs and ways, whilst we boys tried to make fools of them if we could, by directing them to places that had no existence. Again it was always something new to see the soldiers taking a line of convicts to the prison, when one, perhaps, would fall and drag down half a-dozen along with him, or some poor blockhead make a bolt for it, only to be retaken and lashed, or, if refractory, strung up by the neck.

Between 1808 and 1811, Jacky returned to school for six months but was continually truant. Sent by his father to work as a swineherd for a family friend at George's River, he fled after one week, having been beaten by his employer for losing a pig. Longing for a sailor's life, Marmon reluctantly worked as a shepherd at Kissing Point for five months then as a messenger and typesetter for George Howe, an emancipated convict who founded the *Sydney Gazette* in March 1803.[16] Deliberately 'mis-delivering news', 'mis-transmitting messages' and making typesetting errors, 'twice or thrice before going to press', Jacky was dismissed, but he was overjoyed when 'not knowing what to do with me next, my father sent me to sea'.

Marmon and a fellow apprentice, Jack Greenwood, left Sydney in 1811 aboard the *Harwich*, a 500-ton whaler under Captain Simmons. Marmon's *Star* whaling narrative generally follows the abbreviated *Herald* account. Marmon's account of the whaling cruise of the *Harwich*, being fairly typical of the period, was cited by the compilers Sherrin and Wallace in their *Early History of New Zealand*.[17]

I was now a strapping lad of twelve, strongly built, tall beyond my years, and having seen as much 'life' as many a man of thirty. Accordingly, though I say it myself, I was rather an acquisition to the vessel, since I was acquainted with all the parts of the ship, the ropes, the spars, the yards, and could lend a hand, with some idea how best to give my assistance. Besides in the foc'sle, I soon became a favourite. I could sing a good song, spin a fair yarn, and do a reasonable quantity of grog with any man aboard – in a word, I was the right stuff for a sailor.

As Jacky settled into the *Harwich*'s routines, as an apprentice sailor, his days became a repetitive cycle of eating, sleeping and four rotating watches or shifts a day during which one half of the crew were generally on deck. His routines below deck were interrupted by the call of 'All hands' to the sails when gales threatened the ship. Sighting a pod of whales near dusk off the Three Kings Islands, the crew launched their whaleboat. Marmon recalled the action and excitement of witnessing a whale hunt first hand.

Down went the boat with Ned Farne, our harpooner, in the bows ready to launch his weapons when opportunity offered. On came the school tumbling and blowing, throwing jets of water ten or fifteen feet into the air, causing a grand yet terrible scene. At length they got almost within range; the boys were pulling like mad to keep up with the pace the whales were swimming at; we saw Ned rise up in the bows, poise his arm back for an instant, then launch the harpoon straight for the huge back of the fish that was nearest to him.

The aim was true, the missile was buried over the barb in the soft blubber beneath the outer skin and away went the whale dragging the harpoon rope after it so rapidly that they had to pour water upon the side of the boat to prevent it igniting through the friction. Again the huge creature rose to breathe, and another harpoon was driven into it, causing it to rush away. . . . Darkness fell over the scene before they had killed it, and the boat remained by the carcase all night to prevent it sinking. When morning came it was a busy scene on board, preparing to cut it in and try it out. At length the task was completed, and five large [casks] were secured . . .

The *Harwich* remained in the Tasman Sea hunting, chasing and killing whales whose carcasses were 'cut in' alongside, and 'tryd out' (rendered down in try pots) aboard the ship. Their cruise took them from the Three Kings Islands, to Curtis Island, off the coast of Tasmania, Australia, and back to Norfolk Island before being struck by a heavy gale. With one of her try pots swept away and whaling boats damaged, the ship was driven eastwards before bearing up to the Bay of Islands and anchoring off Te Puna. 'We were the only vessel in the bay at the time, though others entered during our stay.' Te Pahi was conspicuously absent. Unjustly blamed for the attack on the *Boyd* at Whangaroa in 1809, he had been killed along with 15 of his people by a retaliatory force of armed seamen from several whaling ships.[18] Although tensions remained high and the onshore camp of the ship's sawyers was heavily guarded, some of the younger seamen mixed freely with Māori. Jacky became increasingly fascinated by and attracted to their customs and way of life.

[A] chief named Taua Makia came aboard to take care of us and watch over our interests, lest we should be swindled in trade or otherwise maltreated . . . but the 'consideration' expected was not large. The skipper ordered a boat to go ashore and bring a load of gravel to serve as shot for our guns since . . . the natives were not to be trusted, for the New Zealanders were not to be trusted even although we had a protector. The news had spread like wild-fire that a ship was at anchor in the bay, and already scores of canoes were being launched to pay a visit to the pakeha, but we loaded our guns and pointing them astern ordered all visitors to keep back, which after a little demur and grumbling they did. Nevertheless, all throughout our stay, they never desisted in their attempts to get aboard, considering it a gross breach of hospitality on our part to deny them the privilege.

Three of us had been wandering about in a bit of bush near the Keri-Keri River, trying to find our way back to the saw-pits when suddenly we issued upon a cleared space, in which were a few houses and patches of cultivation. Before the entrance to one of the whares stood a band of females crowned with chaplets of green leaves and wringing their hands. One of these, an elderly woman who seemed to act as chief mourner upon the occasion . . . advanced in front, and began to throw her arms about, raising her head and eyes to heaven. Whilst doing this in a very plaintive quivering tone she commenced a wailing song, in which she was joined by her companions.

It was the *tangi* or wail for the dead. But at this period I knew nothing of Maori customs or ceremonies, and my very hair began to rise in horror as I thought perhaps they might be celebrating some human sacrifices. Our fear kept us quiet. . . . When the sorrowful song was ended, and the females had entered the *whare*, we noiselessly strove to retrace our steps, and chance favouring us we came out upon the shore a mile or two from where the sawyers were at work. As I afterwards discovered, no duty is so sacred or obligatory as the internment of the dead, no trouble being considered too great, no expense too excessive, no lamentation too extreme to testify to the respect with which the deceased was held on earth, and to raise him in the estimation of the mysterious spirits to whom he had gone.

Taua Makia sometimes went with us fishing to induce the prey to come upon our hooks by the constant chanted chanting of *Karakias* or incantations, supposed to have a very potent influence over the finny tribe. We were [not] very successful when he was with us, since the noise he made and the fishing gear he insisted on employing were neither conducive to lure the fish to our bait, nor to hold them when they were hooked. But this, of course, may have been an ignorant *pakeha*'s prejudice, since many a lusty *kahawai* or *schnapper* have I caught with a hook made from a dead man's bone.

Te Pahi

This Rangihoua chief welcomed whaling ships and the new knowledge, skills and goods they brought. His generosity and enterprise left a lasting impression on Marmon. *R. A. A. Sherrin and J. H. Wallace,* Early History of New Zealand: From Earliest Times to 1840, *Auckland, 1890, p. 42.*

We began to mix a little with the natives when ashore, and I grew more familiarised with their ways. We attended their baptisms, *He Tohi*, and gave presents to the infant, that it never enjoyed; and we consulted the *Niu* or divining sticks whether we should reach home in safety; we were present at their marriage *tauas*, when the bride was carried off by main force, sometimes *minus* her clothing. Finally we were guests at their *hakaris*, or feasts, and could vouch for the excellence of Maori culinary skill.

With her repairs completed, the *Harwich* prepared to weigh anchor at dawn. During the night, Marmon, hoping for a life of ease among Māori, tried to desert by swimming from the ship. He was seen by the watch and on being returned to the ship was berated by the captain, but 'escaped a flogging'. The *Harwich* continued whaling at the Three Kings and cruised the waters around Curtis Island and Moreton Bay before returning to Sydney with half the crew ill with scurvy and dysentery. 'Thus ended my voyage in the "Harwich", perhaps the most pleasant of all my trips.' According to the *Herald*, during Marmon's 1811 whaling voyage his ship also cruised the South Pacific in search of sandalwood, during which a stowaway was discovered.

I forgot to tell you that while we were in Sydney a young woman named Mary Davis had fallen in love with one of our crew, and just before we sailed had stowed away aboard. Our captain did not find it out til we were far out at sea and could not put back. She had been very sickly all the time, and died here. The captain would not have the poor creature buried ashore for fear that the natives would dig her up and eat her, so she was buried in the sea from here to Tahiti.[19]

Although whaling captains sometimes sailed with their wives, having an unattached or 'loose' woman aboard was considered bad luck as she created tensions and potential problems among the crew. Ships departing Sydney were plagued by convicts of both sexes attempting to stowaway. Official measures including issuing passes to all convict visitors and searching or smoking the holds of departing vessels had little effect. The whale ships rarely returned to Sydney until they had a full cargo of oil, and a ship might be at sea for two years or more. Consequently, some women followed their lovers aboard and prostitutes who paid local boatmen to convey them to a ship, looking for 'business', were sometimes hidden by the crew.

In the *Herald* account Marmon describes encountering 'Sal', another female stowaway, on a later voyage aboard a coastal surveying vessel. This was possibly 'Sally' the companion of Sam Collins, a shipmate he describes in the *Star* as frequenting 'Micky Hall's grog-shop'.[20]

On the third day after we left Sydney, I went below to pump off the water, when, behind one of the casks, I saw a woman hiding. I knew her and said, 'What! You here Sal?' I told the officer, who said, 'Send her aft.' She was taken before Captain King who asked her how she got there. She said because she was fond of the boatswain, and could not bear to be left behind, and so had stowed away. Captain King sent her forward saying,

'Go there; keep yourself to yourself, and let me hear no complaints about you.' This woman's name was Sarah Chamberlain, and she kept herself close and very tidy all through the voyage.[21] My first move [at Sydney] was to make for a convenient grog-shop, kept on the sly by one of the military and commence to spend my money, as I considered every sailor should, in a good spree. . . . Just the day before we arrived, a batch of female convicts had come from England in the 'Thames' frigate, and the soldiers had been busy selecting the best looking as companions for a month or two before they were sent to prison. This was winked at in Government House – nay, even the offenders and their paramours were publicly asked to the balls, much to the disgust of Sam Marsden, the parson. . . . [R]um a few years back was a standard currency, and indispensable medium of exchange, in a colony where money was scarce, and many a day's wage have I received in spirits.

The three succeeding years – that is, from 1811 to 1814, when I completed my apprenticeship – were the most active I spent in my life. During the greater part of them I was engaged in whaling, being not

Tangi over a dead chief
Marmon first witnessed a Māori tangihanga or funeral ceremony near the entrance
to the Kerikeri River, Bay of Islands in 1811.
R. A. A. Sherrin and J. H. Wallace, Early History of New Zealand: From Earliest Times to 1840,
Auckland, 1890, p. 47.

three months in Sydney during this time, and upon their conclusion I was rated as a first-class seaman.

A bold and industrious sailor, Marmon was a useful addition to any whaling crew. In the *Herald* he recalled, 'The life was just what I liked, it suited me exactly.'[22] In 1812 Jacky shipped out once more aboard *Harwich*, which successfully hunted right whales in Tasmanian waters. A large sperm whale and five right whales were soon secured, which returned 30 tons of oil and, shortly thereafter, three more right whales in Adventure Bay. 'Next day we lit our try-work fires, and tryd out the oil from the soft white blubber.' Jacky toiled alongside his shipmates at the try works but, being of slight build, never served as an oarsmen or harpooner. The crew had barely completed this task, 'when another school was seen in the bay, from which we cut out two more prizes'. The number of 'fish' sighted and the sheer size of the pods encountered on Marmon's voyages indicate the extraordinary number and variety of whales inhabiting Australasian waters during the early nineteenth century. The *Harwich* sailed on to Hobart to replenish its stocks of wood and water.

Aboard the whale ships danger and adventure were real and almost routine but Marmon makes light of the flensing and the trying-out process, during which the crew worked feverishly to extract oil from the whales' blubber in brick try works before the onset of foul weather. During this procedure, the oil-drenched whale men, who rarely slept, were fortified by extra rum rations and ship's biscuits dipped in hot whale oil. Marmon's seafaring recollections are generally positive and his 'uneventful' voyages omit or downplay the toil, shipboard fires, deaths, injuries, malnutrition, scurvy and the harsh treatment he endured or witnessed as a whale man.

We were allowed to go ashore and found that Hobart grog was the worst that had ever been distilled. From here back to Adventure Bay was our next move, where in a month we caught and tried out no fewer than sixteen whales, our fires never being extinguished until we had filled with oil everything in the ship that would hold it, even to the washtubs, which were the perquisites of the sailors. As we had now on board above 200 tuns of oil, we knocked off whaling, cleaned up our decks, and sailed once more for Hobart Town. Here we remained a fortnight, keeping in right royal style Christmas and New Year . . . every mother's son of us was most imperially drunk for the entire week.

Finally, bound for Sydney with a full cargo of oil, the *Harwich* was struck by a violent gale and blown eastwards for many days. The captain decided to seek shelter and supplies at the Bay of Islands and their old anchorage at Te Puna where Jacky heard of the massacre of the *Boyd*'s crew at Whangaroa Harbour, though he is more likely to have first heard the story from Hongi Hika during the *Harwich*'s visit to the Bay in 1811. A chief of high rank and ambitions, Hongi welcomed contact and trade with Europeans as he wished to access European technologies, particularly muskets to avenge past defeats. In later years Jacky's destiny was to become closely intertwined with that of the great chief.

From the Maoris who came on board to barter pigs, taro, kumaras and potatoes, we heard of the 'Boyd' massacre. Hongi, the chief of the Ngapuhi tribe, came off to our vessel and seemed very desirous to learn all he could about European customs. He was, seemingly, a most mild and amiable savage, with not a trace of the terrible ferocity he afterwards displayed visible in him at this period. He was remarkable only as an ingenious craftsman, – being a skilful carver, and a clever designer of mokos or tattoo marks.

The *Boyd* was an English ship under the command of Captain John Thompson, which visited Whangaroa, north of the Bay of Islands, in August 1809 to load kauri spars. Thompson had unjustly flogged Te Pehi [George], a Māori sailor and senior chief from Whangaroa. Enraged at the mistreatment of their rangatira, the Whangaroa people attacked the ship and massacred the passengers and crew. The *Boyd* was set alight when a chief accidentally ignited a cask of gunpowder. For many years Māori shocked a succession of European visitors with their candid accounts of the *Boyd*, for they always viewed the actions of their countrymen as tika or perfectly correct.[23]

Hongi told this through Eremai, an interpreter, with such an air of satisfaction and approval that Captain Walker considered it safest to

'Boats attacking whales'
Marmon spent most of his seafaring years aboard deep-sea whalers in the
Southern Ocean.
Wood engraving 96 x 167 mm, William James Linton, A-109-046, Alexander Turnbull Library.

depart as soon as possible, lest the chief, not withstanding, his seemingly
pacific character, might seek to emulate the Boyd massacre by attacking
the Harwich. Therefore, to Hongi's disappointment, we left the Bay for
Sydney on the 15th January, after giving him two muskets, some powder
and shot, an axe or two and some knives as a present, we left the Bay for
Sydney. We reached Port Jackson on the 25th January, nothing eventful
having transpired on the voyage.

During a subsequent whaling cruise, aboard the *Harwich*, Marmon
cruised waters around the Antipodes Islands and New Zealand. This
voyage can be dated at 1815, as they encountered the *Trial* and *The
Brothers* from Sydney and the British whaler *Catherine*, which cruised
New Zealand waters each year between 1814 and 1816.[24]

This was our cruising ground. Not a very pleasurable one you will say,
but we do not look to those things in whaling. All the beauties of nature
would not rival a school of whales blowing and tumbling in monster
happiness. This was an entirely uneventful cruise, save that we repeated
our success in whaling, and that poor Jacky Greenwood fell from the
mizzen-top on to the deck and was instantly killed. . . . We buried him

at sea, Captain Walker reading a service over him, and then Jacky was
gone and forgotten.

The unfortunate Jacky Greenwood was 'buried' quickly at sea, for
seamen believed that the souls of the dead would remain with the ship if
the body was kept too long aboard. He was quickly 'forgotten' as sailors
had an aversion to using words like 'death' or 'dead', or talking in any
way that linked them or their ship to bad luck.[25]

Having departed the Antipodes Islands, the *Harwich* cruised around
Curtis Island and New Zealand's East Cape, 'with varying success'
before approaching North Cape 'where we traded with some natives for
pigs and potatoes. The former were good, but the pork tasted very fishy,
as the pigs were fed principally on sea-weed and fish.'[26] At the Three
Kings Islands off northern New Zealand, Marmon learned that Māori
had also attacked the trading ships *Trial* and *Brothers* at Trial Harbour or
Kennedy's Bay near Poverty Bay. The ships had successfully traded with
Māori there but upon their return in August 1815 they found Māori
angry and aggressive. The *Herald* memoir contains the more succinct
summary of events.

[We] fell in with the Trial brig, Captain Hovell, and the Brothers schooner.
The captain of her had been killed at Mercury Bay. The natives had tried
to take the vessel, but were beaten off by the crew, led by the carpenter
an Irish-man named Macklin, who jumped from the hold with a handsaw,
and soon cleared the decks. The natives jumped overboard, but not before
they had killed three white men. It was soon after this that I fell in with
Tapsell, who was a carpenter [and third mate] aboard the Catherine, a
whaler also.[27]

Thomas Kendall, the leading Anglican missionary at the Bay of
Islands in 1815, later claimed that Captain Hovell provoked the attack
by defrauding Māori.[28] The *Catherine's* carpenter was Hans Falk or Hans
Tapsell, a courageous and adventurous Danish sailor. Initially a South
Seas rover like Marmon, Tapsell made regular voyages to New Zealand
and the Bay of Islands during 1803, 1815, 1823 and 1827. He finally
settled at Maketu in 1828, became the principal Pākehā-Māori trader
for the Arawa people and has many descendants in the Bay of Plenty.[29]

After a long cruise to the New Hebrides, the *Harwich* returned to New Zealand's North Cape.

Whilst here, influenced by one of the men, I ran away with him and hide in the bush but hunger compelling us to seek supplies, I was dispatched to forage, whilst my companion kindled a fire, but falling in with some Maoris on the way, they stripped me of my knife, vest, shoes and my hat; they conveyed me back to the ship, exchanging me for 3lbs pounds of powder. Alas, it is true, such was my Maorian value; not even did I attain to the rate of an old musket. However, my previous good conduct stood me in good stead, so again was I exempted a flogging.

Hearing that whales were plentiful around New Caledonia, the skipper at once ran for that island, sighting Norfolk Island on the way. The inhabitants, a robust race of savages of almost negro blackness. They are very hostile to strangers, and would not permit us to land . . . We got here four whales in all, one of which was a sperm, and our success not corresponding to our hopes, we stretched back to New Zealand, going into the Bay of Islands for wood and water. Our friend Hongi came on board, bringing with him a relation, Tapawaiki, as well as pigs, potatoes and kumaras. When we left, we gave him a written character that would serve as a recommendation to other captains coming in, that they might rely on his honesty and friendliness.

From the Bay we ran down past the East Cape, into Cook's Straits, landing in Admiralty Bay, thence still southward past the Chatham Isles, past the Antipodes and Campbell's Island, still on South until we were in the Antarctic Circle. This was almost virgin whaling ground, and we got no fewer than twelve splendid fish, which we cut and tried out with the very iron blistering our fingers from the extreme cold. Still on southward til we came to a vast continent of ice, and on the horizon the grand spectacle of an active volcano rolling its fiery columns to heaven, amidst eternal frost and snow. This was the limit. After securing two more whales, which completely exhausted our means of containing the oil, the order was given 'about ship', and nothing loth we started Sydneywards.

The *Star* places Marmon as a beachcomber at Tahiti and Bora Bora between 1815 and 1816 and aboard the trading ship *Sally* in 1817, bound for the Bay of Islands where he deserted, but there is no record of the

Sally. The *Herald* places Marmon aboard the sealer and trader *King George*, which actually visited the Bay in 1817 and from which he likely did desert, though Marmon states that he sailed on to Bora Bora to live as a beachcomber for two years between 1817 and 1819.[30]

Interestingly, in the *Star*, Marmon later describes successfully distilling 'grog' for his Māori hosts, from a recipe provided by 'a sailor named Bill Green, at Tahiti', which matches the reference made to Green in the *Herald*.[31] Unearthing new documentary records on a number of hitherto unknown Pākehā-Māori during the late nineteenth century, the noted New Zealand compiler and historian T. Lindsay Buick concluded that Marmon indeed first lived among Māori in 1817.[32] Despite the uncertainty surrounding names of ships and the specific sequence of events, Jacky appears to have sojourned as both Tahitian beachcomber and New Zealand Pākehā-Māori between 1815 and 1820 and his departure from Tahiti is worth citing, as an example of Maning's wit at its best.

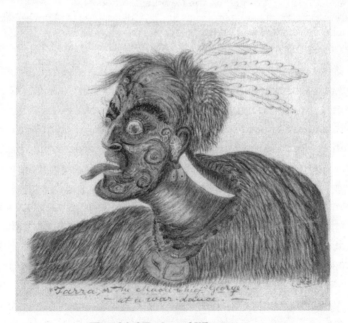

The chief Te Ara of Whangaroa
While at the Bay in 1812, Marmon first heard how the unjustified flogging of this young chief by the captain of the *Boyd* led to the massacre of the ship's crew and passengers.
Watercolour 134 x 149 mm, Augustus Florence, '"Tarra" or Maori chief "George" at a war dance', A-114-002, Alexander Turnbull Library.

Trading on the New Zealand coast
The harsh discipline aboard many ships and the friendliness of Māori encouraged
many sailors to desert and to live among the tribes as Pākehā-Māori.
'*A trading schooner surrounded by the canoes of New Zealanders*', *Dumont D'Urville*, Voyage
Pittoresque Autour du Monde, *Auckland Institute and Museum.*

Right glad I was to see the banana and bread-fruit groves of Papeete
disappear beyond the horizon. Amid such scenes of beauty, where earth
seemed as nearly a paradise as can be realised in life. I had grown mortally
tired – an insatiable longing for my former dare-devil existence had taken
hold of me; in a word reader, I was heartily sick of respectability. Poor as
a church mouse I had set foot upon Tahiti, and as poor I left it, though
my enemies will insist that I left his Tahitian majesty minus fifty yards of
tapa, or native cloth. Reader it is a malicious slander. If I did appropriate
the cloth, it was in lieu of my wages, with interest and compound interest
up to date; only as I was rather hurried in my departure, and forgot to
give his majesty a receipt, he fears I may, like a dishonest tailor, send in
my bill again, therefore I am accused of stealing it.

Sometime during 1816, either aboard an unnamed whaler, or in
1817, aboard the *King George*, Jacky's luck deserted him when he was
falsely accused of shirking by the bo'sun and flogged. Before this event,
Marmon seems to have accepted without rancour the hierarchical

nature and harsh discipline of Sydney convict society and shipboard life. The shock and indignity of the ordeal prompted Marmon to desert and 'go native', in New Zealand. It also marked the beginnings of a bitterness and antipathy towards authority that intensified during his life as a fugitive and Pākehā-Māori.

In some mysterious way or other, I had offended the old bo'sun of our ship, and he had persecuted me with most relentless malice. Nothing I could do was right, the rope's end was my daily sauce, and complaints about my laziness were continually being carried to the captain. At length one day, irritated by their constant recurrence, he said, when another of my misdeeds was laid before him, 'String him up and give him a dozen.' This was just what the bo'sun wanted, in a trice he strung me up to the mast, and a good round dozen I received, being only released when nearly fainting with pain and shame.

Between the 1790s and the Treaty of Waitangi in 1840, several thousand sailors seeking escape from harsh discipline and hardship deserted their ships to live for a time among Māori.[33] Given the strict maritime hierarchy aboard ship where a bo'sun's word was law, Marmon had little control of his own destiny. His decision to abscond and live among Māori was shaped by additional factors. Aged 19, Jacky had served 10 years before the mast and, given his youth, slight build and limited education, his prospects of advancement in the whaling trade were limited. The harsh, monotonous work and Spartan home life of a labourer or odd job man in the convict settlement of Sydney held even less appeal. Life at sea had long provided Marmon with action and excitement and life among Māori offered further challenges and adventures.

Many early sailors encountering Pākehā-Māori on the coasts of New Zealand were impressed by their importance and independence. Visiting North Cape aboard the *King George* in 1817, Marmon watched an escaped convict named Jim Price accompany his rangatira aboard the ship in the standard Pākehā-Māori role of trading intermediary. Alternately translating for, and advising, his chief and the ship's captain, Price helped set the terms of trade. By joining Māori, Jacky might also, like Price, attain influence and status among both races.

Long attracted to Polynesian ways of life, and having recently lived as a Tahitian beachcomber, he was hardly embarking on a new, untried way of life. Marmon's practical skills, learned at sea and while 'odd-jobbing' in Sydney between voyages, were useful in Tahiti, and, as a regular visitor to the Bay of Islands, Marmon was confident that these skills would serve him well among Māori.

CHAPTER TWO

Gun-trader, 1817–20

Jumping ship at the Bay of Islands in 1817, Jacky Marmon lived as a Pākehā-Māori on the Kerikeri River for more than two years. His hosts and protectors were a hapū of Hikutu settlers from the Hokianga. Jacky was one of 10 Pākehā-Māori believed to be living in tribal New Zealand during the 1810s.[1] Early Pākehā-Māori were mainly located at Hauraki (Thames/Auckland), Murihiku (Foveaux Strait), and at Tokorau (Bay of Islands). On the Kerikeri, Marmon lived like a Māori, but as an embryonic gun-trader with commercial motives, he did not fully assimilate Māori values. To succeed as a trader, however, he was obliged to modify his speech, language and behaviour, but his basic attitudes and values remained unchanged.[2]

In 1769, Captain Cook had found the true Māori communal unit to be a small, mobile group which used the resources of an area on a rotational basis with other similar groups. The arrival of Europeans and the desire by Māori to acquire flintlock guns, however, compelled these loose groups to band into hapū or subtribes both for defence against other hapū and as a method of stockpiling supplies to barter for muskets and munitions.[3] Marmon's arrival coincided with the fiercely competitive intertribal arms race at the Bay. During the early 1800s, visiting whale

Scouring a flintlock musket
The Bay of Islands hapū competed fiercely to acquire muskets. New owners spent much time in cleaning and polishing these status weapons.
Augustus Earle, 'Two New Zealanders Squatting', PIC-AN2854233, National Library of Australia.

ships engaged in a lucrative trade, bartering a few antiquated muskets for substantial cargoes of provisions. Typically, Ngāpuhi exchanged eight large pigs and 120 baskets of potatoes or one ton of dressed flax with the whaling skippers for a single, cheap flintlock musket valued at between five and 10 shillings, a rate of exchange that was fixed and considered fair by both sides.[4]

The guns acquired by Ngāpuhi came mainly from English and colonial Australian vessels and the occasional American ship that refitted, reprovisioned and bartered for the services of Māori women and cargoes of flax and timber at the Bay. These vessels, and trader Pākehā-Māori like Marmon, were end links in a chain of gun distribution that stretched back to the great English industrial cities of Birmingham and Leeds. Here, gun makers on government contracts and a multitude of subcontractors used the factory system to assemble flintlock guns from an array of interchangeable parts. These included more robust and reliable military firearms for the British army and navy, and cheap substandard guns of 'plain iron' or 'sham damn iron' for the African and

Pacific trade. By the end of the eighteenth century, Birmingham's gun makers alone had already manufactured and consigned more than five million weapons to 'the native trade'.[5]

Gun making and gun trading were among the most profitable industries spawned by the Industrial Revolution. The eighteenth and nineteenth centuries witnessed the irrepressible spread of gun trading around the globe. Europe responded to the insatiable demand for its destructive firearms from indigenous people for use in their local wars by exporting firearms before imposing itself on the survivors. So lucrative was the trade in cheap iron guns for manufacturers, ship owners and colonial trading houses that production continued unabated during the American and Napoleonic wars, with output in some industrial centres outstripping the production of military firearms.[6]

Determined to gain military advantage and settle old scores, ambitious Ngāpuhi rangatira used every means possible to obtain muskets, shot and powder ahead of their rivals and enemies. Trained in the use of flintlock guns from age six, and possessing diverse practical skills, useful European runaways like Marmon became prizes for which the chiefs fiercely competed. During the intertribal Musket Wars of the 1820s and 1830s, practical knowledge of loading, firing, maintaining and repairing muskets was diffused among the tribes by Māori themselves. In the contact period, however, early culture-crossing Europeans such as Marmon were expected to share this knowledge with Māori at the Bay. Such was the demand by Māori for competent 'mechanics' that one visitor to the Bay complained that the warriors were

constantly pestering the Europeans by bringing them sick muskets (as they call them) to look at and put to rights, and are quite surprised that we cannot 'make them well again'. They cannot be made to comprehend that every white man does not know how to make a musket or at least repair it.[7]

Bound to the tribe by marriage and adoption, useful Pākehā were carefully protected, nurtured and assimilated into tribal life. As advisors, trader go betweens, instructors and armourers, Marmon and his peers played an important role in expanding and servicing the arsenals of northern chiefs whose incessant military alliances, raids and major campaigns after 1818 forged the fiercely aggressive Ngāpuhi tribal confederation.[8]

We lay off Te Puna, a little way above [Rangihoua] where were the mission buildings founded by Parson Marsden, and I could see everything that went on ashore, until sometimes I was tempted to make a spring for it and swim to land. . . . After we had taken in our cargo of flax the captain prepared to return but on the night before he sailed I found means to slip overboard, and, holding my swag in my teeth, to swim ashore. I concealed myself in a clump of high ti-tree until the Sally sailed, when I at once issued from my hiding place and proceeded towards the mission buildings. . . .

I concluded the best thing I could do was to go to the parson, represent myself as a convert who had been obliged to leave my vessel through the prevailing wickedness on board, and get them to give me food and work. The thought was father to the deed. I drew my visage to a befitting length and told my story, after which the parsons made as much work about me as if I had brought them a thousand pounds.

Marmon's Pākehā-Māori narrative has been challenged by several historians as the journals of Anglican missionaries living at the Bay and Kerikeri make no reference to him until 1827; but neither do their journals mention the Pākehā-Māori James Burns at Waitangi or John Rutherford at Otuihu Pā who also left accounts of their lives among Māori at the Bay. Thomas Kendall, the senior missionary at the Rangihoua station, supervised a succession of runaways employed as general hands at the Rangihoua mission following its establishment in 1815, but does not name them and, because so many turned out to be drunkards and trouble makers, he refused to employ these men after 1820.[9] The journals of Anglican and Wesleyan missionaries, visitors and early settlers contain many references to runaway convicts and sailors living among the tribes but again they, too, are rarely identified by name, which is an eloquent silence. Having slipped back down the scale of civilisation by living among and becoming like Māori, Pākehā-Māori became an invisible population in the eyes of transplanted Englishmen among whom religious, racial and class prejudice was entrenched.

Furthermore Marmon was not just a Pākehā-Māori; he was Irish and a Catholic.

I had now a full opportunity of studying Maori life and customs. . . . Undoubtedly the Maori is the finest of all native races. The nearest approach to him is the Marquesan or the Tongan, but neither of these have the same suppleness of frame nor the active intelligence possessed by the New Zealander. To see a *rangatira* (chief) in his 'Sunday best' with his cloak of kiwi feathers, thrown over his *pekerere*, his head plentifully daubed with red ochre, and adorned with nodding *kotuku* plumes, his face a maze of tattooing, yet very expressive either of friendship or hatred, his frame as lithe as the eel he worships and eats, is to be convinced of the truth of my assertion.

Marmon's *Star* memoir constantly casts light on contemporary Māori affairs, customs and events. He recalled during his 1815 visit to the Bay, and again in 1817, how local rangatira were becoming more discerning about the types of Pākehā arriving among them. Rather than welcoming every European as a representative of a strange and exotic race, surplus, useless or troublesome runaway sailors and convicts from the Australian penal colonies were seized and sold by the chiefs to ships' captains, whose vessels were chronically short of crew. The standard rate of exchange was one musket per runaway.[10]

The Maori chiefs who at first were inclined to secure me and sell me to the first vessel that came in to the bay, when they saw how welcome I was at the mission, one and all came and hungied – rubbed noses – with me, contending which should secure me as his *pakeha*, but I was in too comfortable a billet to leave it easily, notwithstanding, Hongi [Hika], Korokoro, Muriwai, made me most tempting offers, Kawiti, also from the Hikutu hapu, offering me his two daughters as companions. But of course as a religious man such a bribe would have no inducement for me apparently, though I managed, for all that, to make love to the girls on the sly. Here I was, therefore, in April 1817, established in New Zealand as parson's man. . . . My work was not heavy. I had to cut wood, bring water, do a little fishing, and manage the little fishing boat, that would run over to Kororareka, or up the Keri-Keri as the occasion required.

Established below the great pā at Rangihoua, the Anglican mission was located near an anchorage favoured by whalers who had first been welcomed by Te Pahi. The main centre for Pākehā–Māori contact in this period, Rangihoua drew many of the great chiefs and their armed retainers wishing to obtain guns for their grand 1818 campaign against Ngāti Porou on the East Coast. Marmon found the local gun trade dominated by several resident Pākehā-Māori scattered around the Bay. From the swamps and creeks of region, Māori cut, dressed, transported and bartered muka (flax fibre) for muskets and powder with these traders, who in turn bartered the flax for additional muskets from the shipping.

[Maori] worked with a will, preparing flax for the traders and as their only instrument of preparation was a pipi shell, it was most tedious. Besides, they would accept no other commodity in exchange save muskets and ammunition and for one ton of prepared flax they would receive one musket, some idea may be formed of their arduous task. I thought it was as well to do a little business on my own hook here. Having smuggled

Rangihoua Pā and mission station, Bay of Islands
Marmon worked here for a time as a general hand for the Anglican missionaries and also as an independent gun-trader.
PIC.AN2255627, National Library of Australia.

a gun or two from the vessels that came in, I bought up all the flax, for which I demanded from the traders two muskets, though I still paid the natives only one.

With just 200 precious muskets dispersed among New Zealand's coastal tribes by 1817, Māori at Rangihoua willingly paid Marmon's inflated prices. Notions of racial superiority drove the New Zealand gun trade, particularly the belief that 'inferior' people should make do with inferior guns that would have to be replaced regularly. Marmon and his fellow Pākehā-Māori quickly realised that the common toa (warrior) actually preferred cheap trade muskets.[11] By 1817, leading chiefs such as Hongi Hika and Korokoro had obtained good-quality flintlock muskets and pistols directly from the ships' captains or during their visits to Sydney. The primary evidence, however, reveals that before the mid-1820s, shoddy muzzle loaders of plain iron were more eagerly sought by the warriors than more reliable black powder military muskets like Brown Bess, for the former were cheaper to buy, flashier in appearance and simpler to repair.[12]

The preference for Marmon's trade guns of 'plain iron' by Māori was also founded on their light weight and short barrels, which made for ease of aiming. The tribesmen found the wide .50 to .70 calibre bores of the English guns ideally suited to birding, wildfowling, pig hunting and man hunting, as gravel and pebbles could be easily substituted for birdshot and musket balls. Additionally, the warriors disliked the heavy recoil of military muskets like Brown Bess, which were suited to powerful, finely grained black powder. Expensive black powder often burst the thinner barrels of trade guns, designed for low strength, coarse grained 'lighty' or trade powder carried by visiting whale ships.[13]

From the early contact period, the pū or musket held a powerful mystical and psychological appeal, for it could deliver thunder, fire, smoke, lightning and occasionally sudden death from a distance and metal was a marvel that fascinated Māori. The trade muskets bartered by Marmon were deliberately 'tinselled off' by the English gun makers to captivate indigenous people like Māori who constantly polished the barrels, butt plates, broad lock plates and exaggerated escutcheons.[14] Individually named and with the woodwork intricately carved, flintlock guns were incorporated into a number of tribal rituals. Displayed with flamboyance during haka, possession of these glittering weapons increased the mana of their owners while unequivocally stating the military and economic capabilities of the hapū.

Whilst assiduous in my attention to the mission, I yet strove to identify myself as much as I could with the natives, as I soon began to get tired of the Joint Stock Preaching Company, and longed to cut respectability for a free and easy life in the Maori whares. I picked up the language as thoroughly as I could, I became acquainted with as many chiefs as possible whom I could oblige in a good many ways, I went to their *kaingas* (villages) at Kororareka and Keri-Keri; joined in their *tangis*, paid respect to their *tohungas* (priests), and more than all, when I could get any rum, I gave a drink all round, until I was regarded as only a step behind the missionaries, and an infinitely better fellow.

Disillusioned with life as a common sailor and mission odd jobber, Marmon carefully prepared his way before crossing cultures. From previous visits to New Zealand, he knew that life among Māori would provide an opportunity to improve his status and personal wealth. Marmon's plans were unexpectedly advanced when a secret affair he had been conducting with Tūī, the daughter of the chief Kawhitiwai, was discovered. (Maning rewrote their names as Tiu and Kawitiwai or Tawitiwai). Her father complained that 'every *rangatira* had a *pakeha* except him' and that 'he wanted utu (recompense) from me for fooling his daughter and making her a tūtūā (nobody) in the tribe'. Kawhitiwai launched a taua muru or plundering party against Marmon and his missionary employers, the event drolly conveyed by Maning.

[W]e heard a terrible sound of yelling and hasty foot-steps approaching. The Maori children cried out to us, 'The *taua*, the *taua*,' but before we had time to remove anything from the yard it was filled with naked armed savages, bent upon plunder. The scene almost defies description. In one corner was one parson holding hard to a pair of blankets and an iron pot against three Maoris who were struggling to secure them; in the opposite corner another of the missionaries, with his heels in the air, was yet battling bravely to retain possession of a pair of inexpressibles and a hat.

The chiefs Waikato and Hongi Hika with Thomas Kendall
At Rangihoua, Marmon was employed by the missionary leader Thomas Kendall
and first encountered the Ngāpuhi fighting chief Hongi Hika.
*Oil, 720 x 920 mm, James Barry, 'The Rev Thomas Kendall, and the Maori chiefs Hongi Hika and
Waikato', D-P618-G-CT, Alexander Turnbull Library.*

Entering the yard Hongi Hika restored peace and resolved the impasse by using Māori divining-sticks or niu. Hongi proposed to throw the sticks and if the one marked as Marmon's fell under that assigned to one of the chiefs wanting to acquire him, Marmon was to go with that chief as his Pākehā 'to which for the sake of peace the parsons and I consented'.

The niu sticks were cast and Marmon's fell directly beneath that of Kawhitiwai's.

The moment Tawitiwai found I was going with him, his manner entirely changed. He hungied me until I imagined every bone in my nose was broken, and immediately presented me with his *heitiki*, or neck ornament, as a mark of his esteem. Having collected and packed up my swag, which his *wahines* (wives) carried down to his canoes for me, I bade farewell to my parson friends and pushed off for Kawitiwai's *Kainga* on the Keri-Keri River.

The great secret of the Maori ambition to have a resident *pakeha* amongst them was the desire to possess all the methods of warfare and offence known to him, so as to confer on the tribe he honoured with his presence greater success in their constant conflicts, for fighting was, to Maori, the chief ambition of life. Each winter he cultivated his taro, or kumaras, with the utmost diligence, so that the entire summer might be devoted to fighting.

Marmon recognised that his successive Māori patrons were prepared to respond creatively to European military technology and that he was valued and protected by them for any knowledge he might have about musket repair, maintenance and marksmanship. Though, eventually, European guns were fully acculturated into Māori warfare, ultimately the musket chiefs found nothing useful in other European forms of warfare and did not seek to imitate them.

We sailed up the winding Keri-Keri for some distance. . . . Our arrival was proclaimed in the *kainga*, every man, woman and child hurrying to the river bank. Amidst a babel of discordant sounds, we landed, every voice shouting at its utmost pitch, '*haere-mai, haere-mai*, welcome, welcome,' every dog worth a bark joining in the chorus, nay, even the very pigs swelling the concert by intermittent squeals. After prolonged *hungieing*, Tawitiwai demanding silence, delivered a speech to the following effect, whilst he walked up and down slapping his sides and brandishing his mere:- 'My children, I have brought you a *pakeha*; he is mine, and see that you treat him well, or what will he think of you? Give him plenty kai (food) and a whare, and other pakehas will come and you will have plenty *pu* (muskets) and *paura* (powder). He is mine; I have won him with the *niu*; look well after him.'

Then again arose the fiendish yells of *haere-mai*, during which Tawitiwai's beckoned his daughter Tiu, who approached me with a rougish smile of recognition. She was dressed for the occasion in a large cloak adorned with *kiwi* feathers, which was fastened on the left side, leaving the left arm and neck uncovered. She wore earrings of sharks' teeth and a *heitiki* of polished greenstone. Altogether she was a very pretty girl, whom any epicure in beauty might long for. She was made over to me as my principal wife, *he wahine matua*, but as it was supposed the *pakeha* was by nature rather of a free-lover four others were added from lesser individuals, being called in distinction from Tiu, *nga muri manu*, the birds that followed. Of course such an event as the arrival of a *pakeha* amongst them could not be passed by without a great *hakari* or feast, followed by athletic sports such as *he pui* or skipping rope, *te takaro ringaringa* or wrestling, *te para mako* or dart throwing, in which great skill was displayed by all competitors. It was nearly dawn before I betook myself with my wife-in-chief to the *raupo whare*, henceforth to be my home.

Polygamous marriages to the daughters or sisters of a chief provided a powerful incentive for early runaways to remain with a tribe. Marriage generally brought the newcomer a house, lands, status and kinship ties with other influential whānau within the hapū. For Marmon, marriage to Tūī and her sisters helped provide protection from hostile tribesmen and arrest by ship's captains or the missionary magistrates. It also ensured that his transgressions of Māori law were tolerated by his kin, who jealously guarded and protected their newfound source of wealth and power. To be effective as a trading intermediary it was imperative that Marmon quickly master the rudiments of the Māori language. Behind every successful trader Pākehā-Māori was a Māori woman, usually a chieftainess, and Tūī, Marmon's main wife, helped him learn the new language and guided him as he negotiated the laws of utu, muru and tapu and relationships within the hapū.

In their memoirs, published as *Old New Zealand*, and *Pakeha Rambles in Maori Lands*, shortly after the New Zealand Wars of the 1860s, the Pākehā-Māori traders, Frederick Maning and Charles Marshall, imply a solitary and strangely puritanical existence among Māori.[15] They never acknowledge their Māori wives, perhaps because, as Pākehā-Māori, they had been obliged to choose sides during the New Zealand Wars. (They chose the British/settler cause and recrossed cultures.) Perhaps, too, they were sensitive to the needs of wartime settler readers, whose Victorian values of home and family were threatened by Pākehā-Māori who cohabited with Māori women. Unconcerned with maintaining a reputation among Pākehā, in the *Star* memoir, Marmon acknowledges two polygamous and several monogamous marriages, and as we shall see, was the only Pākehā-Māori to leave a detailed account of a cross-cultural love affair.

'A New Zealand Girl'
Useful European runaways were bound to the tribes by marriage, generally to a
sister or daughter of the leading chief.
Aquatint on page, 220 x 137 mm, Augustus Earle, PUBL-0022-258, Alexander Turnbull Library.

The first Pākehā to live among the tribes had great novelty value.
This was founded partly on their strange habits and appearance but,
particularly, the colour of their skin, eyes and hair. For Kawhitiwai and
Hikutu, Marmon was not just an exotic curiosity but a status symbol,
whose presence as a representative of a technologically advanced
culture enhanced the mana or prestige of his hapū. According to one
nineteenth-century observer, the first Pākehā acquired by Māori were
'kept and fed on much the same principles as curious animals are kept in
England'.[16] As both tribal pet (mōkai), and adoptee (whāngai), Marmon
was nurtured by the tribe, treated with great kindness and provided with
partners to accommodate his sexual needs. Not required to perform
menial tasks, he shared the same food as his chief, served twice a day
from the hāngi or earth oven by Kawhitiwai's slaves in simple baskets
plaited from green flax.

My patron – or so I must term him now, I suppose – seemed to regard
me as a sort of pet animal to be treated with especial forbearance and

kindness, though also to be remorselessly swindled if opportunity arose. For what other use according to native ideas, was a *Pakeha*. . . . So long as he patiently endured swindling he was a very excellent man; but let him begin to swindle, or rather let him be found out, and Taipo [evil spirit] himself was an angel of light [compared] to him.

Though not required to toil in the fields as did some useless or superfluous Pākehā enslaved by Māori, Marmon was expected to make fresh cartridges and to check and repair the firing mechanisms of the few muskets then owned by Kawhitiwai's warriors. Trading was one of his main mediating tasks and from this position he was able to anticipate the needs of Māori and Pākehā and make himself indispensable. Nevertheless, as a mōkai, Marmon was subject to a cramping surveillance by Kawhitiwai. Refused permission to board the shipping at the Bay to trade lest he run or be arrested for desertion, Jacky was obliged to conduct trade through the Pākehā-Māori living near the Bay's deep-water anchorages. As a sailor, Marmon had previously traded in smoke-dried Māori tattooed heads [mokomokai], which generally fetched £10 apiece.[17] While his principal item of exchange was flax, Marmon again bartered mokomokai along with fine cloaks, Māori curios and weapons on behalf of Kawhitiwai and other members of the hapū. With just 10 to 12 ships calling at the Bay annually during 1817 and 1818, there was ample time to enjoy a leisurely existence on the Kerikeri.[18] His descriptions of everyday life among Māori indicate a liberation of spirit and a sense of well-being.

Thus commenced my life as a *Pakeha-Maori*. It was quite in accordance with my restless disposition and dislike to the usages of society thus to be without its pale, to go where my spirit listed, to do whatever I desired. Thus my life for two or three years may be summed up in a few sentences. I lived quietly with my wives, raising quite a colony of children. I went out fishing in the bay for kahawai whenever the thought struck me, I did a little potato-planting and kumara cultivation in the season, I snared or shot birds, I tried boat-building, and when all things failed had my pipe to fall back upon, though tobacco was represented by dried koromiko leaves.

I agreed pretty well on the whole with my wives, though Tiu turned out a perfect Tartar, with a temper like a bear with a cold. Angels have turned to devils before. Kawitiwai was frequently away on war expeditions, at which time our settlement was drained of all the young men, its defence being left to women and warriors too aged now to fight. I had two or three pretty sharp quarrels with my patron, when I considered he wanted to over-reach me, and invariably held my own, declining to accept any compromise; and in almost every case got my own way.

I consulted the *tohungas* (priests) as regularly as my Maori brethren, and professed to exhibit as great awe as they, when the low whistling moan on the roof announced the presence of a spirit from the realms of Te Reinga. My only regret was that our supply of rum was very limited, until following out the directions I received from a sailor named Bill Green, at Tahiti, I succeeded in distilling some pretty fair grog from potatoes and maize, when the entire settlement got drunk for a week. Ah, those were happy days for me.

A survey of pre-Treaty literature reveals 13 Pākehā-Māori known to have been adorned with the face tattoo or tā moko. The patterns were incised into flesh which was reputed to be far more agonising than the puncture method employed by tattooists elsewhere in the Pacific. Tā moko was a means by which the Europeans entering tribal life could exhibit their courage and acquire mana, and enabled chiefs to link their Pākehā to the tribe. Most tattooed Pākehā-Māori were fully assimilated culture-crossers who fought as Pākehā toa or white warriors in intertribal battles. Like many new traders, Marmon may have felt superior to his hosts both racially and socially and with his hapū already acknowledging his sailor tattoos as proof of his courage and endurance, Marmon chose not take tā moko during his first sojourn among Māori.

As I had amused myself at sea in tattooing my arms and legs according to various devices, I was considered rather a hero, since the *moko* or tattooing as executed in New Zealand is a most painful and agonizing operation, calling for a great amount of pluck on the part of the victim. In fact, so excruciating is the suffering, that only a small part can be completed at a time, and it is customary, when any noted spark is undergoing the moko, for his sweethearts to sit beside him chanting . . . a karakia (spell) . . . to deaden the pain.

I did a pretty brisk trade in flax and pigs, bringing many traders up the Keri-Keri, when it got to be known I was there, thus vastly increasing the importance of Tawitiwai's *hapu*. I still continued to raise the price of flax in muskets, so that by the end of two years' time I found myself in possession of twenty muskets to the good. These I had to secrete with great care, as were it known I had them near me, a taua would be at once organised on the most frivolous pretence, and I should lose my hard-earned gains; for Kawitiwai was terribly jealous of his authority, and were he to dream that I was more powerful than he, I should be stripped to the very skin, father-in-law though he was to me. Some of the muskets I concealed under the roots of a gigantic *totara* tree that overhung the river, and was avoided by everyone, as the abode of a fearful Taniwha or water-demon, which was constantly on the watch to entrap fishermen or sailors; Others I buried under layers of *ti-tree* until required, selecting the loneliest and densest parts of the bush for my purpose.

Māori village (kāinga) with swing and pā
On the heavily populated Kerikeri River Marmon lived with and traded guns for his
chief Kawhitiwai and Hikutu, his adoptive hapū.
A. S. Thomson, The Story of New Zealand, London, 1859, p. 209.

During the years 1818 to 1824, when the Ngāpuhi inter-hapū arms race was at its most intense, muskets, shot and powder were the only items they would accept as trade goods. 'Why . . .' recalled Marmon in the *Herald*, 'you could get a chief killed for three muskets.'[19] His store of 20 muskets typically comprised a variety of modern and antiquated flintlock guns in various states of disrepair. The trashy, mass-produced trade musket predominated, but, like other traders of the period, his stock will have included a few double-barrelled muskets and shotguns (tūpara), blunderbusses, pistols and perhaps one or two cast-off sporting muskets, military muskets and muskatoons, the last being a short, heavy-barrelled naval musket with an enormous bore.

Blunderbusses were keenly sought by the toa, and Marmon had a keen competitor in his neighbour and former employer Thomas Kendall, an avid gun-trader who obtained eight of these weapons from the whaler *Martha* in 1818.[20] The bell-shaped muzzles made for fast, easy loading; the brass barrels resisted the corrosive effects of salt water, and the standard Māori load of lead balls, pebbles and glass produced ruinous casualties at close range. Double-barrelled guns or tūpara were valued for their capacity to fire a vital second shot. Tūpara and flintlock pistols were initially status weapons, carried primarily by the chiefs, who often gifted them to potential allies, or to senior chiefs, as tributes.[21]

In 1818, Marmon witnessed the departure of Kawhitiwai and his warriors, some armed with precious muskets, in one of two huge marauding taua that left the Bay of Islands. Led by Hongi Hika and Te Morenga, these amphibious expeditions set out to attack Ngāi te Rangi at Tauranga and Ngāti Porou on the East Coast. The chiefs were seeking utu for the deaths of their relatives, two Ngāpuhi chieftainesses, kidnapped by the pirate crew of the *Venus* in 1806. Eventually exchanged by the crew for fine cloaks with men of Ngāi te Rangi and Ngāti Porou, both had been killed, cooked and eaten.[22]

Thus were the Ngapuhis . . . plunged into the bustle of preparation for another war . . . the Ngatiporous were in themselves a very strong tribe besides being closely allied to the Ngati Kahungunu . . . and the Rangitani of Ahuriri in Hawke's Bay, who were celebrated for their ferocity and warlike character. . . . One thing I resolved was that, if I possibly could I would avoid going . . . because I hoped to do a good trade in flax when everything was quiet.

The 1818 expeditions that Marmon's hapū joined were unique, firstly for the numerical strength of the taua, for these were the first great predatory Ngāpuhi musket taua founded on extensive intertribal alliances, and secondly for the reliance of these expeditions on the psychological effects of gunfire to break and conquer the rākau or conventionally armed forces arrayed against them. Te Morenga's force, for instance, though 800 strong, carried just 35 muskets.[23] The trade muskets supplied by Marmon and his fellow traders at the Bay changed the character of Māori warfare and upset the established intertribal balance of power. Predatory raiding between 1818 and 1821 was characterised by taua numbering 200 to 1600 toa armed with limited numbers of muskets. These precious weapons were used to shoot enemy rangatira, the warriors either fleeing the battlefield in panic or standing bewildered by the sound and effects of gunfire to be slain or enslaved.[24] A recent and priceless acquisition, Marmon was not permitted to accompany Kawhitiwai and his warriors on military expeditions.

Operating independently, Hongi and Te Morenga's forces ravaged the Bay of Plenty and East Cape regions and Marmon recalled their eventual return, following 'the capture of no less than eight *pahs*, among these Maraenui, beyond Opotiki, then Awatere, then Wharekahika, East Cape, and Waiapu'. Horrified missionary eyewitnesses recorded that the expeditions also returned with some 2000 prisoners and canoes filled with the tattooed heads of their enemies.[25] By late 1819, the novelty of Marmon's Pākehā-Māori existence was waning and, as a consequence of several unfortunate incidents, he became disillusioned with Māori way of life.

But do not imagine, reader, that my life here was wholly devoid of care. When a man has a superfluity of any thing, the very abundance of a good thing becomes a nuisance. I had an excess of wife and their constant complaints, uttered by five distinct organs of speech, were in the long run, wearisome. Perhaps I have no romance in me, but I was mortal enough to consign them all to the – a week after I became the happy

Trading scene

As the principal trader for Hikutu, Marmon bartered with neighbouring hapū. He also exchanged flax, pork and Māori crafts for guns, powder and general trade goods with Pākehā-Māori located at the Bay of Islands.

Sepia, ink and wash 260 x 360 mm, John Williams, 'Maori bargaining with a pakeha', D-Po79017-A-CT, Alexander Turnbull Library.

possessor of them. Again, my bargains did not always go straight, either with the traders or the natives, and a man gets soured as his bad debts increase.

Runaways entering tribal societies to acquire opportunities and positions denied them in European society found the world of Māori an equally hierarchical and competitive one where concepts of mana or status were paramount. Though they were essential for the prestige and survival of their hapū, Pākehā-Māori were not exempt from regular challenges to their influence and mana from males within their own hapū. As key advisors who could explain Europeans and their strange customs and technologies, Pākehā-Māori undermined the traditional influence and status of the tohunga. The *Star* memoir details several challenges to Marmon by tohunga intent on undermining his influence and to enhancing their own mana. The first challenge by Iwitangi, advisor to Kawhitiwai and chief tohunga for the hapū, provides some understanding of the stresses and pressures Pākehā-Māori could create for tohunga when first entering Māori communities.

My chief cause of annoyance was from one of the natives, who had conceived a mortal hatred to me, not from any injury I had done him, but from the loss of *mana* (influence) he sustained on my arrival at the settlement. He had formally been a favourite with Tawitiwai, and being a *tohunga* was perhaps in many ways useful to him in making the will of the gods to coincide with the will of the chief in matters affecting the welfare of the hapu; but after my arrival Kawitiwai consulted me more than Iwitangi and thus drew upon me the wrath of the neglected soothsayer.

Not that this would have troubled me much, but he was able in many ways to frustrate my wishes in regard to many things. If I wanted to purchase a few acres of land to cultivate as my own property, when the gods were consulted as to the propriety of the action, the reply was that the land of tribe must not be alienated; if I wished to take a journey any place he had always a convenient vision warning him to prevent me going; if I was ready to strike a bargain with the traders he would step in and prevent it, and although frequently I told him to go to the devil, concluding the bargain, I did not wish to come to any rupture with the religious spirit of the Maoris so more often I yielded. The tohunga saw this and traded on it.

Emboldened by the success he sometimes gained he determined upon a further stroke to effect my downfall. We were seated at a solemn *hakari* in honour of Kawitiwai's marriage to his sixth wife, when suddenly the *tohunga* started and seemed very uneasy. He stared long and earnestly at me, so that I almost expected what followed, when his body became violently shaken as if by some invisible spirit; he fell on the ground twisting and turning as if in pain, his eyes rolled in their sockets, his arms swayed ceaselessly to and fro, his legs twitched and kicked as if through cramp. He was supposed to be under the influence of the god, and a dead silence prevailed until it would be heard what was the will of heaven.

'Oh Ngapuhis, you are under the wrath of Maui. He is sore displeased and has vowed enmity against you and why has he done so? Because ye have received a pakeha who is distasteful, a scoffing *pakeha*, who laughs at Maui. Sacrifice him to Maui that his wrath may be appeased, and he smile upon you once more.' The symptoms of divine possession disappeared, and the *tohunga* rose, casting a swift glance of triumph in my direction.

In an instant Kawitiwai sprang to his feet, with every feature distorted with rage. He rushed up and down outside the circle of feasters, clapping his hands together, and ever and anon stopping to stamp his foot. 'Maui is a great deceiver. He deceived his brothers – Atamai the liberal one, Toa the strong one, Mohio the wise one – and he has been playing tricks on our *tohunga*. Ah Maui, you are in our *tohunga* just now and I will give you a lesson so that you will not forget Tawitiwai.'

With these words he seized the unfortunate *tohunga* and beat him most unmercifully, protesting all the time it was not Iwitangi he was beating, but Maui, to teach him better manners towards the *pakeha*. When it was over, the soothsayer slunk away, most crestfallen, conscious that he was most exquisitely fooled, convinced also that if he would wreak any spite on me, it must be through his own agency, not through Tawitiwai. It was my turn to crow now, which you may be sure I did most exultantly.

This incident rendered the hatred of the tohunga towards me utterly ungovernable. In every way he could think of he persecuted me, and although I affected to laugh at him, yet I refrained from giving him a sound hiding until I had sufficient reason. This came before long. I mentioned that I was obliged to conceal my muskets lest I be considered too wealthy, and although I used every precaution to ensure secrecy, yet Iwitangi had got some inkling of this, had watched me, and finally succeeded in robbing me of five muskets, which he disposed of for flax. Suspecting who was the thief, I watched for some days, and at length detected him in the very act of abstracting a musket from the roots of the totara tree. He tried to fly, but in an instant I was on him, threw him on his face, and thrashed him till my arms ached. 'Now,' I said, 'go and try stealing from me again, do.'

I imagined that I should have the entire tribe up in arms against me. But no, he was not liked, and besides was much too ashamed of the occurrence ever to breathe it to a soul. But even this lesson was not sufficient to drive the devil out of him, it only added fuel to the fire of his hatred, until at length he made up his mind to kill me so as to regain his lost influence with the tribe and Tawitiwai. . . . Karakias (spells) had no effect on me, his maketu or witchcraft as little. In vain, did he procure

A Ngāpuhi warrior displaying a pū or flintlock musket
With their capacity to deliver thunder, smoke and fire, muskets were rapidly
incorporated into a variety of Māori rituals including haka and tangihanga.
*E. H. McCormick (ed.), Markham, Edward, New Zealand, or Recollections of It,
Wellington, 1963, p. opp. 56.*

portions of my food or clothing, bury them, and repeat spells over them, under the idea, as they decayed, would I also. Devil a bit, I got stronger every day, and more capable of giving him a bigger thrashing should he become disagreeable again.

At last he made up his mind to shoot me. I had been down to the Mission Station at Rangihu to see Parson Marsden, who was thinking of opening a station on the Keri-Keri [1819], and had brought out a man named William Puckey from Sydney to undertake the building work. My road by land lay through very thick bush, capable of affording first-rate concealment to any murderer. Therefore here it was Iwitangi determined to make away with me. I was pushing on as rapidly as I could so as to reach the *kainga* before nightfall, when suddenly the *tohunga* stepped out from behind a gigantic *kauri*, and saying, 'I have you now Pakeha,' presented a musket at me and fired. Three inches more and this veracious history would never have been told. The ball carried away the lower part of my right ear and buried itself in a tree right behind me. In an instant I was on and had floored him. . . . Both of us could not live and I was thoroughly sick of the persecution to which I was exposed. Therefore, placing my knee on his chest to keep him from struggling I primed my pistol, placed it to his ear, and fired. There was a terrific convulsion and a shriek, and the *tohunga* was a corpse.

I took the musket from him and pursued the journey, reaching the Keri Keri towards nightfall, feeling an uncommon relief in having disposed of my adversary. After a day or two, speculation began to arise, where was the *tohunga*. Some of the natives wanted to consult the gods, but the one way of access was denied them through his absence. At length two of the Rangihu natives coming through the bush found his body, and brought in word to the settlement. Three of the members of my tribe with myself were commissioned to go and bring the body to the settlement, we being declared *tapu tango atua*, or unclean for the time being. This we did with great apparent grief. On it being ascertained that Iwitangi was shot through the head, suspicion was directed at some of the Aupouris or Whangaroa Maoris who had a deadly hatred for Kawitiwai and his *hapu*, and without delay, an expedition was to be organised against them. But in the meantime the rites of burial were to be given to Iwitangi.

It was during his 1815 visit to the Bay aboard the *Harwich* that Marmon realised that the tangihanga was the crucial ceremony in Māori culture and how it placed obligations on all members of society. At Iwitangi's funeral, he witnessed the prolonged wailing over the deceased tohunga by the women who lacerated their heads, faces and breasts with shells. The men meanwhile chanted 'for the soul of the dead' and fired off their muskets which indicated that, by 1817, the pū was perceived to have mana that could be transferred to the deceased.

The body in the meanwhile lay in state under a kauri tree, clad in fine mats, adorned with feathers, his arms being laid beside him. After the spade was made the corpse was instantly interred, being conveyed to the wahi tapu (burying ground) by the three bearers who brought it to the settlement. During all this time we could not help ourselves to food, but had to be fed, as any vessel we touched would have been rendered unclean, nay, our very food would have turned to poison within us. When all was over then came the tangi or lament, after which Iwitangi was left to his long sleep.

Marmon was the first Pākehā-Māori to describe how Māori accul-turated European muskets into their tangihanga ceremonies. Muskets were initially perceived by Māori as possessing a life of their own, being charged with supernatural qualities sufficient to cause death or injury among the living but also to ensure safe passage for the spirits of deceased rangatira or tohunga by driving off the atua or vengeful spirits.[26] The warriors charged their weapons with double or triple loads of paura mamae (sacred gunpowder), previously blessed by the tohunga. Fired in sequence or as volleys, the marae was wreathed in smoke, giving the ceremony a surreal aspect. Following the dramatic increase in shipping and the number of guns traded to Māori after 1818, the tangihanga became a spectacular ceremony, the crash of musketry according the deceased the prestige they had enjoyed in life.[27]

When Marmon lived on the Kerikeri, Māori understanding of the destructive power of European firearms outside the Bay of Islands and Murihiku or Foveaux Strait was still being arrived at gradually. Between the battle of Moremonui in 1807, when Ngāpuhi first attempted unsuccessfully to use muskets offensively, and 1818, the year of their first large-scale musket expeditions, guns were acculturated into a variety of established food-gathering activities and peacetime rituals. These included the welcoming and farewelling of visiting chiefs and Europeans and saluting the arrival and departure of ships.[28]

During his residence on the Kerikeri, Marmon occupied a middle ground between the cultures. In his desire to become a successful gun-trader he compromised, adopting a Pākehā-Māori lifestyle which combined elements of both cultures. Living among Māori on Māori terms and being dependent on Kawhitiwai and his people he had been obliged to demonstrate an outer conformity. Yet, so vital was Marmon to his hosts that his sexual transgressions and the killing of Iwitangi were overlooked. In *Old New Zealand*, Maning states that the treatment of Pākehā-Māori by their chiefs and their mutual trade dealings were regulated by the restraint of public opinion and the danger of the trader running away.

Should he, by any awkward handling of this sort, cause the Pakeha at least to run for it, the chief would never hear the end of it from his own family and connections, pakeha being, in those glorious old times,

'One of the Hill Chiefs'
Ambitious musket chiefs like Kawhitiwai were confronted with a dilemma –
how far to apply Māori social sanctions to control their Pākehā without driving
him from the tribe.
Robert Marsh Westmacott, 'One of the Hill Chiefs N.Z.', PI.NLA.PIC-AN3458440,
Alexander Turnbull Library.

considered geese who had laid golden eggs, and it would be held to the
very extreme of foolishness and bad policy either to kill them, or by too
rough handling, to cause them to fly away.[29]

Ultimately, it was the application of Māori customary law to their Pākehā that drove Marmon from the tribe after all his store of muskets, painstakingly accumulated over more than two years, were seized. Marmon's experience highlights the dilemma that confronted many chiefs in the era preceding the commencement of organised colonisation in 1840 – how far to apply Māori social sanctions to control the Pākehā without driving him from the tribe. Bound by the law of muru to plunder the property of his own Pākehā, Kawhitiwai lost Jacky Marmon, the source of his tribe's growing military power and material wealth.

[S]carcely was I settled down to quiet enjoyment of happiness when another cause of trouble [arose]. Tiu, my principal wife, was standing under a tree during a great storm of wind and rain, when a large branch broke away, and descending on her crushed her to death. . . . This dispensation of Providence, according to Maori law, indicates the wrath of heaven against the unfortunate husband; therefore it was only proving themselves good, *religious* heathens, anxious to *keep square* with the celestial powers that be, to organise a *taua muru* to sack his house and belongings whilst he sits by and considers himself the more highly honoured the more thoroughly they destroy everything they can lay hands on.

Scarcely was my wife buried, and that with all due solemnity, as became a chief's daughter, than the mob of plundering friends appeared, and in five minutes left me without a stick or stitch in the wide world. In an evil hour I had brought my muskets into my *whare* so that they were a grand prize to the human vultures. I was, therefore, not only destitute, but had not a single commodity to trade, with which to better my position.

Sitting in my sacked whare that night, I commenced to review my position. Maori life was all very fine, but was apt to be monotonous, and my three years' experience had made me feel very tired of it. Yet what was I to do? Go back to Sydney I could not, to go to the mission was, if anything, a shade worse, to change my quarters to some other tribe was only to run the chance of being cooked or at least live over again the existence I had lived at Keri-Keri. Ha! I have it. There was a ship sat this time in the Bay, bound for Van Dieman's Land, why should I not get passage in her, and see what was to be done in that colony. . . . This was my determination, therefore, at night when the settlement was buried in slumber, I took a little money I had saved, stole out, unloosened a canoe from the landing-place, and noiselessly paddled down the river for the Bay. Before day dawned I was off Te Puna, where the 'Fanny' lay.

The *Fanny* is untraceable but a ship with the near-sounding name *Anne* was at the Bay at this time.[30] Kawhitiwai and his fellow chiefs at the Bay took great care in housing, feeding, breeding and monitoring the activities of their first Pākehā. Regarded as the property of the tribe, Marmon had not been permitted to trade with rival hapū. The decision to leave the tribe was considered a great affront to chiefly mana and was fraught with danger. When Marmon met John Rutherford, the chief Pomare's Pākehā-Māori on a Māori battlefield during 1825, Rutherford claimed to have lived as a virtual captive for almost 10 years before eventually escaping to Sydney aboard an American brig.[31] Marmon, too, was obliged to secretly escape his tribe. Entering the world of Māori was not difficult for Pākehā, but exiting it was difficult and occasionally fatal for Pākehā-Māori, particularly as the intertribal wars gathered momentum after 1818, and the possession of a gun-trader became a condition of survival for the tribes.[32]

But Tawitiwai had not been so blind as I thought. Finding he could not sleep he rose and directed his steps towards my *whare* to have a *korero* (talk) until sleep overtook him. He found the bird had flown, at once dropped to the conclusion that I had made tracks. Accordingly he also took a canoe and paddled for Te Puna; but I had too great a start. Before he came in sight I had boarded the vessel and been accepted by the captain as a sailor, to whom I told a fictitious yarn about being wrecked. When Tawitiwai came up he, of course, could not board, as to keep the natives away all ships at that time, spread a netting round the sides, lest a large number of Maoris being on board at once they should seize the vessel, as had been done at Mercury Bay and the Thames.

My former patron, of course, used all of his eloquence to induce me to return but in vain. I had had enough of him, and longed once more to commence my travels. So with bitter reproaches on my ingratitude . . . he was forced to go ashore to seek consolation from the missionaries. After a day or two, the cargo being completed, we sailed for Hobart Town, I very glad to have a change of scene. And yet a singular fatality always brought me back to the Bay, for wander where I will . . . I am always brought back to thy shores, oh Takiraw or the Hundred Isles.

The *Herald* places Marmon 'on several voyages to and from Tasmania' in 1820.[33] The *Star* has him living in Tasmania for much of 1820, where he 'remained some time in Hobart Town doing odd jobs so as to keep myself alive, but getting tired of this hand to mouth existence' became a bushranger. After this dubious and unverifiable adventure, he joined, according to the *Star*, the *Himalaya* bound for Calcutta. Marmon looked forward to his visit to India 'but when we were ten days out from Hobart Town a heavy south west gale sprang up, which lasted for ten days'. The ship put into the Bay of Islands where 'amidst old scenes and associations, the longing for my pakeha-Maori life returned, and I deserted the "Himalaya", once more to resume it.'

To modern readers, Marmon's *Star* and *Herald* memoirs may read like fiction, but regularly changing one's identity and roles was a feature of frontier life and he was one of many itinerant European seafarers who consciously fashioned and refashioned new identities for themselves among the islands of Polynesia. Sometime during 1820, having sailed from either Hobart or Sydney as a deckhand, Marmon again 'ran' from his ship at the Bay of Islands to resume his Pākehā-Māori existence on the Kerikeri River. This time his commitment to Māoritanga would be absolute.

CHAPTER THREE

Tohunga Pākehā, 1820

Pursuing enquiries about Marmon in Auckland during 2003, I contacted a Māori researcher, recently returned from Hokianga following her own investigations into resident Pākehā-Māori. She had in her possession a family heirloom, a yellowed and spotted nineteenth-century photograph, reputedly of Jacky Marmon, that was never to be loaned or copied. The photo revealed the image of an elderly, weather-beaten Pākehā male with medium-length, black hair, flanked by two taller, light-skinned, young Māori women with long, flowing tresses. His companions were not adorned with the moko kauwae, or women's chin and lip tattoos, but the Pākehā's long, coarse features bore indistinct, regular lines or furrows akin to a faded moko pattern. Overdressed by the photographer in formal nineteenth-century European costume, one woman appeared uncomfortable and perplexed, the other dignified and indifferent. The Pākehā, too, seemed awkward in his dark suit and constricting collar, but his piercing eyes stared directly and chillingly into the camera.

Several Pākehā-Māori were initiated into the Māori priesthood, and Jacky Marmon lived and practised as a tohunga Pākehā among Ngāpuhi at the Bay of Islands and Hokianga between 1820 and 1838. Tohunga Pākehā generally practised as seers, interpreters of dreams and healers, but Marmon accompanied Hongi Hika on Ngāpuhi's first great musket campaign in the unique role of war tohunga. The *Star* editor exaggerates Marmon's tohunga experiences for the entertainment of its readers, while the *Herald* editor casts him as a 'rational' European sceptical of tohunga practices.

In the absence of supporting evidence from European eyewitnesses, some historians have questioned the veracity of Marmon's tohunga claims.[1] Yet it was as much for his tohunga status as his reputation as a cannibal that Marmon was and is remembered by Māori and Pākehā at the Bay and Hokianga. Such a role was also in keeping with his predilection for manipulating Māori social conventions and superstitions to enhance his personal mana and to gain material advantage.

Two later references by contemporary writers to Pākehā-Māori at Hokianga who made religious conversions may well apply to Marmon and to his fugitive companion Jim the Boy. During the early 1830s, the itinerant Jewish trader Joel Polack met a 'European' at the Hokianga who religiously observed Māori rites surrounding the hauhunga ceremony, where the bones of important deceased personages were scraped clean before being interred. This individual 'had resided many years in the country [and] had, in part, effected a great change in his opinions, for he had heard the native priests promise many of the things that had actually come to pass'.[2] In *Old New Zealand*, Maning wrote: 'Indeed, I have in the old times known several pakehas who thought there was "something in it", and two who formally and believingly consulted the oracle and paid a high doucer to the priest.'[3]

Marmon's decision to rejoin Māori in 1820 was calculated rather than spontaneous. Under the tuition of one of the *Himalaya*'s crew, Ben Bolt, 'a man of great knowledge and education, but a slave to drink', Marmon claims to have acquired proficiency in the arts of 'Second Speaking' or ventriloquism, 'the secret of mesmerism and the preparation of herbs and simples'. Marmon's claim is interesting as it coincides with a note in the journal of the Anglican missionary William Yate that 'a seaman skilled in ventriloquism' had made several voyages to New Zealand in this period.[4] Having ignored Kawhitiwai's entreaties and escaped his hapū in 1819, Marmon ensured that he re-entered Māori society with a set of skills that would impress his former chief and hapū and ensure their forgiveness and acceptance.

Fleeing the restrictions of colonial life to live amc
Kerikeri River between 1817 and 1820, Marmon
onerous laws and standards of conformity among
to gain real power among Māori, Marmon needed in a
change himself. Mākutu or magic was part of the social sys.
Māori and helped preserve social order but, more significantly, it was
a weapon that could be employed advantageously by the weak or the
calculating. In late 1820, determined to acquire semi-autonomous
status as a tohunga Pākehā, Marmon committed himself fully to Māori
living which, despite his ulterior motives, led to a major psychological
and spiritual transformation.

I knew now that my position amongst the Maoris would be totally different. I was in possession of secrets they could never dream of, and if I did
not become a great *tohunga* it was my own fault. A Maori never looks
at causes, only effects, and I was convinced that in a short time I should
have acquired an ascendancy over their minds which no *Ariki* (Great
Chief) or *tohunga* could under any circumstances have possessed.

The first man I met ashore was Parson Marsden, who was still pushing on the Mission. He wanted to know what I intended doing. I replied,
'Resume my former life.' He offered me the billet I held before as servant
to the Mission establishment, but I refused it as there was too little freedom attached to the office; but I said until I made all my arrangements I
would work for food and shelter. This was agreed to, and I commenced
my duties again. Parson Kendall had gone home with Hongi, who was
being received with great honour in the Old Country, so that Parsons Hall
and Marsden were all in the Mission station at that time.

Samuel Marsden was indeed resident at the Bay of Islands between
February and December 1820 when Thomas Kendall and Hongi Hika
were visiting England. Known in Parramatta, New South Wales as 'the
flogging parson', Marsden, who held a magistrate's commission and the
power of arrest, was also known to befriend certain convicts and sailors
and he likely encountered Marmon at Rangihoua while preparing to
establish the new Anglican mission on the Kerikeri River. The English
gentleman rover Edward Markham, who visited the Bay and Hokianga
for 10 months during 1834, confirmed Marmon's presence at the Bay

Samuel Marsden
Although a missionary magistrate with powers of arrest, the Anglican leader
Rev. Samuel Marsden often befriended certain convicts and sailors.
E3443/42, Hocken Library, Dunedin.

in 1820. Employing the Pākehā-Māori as his interpreter, Markham's journal entry for 30 June 1834 includes a reference to 'Jacky Marmont, a noted character who had been on the island for fourteen years, and speaks [Maori] better than even the missionaries do'.[5]

Marmon's duties at the Rangihoua mission included collecting mail and supplies from incoming ships. The crew of one vessel, the *Pretty Jane*, however, recognised Marmon as a runaway and planned to seize him and claim a reward from their ship's captain. Under the guise of friendship, these 'jolly dogs' invited their intended victim aboard and plied him with rum. Narrowly escaping their carefully laid trap, Marmon, shocked and aggrieved by this betrayal, resolved to move back to the safety of the Kerikeri River and the kāinga of his former chief Kawhitiwai.

This was the last time I put faith in my own race the *pakehas*. Henceforward I am a Maori in thought, word and deed, since among the savages I have found more true faithfulness, man to man, than in the boasted European. There is no honour in them. Their hearts are as false as a rotten *kumara*. No more of them for me, their very language I abhor, and would not use it were it not to shower my maledictions on them. I resolved what my plan of action would be, to return to Kawitiwai's kainga. As I was in want of food and rest, I proceeded towards my former residence, the iron of man-hatred having entered into my heart, and only desiring a place to lay my head to end my days in seclusion and obscurity.

Marmon's return to the Kerikeri River also coincides with two intriguing entries in the journal of the Rev. John Butler. Then based at the Kerikeri mission station, which was under Hongi Hika's protection, Butler's entry for 7 April 1820 included the note: 'Mr Marsden has sent down [from the Bay], an emancipated convict, the notorious John . . .

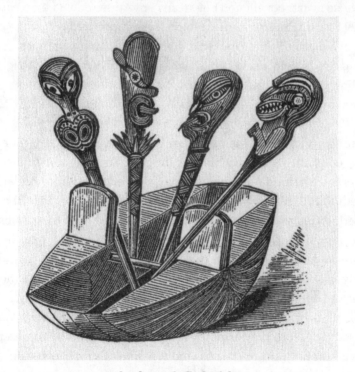

A tohunga's God sticks
Carved niu or divining sticks became part of Marmon's own tools of trade when he practised as a tohunga Pākehā on the Kerikeri and, later, at Hokianga.
R. A. A. *Sherrin and J. H. Wallace*, Early History of New Zealand: From Earliest Times to 1840, *Auckland, 1890, p. 515.*

he has . . . threatened to knock out our eyes and committed fornication among the natives.' This probably meant that the newcomer had taken a Māori wife or wives. Butler later noted how this man later 'fell into a most violent rage, cursing and swearing. . . . He had been out drinking rum with some sailors belonging to the Sarah.'[6] Butler's references to a fugitive with a plausible story, over fond of drinking with visiting ship's crews, prone to violent rages, cursing and threats to knock out the eyes of disapproving missionaries, sounds very much like 'the notorious John Marmon', who admitted using many aliases.[7]

I felt I must be, even more than before, a Maori in habits and actions, even in sympathies and feelings. I had acquired accomplishments of *second speaking* and mesmerism to astonish the natives, and I hoped to be regarded ere long as *the* great *tohunga*, whose advice must be asked, and whose favour conciliated before any enterprise could be engaged in, not only by the small *hapu* with which I was connected but by the entire Ngapuhi *iwi* (tribe). Can you blame me, reader, if I traded on superstition to live in ease, when it is known that half the world lives upon religiously swindling the other half. Give a parson an inch and he will take an ell has been proved before now, and upon this principle I worked the Maori.

Maning's address to the reader in the above quotation typifies the way he constantly inserted himself into the *Star* memoir to attribute motives for Marmon's actions. Maning's determination to undermine the credibility of Marmon's tohunga narrative was motivated by the need to entertain his readers and by envy. Interviewed in 1881 at Auckland by the compiler Dr Thomas Hocken, Maning hinted that he had been initiated into the Māori priesthood, an achievement considered unlikely by some writers.[8] However, recent evidence unearthed by a Maning descendant, the Australian researcher and writer John Nicholson, does confirm Maning's tohunga status. In the *Star*, Maning disguised the depth of Marmon's religious conversion by representing him as a rational culture-crosser who remained European in values and motives.[9] He further devalued Marmon's accomplishments as a white priest by sensationalising and fictionalising much of the *Star*'s tohunga reminiscences.

Day was just breaking when I reached Kawitiwai's settlement, but everything was still except the intermittent growlings of the dogs as they saw me emerge into the clearing. None of the inhabitants saw me arrive, or if they did so, gave no sign of it, thinking perhaps, I might be one of the mysterious *Mohero* (the earliest inhabitants of New Zealand before the Maoris came from Hawaiki), or a *Patupaeareke* (wild man) strayed from his mountain fastness. I sat down on a fallen tree near the landing-place, and began to arrange my line of action to increase my influence in the tribe.

Marmon remained seated until Kawhitiwai and the hapū had assembled. Using ventriloquism, Marmon convinced them that during his absence he had visited his late, beloved wife Tūī, in the spirit realm of Te Rēinga where she told him, 'I must return to you and be your tohunga, that you might not be left without a mediator between you and the gods.'

By 1820, te ao tawhito (the ancient world) was slowly and unevenly shifting on its axis and at the Bay of Islands the Māori were periodically decimated by introduced contagious diseases and occasional defeats in rākau–musket battles.[10] New people, plants and technologies were coming ashore. Young Māori males were returning from whaling voyages with tales of the extraordinary things they had witnessed. People went hungry as crops and pigs were made tapu for the musket trade and musket armies and, at times, the Bay came to resemble one vast armed camp. There was a strange blending of people and cultures. On the beach at Kororareka, one might see a chief in a European suit, wearing a brace of flintlock pistols, a tattooed European in a Māori cloak or a group of returned Māori seamen in sailors' dress.[11] It was during this period of upheaval and adjustment, when Tū, the ancient god of war, seemed supreme, that Marmon was able to establish his place among Ngāpuhi as a tohunga mākutu (wizard) and tohunga matakite (seer).[11]

[T]awitiwai came to me now with great humility, and desired to know what house I would have. I told him I should again resume possession of the house I had previously inhabited, and to get its occupants out as quickly as possible. The *kainga* had received an addition of about seventy men, women, and children since I left, and was, therefore, now a large place.

My former household was completely broken up. My wives had been given to other husbands, and the little patch of cultivation I had had round the house was let go to ruin. However, these evils were easily cured – the one by demanding any female I might fancy, who was un-married, for who would despise an alliance with a *tohunga* and also a *pakeha*; the other, by a little work and the assistance of the women of the tribe (for they were the workers, the men attending only to fishing and to war). Having got these preliminaries arranged, I settled down as I fondly hoped, to a life of ease and quietness.

Unlike Maning and Kimball Bent of Ngāti Ruanui at Taranaki, Marmon never claimed in his reminiscences to have been formally trained as a tohunga. Yet, his enduring reputation as 'the white tohunga' suggests otherwise, and there is some hint of formal training in the introduction to the *Star* memoir where he claims to have been 'initiated' into the great tribal secrets of Māori. Tohunga knowledge was tapu or sacred knowledge. Carefully guarded and taught only to descendants and those considered worthy, it was rarely shared with Pākehā, for they did not seem to have a system of tapu, nor did they regard things tapu to Māori with respect.[12]

Marmon had initially won acceptance and status by conforming to customs and by attending the religious rites and ceremonies of the tribe. He had taken great pains to show respect for the Māori priests and his determination to live like a tangata Māori (a Māori male) and his skills in ventriloquism, mesmerism and healing impressed Māori. Furthermore, Marmon seemed immune to rewharewha (introduced diseases), mākutu (black magic) and, remarkably, was able to transgress tapu without fear of retribution from the Māori atua (evil spirits).

Tohunga were always receptive to, and respectful of, any special knowledge or skills newcomers might possess. During a visit to Hokianga during the 1830s the British Resident James Busby stumbled upon a clearing in the bush where several Negro crewmen from a visiting American whaler were struggling by means of sign language to instruct a group of tohunga 'in some magic rite'.[13] At the Bay tohunga showed the missionaries great tolerance. Holding their rivals in high

Kerikeri Basin

As the new mission station at Kerikeri thrived, some of the missionaries sought to
undermine Māori confidence in Marmon's tohunga Pākehā status.
William Yate, An Account of New Zealand, *London, 1835, p. opp. 172.*

regard they referred to them both as tohunga and atua tāngata (religious
experts and men of supernatural powers).[14]

The missionaries often blamed the degenerate behaviour of their
Pākehā-Māori enemies for obstructing their efforts to Christianise
and civilise Māori, and Marmon, who authenticated Māori culture by
becoming a tohunga Pākehā, was an obvious target for their propaganda.
During the 1830s, Joel Polack and another visitor to the Hokianga,
George Hawke, perhaps having heard of Marmon's tohunga powers,
refer in their writings to a seaman, 'a scoffer at religion', who taught
his skills in ventriloquism to Papahurahia, a young Māori who later
became the renowned Hokianga tohunga and prophet Te Atua Wera.[15]
It is unlikely that Marmon ever shared his skills with Papahurahia.
Missionary sources indicate that conversing with the spirits of the
dead was an ancient and widespread tohunga art and Papahurahia was
descended from a long line of famous wizards and sorceresses.

Tohunga Māori shared their secret knowledge with Marmon
because of the depth of his commitment to tikanga Māori and, like the
missionaries, he, too, was a valuable repository of European knowledge,
powers and skills. Tohunga treated all kinds of sickness, battle wounds
and accidental injury, but by the 1820s the old rites and ceremonies

seemed powerless in the face of introduced diseases and wounds inflicted by flintlock guns. Christian missionaries and Pākehā-Māori, however, were more successful in curing the new illnesses and battle wounds.[16] The Māori priests also chose to share some of their secret knowledge with Marmon because they were attempting solutions that included preparing selected newcomers as new mouthpieces through which the old gods could speak.

The formal spiritual information acquired by Marmon was tapu knowledge, orally transmitted in the whare wānanga or house of learning. Like Kimball Bent, Marmon spent hours daily as a tauira (pupil), attending this lodge of instruction in esoteric Māori lore, and through prodigious feats of memory learned countless karakia or incantations for all occasions.[17] Karakia were recited in a peculiar voice similar to intoning where the words flowed on in a rapid stream, broken only by the need to breathe. Mistakes during delivery could cause the priest great misfortune and even death. Marmon also learned about the merits of different native herbal medicines, minor surgery and mirimiri (massage), to treat illnesses that were clearly due to physical causes, though this type of treatment was limited because of the widespread belief that illness was spiritual in origin.[18]

I have often been asked what were the duties of a tohunga, and how I being a European could perform them. Prayer and medicine were the two great duties of the tohunga; the former comprised in karakias suitable for every emergency; the latter in a knowledge of roots and the preparation of simples. A tohunga must be able to rule the winds, to make them blow from a quarter suitable for fishing; he must restrain the evil spirits; both practise and destroy the power of witchcraft; hold converse with the gods and raise the dead. He must be able to tell the future, and control the powers of nature. These seemingly can be accomplished by any man with a reasonable amount of shrewdness; for very little art is required to dupe a Maori in matters connected with his religion.

The explanation of omens or aituas was another branch of his office. Everything out of the common was supposed to have a meaning, and to be sent as a warning. The flash of pain through the body, a sudden awakening out of sleep, a day-dream, were all matters requiring explanation; and a token of a tohunga's power was to refer them to the operation of some divinity. Therefore, reader, it ought to be no matter of surprise to you to learn that a European became a tohunga when if a reasonably clever conjuror went to Maori land he would at least be worshipped as a new god.

In the *Star*, Maning appeals to the anti-Māori prejudices of his readers by suggesting that the tohunga Māori were little more than clever conjurers just as some later nineteenth-century writers dismissed the tohunga as 'juggling deceivers', 'hypnotists' and ventriloquists. Like Polynesians elsewhere, Māori endowed their gods with human attributes, believing that their tohunga could communicate with the gods while in a trance. The missionary leader Samuel Marsden who attended tohunga performances during the 1820s was reluctant to pass judgement, writing: 'Whether Satan is permitted to practise an oral deception in support of his spiritual domination . . . I cannot tell.' He concluded: 'This is a subject of such a mysterious nature that I cannot make up my mind either to disbelieve what is so universally credited in New Zealand.'[19]

Dr Edward Shortland, a Māori scholar and linguist who made an intensive study of Māori religion during the 1840s, also reserved his judgement, reporting in 1854:

Atua [gods or supernatural beings], sometimes communicate their will to men in dreams, sometimes more directly with them while awake. Their voice however is not like that of mortals; but a mysterious kind of sound, half whistle half whisper. This I have myself heard, having once been honoured by a conference with the spirits of two chiefs who had been several years dead.[20]

In earlier years Maning himself had been impressed by the powers of the tohunga Māori. As a sceptic, he once attended a séance at Hokianga where Papahurahia called up the spirits of deceased Māori. After successfully frustrating Maning's attempts to confound it, the atua (god or supernatural being) departed. Maning reported, 'I began to feel in a way surprising to myself that there was something in the matter. . . . A ventriloquist said I! – or – perhaps the devil!'[21]

In demonstrating the intimacy of their communion with the gods, tohunga also caused men, including Pākehā, to witness wonderful occurrences. One notable incident related throughout tribal New Zealand occurred at Rotorua during the early 1830s, when the missionary Rev. Chapman and Te Unuaho, the great Ngāti Whakaue tohunga, debated before a large Māori audience. Successfully countering Chapman's arguments, Te Unuaho concluded the debate stating, 'Now you shall see the work of a tohunga.' Picking up a large, dead leaf and intoning a karakia, the astonished Chapman watched as the withered brown leaf became fresh and green. Māori eyewitnesses state that 'the missionary fled, leaving the victory to his Maori brother'. Lieutenant-Colonel Gudgeon, who heard the story at Rotorua during the wars of the 1860s, wrote huffily, 'I cannot believe that the orthodox preacher fled, my experience would have led me to believe that [he] would have accused Te Unuaho of dealing with the father of all evil, and by this means converted his defeat in [to] victory.'[22]

The senior Ngāpuhi tohunga Tohitapu
In the *Auckland Star* memoir Frederick Maning inserted a fictitious clash between
Marmon and this senior Ngāpuhi tohunga.
'*Tohitapu, chief and tohunga of the Roroa*', L. M. Rogers (ed.). The Early Journals of Henry
Williams, 1826–40, *Christchurch, 1961.*

Settling into 'a life of ease and quietness' on the Kerikeri River, Marmon recalled, 'the missionaries having formed a station on the Keri-Keri, a little way from our *kainga*, were unceasing in their efforts to prove to the natives I was an imposter, in which, I must add, they entirely failed'. In 1821, the chiefs Hongi Hika and Waikato returned from London and Sydney with missionary Thomas Kendall, bringing with them a huge consignment of muskets and munitions. Having acquired new weapons, Hongi, like any good general, sought opportunities to use them in the field. His desire to restore tribal mana lost through previous defeats was the catalyst that launched the first great Ngāpuhi musket taua and carnage on an unprecedented scale. During a recruiting tour of the Kerikeri River tribes Hongi insisted that the famed tohunga Pākehā Te Manene become his war tohunga and serve him as psychic, barber and healer of wounds.

It was this great chief that again sent me adrift upon the world, for coming up to our *kainga*, of which he was the real head or *Ariki*, Tawitiwai being merely a subordinate *rangatira*, he demanded that I should accompany him on his expedition as his *tohunga*. The fame or *mana* of my supposed intercourse with the gods, and my fabled return from Te Reinga, had reached him, also my skill in hair-cutting and surgery, all falling in within the province of the *tohunga*, and he wished to know whether the statements of the missionaries or my own were correct. For this reason he had come to Keri-keri, as well as to stir up his braves for his great expedition. . . .

A great feast was prepared for him in the *whare-puni* or guest house. Fish, pork and vegetables were present in the utmost profusion, but the dish of honour was a roasted *cookey* or female slave, with which to inspire the warriors with courage. This was my first experience of human flesh, and as served up by the Maori cooks was very passable. When chopped up with kumeras and potatoes, it resembles a rather fatty stew. I can assure my readers, whose noses I can perceive are wrinkling with disgust, that when you have to do a thing the best way is to do it is with seeming satisfaction. I was regarded as a dauntless *tohunga* and a *pakeha* to be retained in special honour, because I disdained not the most refined dish a Maori warrior can set before his guest.

Some tohunga were highly competitive, protective of their powers and reputations and intolerant of strangers and upstarts. Kimball Bent recalled how, as a healing tohunga, he escaped these challenges but noted how the Hauhau warrior prophet Titokowaru destroyed the credibility and mana of rival tohunga by placing a basket of potatoes on their heads. This act destroyed the tapu of his rivals, but no tohunga dared to attempt the same trick with Titokowaru.[23] During his second sojourn at the Bay, Marmon faced several challenges by rivals who sought to destroy his reputation, take his muskets and thereby diminish the mana of Kawhitiwai and Te Hikutu. Jacky was expected to maintain his own, and his chief's, mana by asserting his rights and exercising his powers to see off these challengers.

With [Hongi], there was a chief of the Koroa named Tohitapu, a great *tohunga*, whose power of *maketu* or witchcraft exceeded that of any other priest in New Zealand. He had come, as he hoped to humble the pride of the Ngapuhi tohunga, and when Hongi, after the feast, desired to consult with the gods about his expedition . . . he seated himself beside me with a satirical smile, as if to say, '*What a fool you will make of yourself.*' This rather nettled me, and I determined, if possible, to surpass all former efforts at *second-speaking*.

The natives seated themselves in a half-circle round me. Hongi being directly opposite to me, with Tawitiwai by his side. But I was determined to deviate entirely from the usual Maori method of consulting the gods or the dead, which Ben Bolt calls *evocation*, and to proceed according to a plan of my own. Therefore, I lit a small fire before me of *rata* stems, half withered flax, dried *kahikatea*, all of them very smoky materials, into which I threw at intervals pieces of kauri gum to diffuse an odour throughout the house.

Every eye was fixed on me, a dead silence prevailed; I wrapped myself in my pekerangi (blanket), drawing it over my head and leaving only my mouth and nose exposed. I then commenced to slowly rock myself to-and-fro, crying in a low, wailing tone upon the several deities in the Maori calendar, 'Oh! *Tiki*, maker of man, be present to help us. Oh! *Rehua*, god of the rainbow, be present to help us. Oh! Tawiri-matea, father of winds, be present to help us. Oh! Maui, god of war, be present to help us.

B.BURNS.

A NEW ZEALAND CHIEF.

The Pākehā-Māori Barnet Burns

Like Burns of Ngāti Kahungunu, Marmon gradually discarded his mix of Western and indigenous dress for full Māori costume.

Wood engraving 120 x 150 mm, 'B. Burns. A New Zealand Chief', London, R. & D. Read, 1844, PUBL-0074-26, Alexander Turnbull Library.

During séances, particularly when communication was desired with a deceased relative, tohunga from their trance relayed, as mediums, the voices of the deceased in the kind of whistling sepulchral tone described by Shortland and believed by Māori to be the natural tone of the voice of the dead. Consequently, whistling was considered to be offensive to the gods and, in old New Zealand, cheerful Pākehā were sometimes surprised to find themselves admonished by their hosts.[24] In this state of trance, some tohunga exhibited furious raging, their body and limbs convulsing, eyes protruding, foaming at the mouth, and giving utterances in strange tongues. On coming to, they would relate the message, sometimes in the guise of a song.[25]

Again there was a dead silence in the guest-house, broken only by a low, whistling sound on the roof, betokening the presence of spirits. 'Whom wish you, oh! Ngapuhis, to return unto you from Te Reinga? Whom wish you to come to open the book of the future?' Tohitapu began to look grave when he heard the audible presence of the spirits, and when I fearlessly vaunted my power to call up whomsoever they wished. Hongi immediately enquired if the Atua or spirit of his ancestor, Ruarangi, could be summoned. I replied it would, and straightaway a scratching noise was heard, gradually increasing til heard by all. Then, in the same low, whistling tone, the question was asked, 'What do you call me for?' Hongi leaped to his feet, exclaiming, 'It is the voice of Ruarangi.'

To the request to know if the expedition . . . would prove successful, the spirit replied, 'It will if Hongi put faith in no man but himself.' To his question if he should live long, the answer was, 'Beware of the fatal tree of Whangaroa.' After this, conceiving that the performance had lasted long enough, and fearing further questioning which might not be so conveniently to evade, I feigned to be possessed of the god Maui and passed into strong convulsions, uttering meantime incoherent sentences about the expedition.

Among tohunga, certain elements were essential to place their subject into a hypnotic trance, particularly force of will which dominated the subject, compelling their eyes to become fixated on the eyes of the mesmerist. Marmon initially retained his belief in the cultural and racial superiority of Europeans which must have greatly assisted him in successfully staring down his opponents, or 'overcoming [their] spirit through the strength of mine', before mesmerising them and destroying the power of their spirit or mana.[26]

Hongi, though awe stricken, seemed incredulous. Accordingly I determined to mesmerize Tohitapu as a convincing proof of my divine mission. Rising suddenly, I approached my patient, gazing steadfastly into the pupils of his eye . . . whilst I made the passes. In a few seconds I had triumphed. I showed my power over Tohitapu, caused him to dance, to sing, to weep, as I chose, finally freeing him from the influence, when every mind in the audience regarded me as the very incarnation of the *Taipo* . . . [Tohitapu] had thought to put me to shame before the *hapu*, but instead I had completely overcome his *atua* (spirit) by the strength of mine. Although he was a most unforgiving, hot-tempered man, ready to take offence upon the slightest provocation, he seemed to consider it useless to display any of it towards me, since I had acquired such power over him. And Tawitiwai, who before had been impressed with a salutary dreads of me, now absolutely begged Hongi to take me from the *kainga* and grant him a *tohunga* of less power. . . . After some conversation I agreed to go with Hongi on his expedition, if the omen of the tieke (a little bird) should be favourable, and on the condition that I should not fight unless I chose.

Maning's inclusion of Tohitapu to this séance was another device intended to undermine the credibility of Marmon's tohunga reminiscences. While Marmon clashed with and overcame challenges by lower-ranked priests, it is unlikely that he ever destroyed the mana of Tohitapu. A member of the Roroa hapū, Tohitapu was one of Ngāpuhi's most senior tohunga, famed for his mākutu or bewitching powers and regarded as one of the most ferocious fighting rangatira of his day. References to this tohunga in missionary writings consistently represent him as a man of great intelligence, tolerance and undiminished mana before his death in 1830.[27] Nevertheless, Marmon's descriptions of these contests have value for they shed light on his performances as a seer and medium.

The contests between Marmon and his rivals may have been grounded in evolutionary psychology and the primitive biology of dominance and submission where some people are able to dominate others by staring fixedly at them. Marmon's bright blue eyes are a genetic trait still occasionally evident among his Māori descendants. Perhaps, like Lawrence and the Bedouin, Marmon was advantaged by his blue eyes and fair skin which unnerved his Māori rivals when they were suddenly reminded of blue sky seen through the sockets of a bleached skull.[28] Once submissive, his subject was taken into a deep hypnotic trance by continued fixation of the eyes, by a combination of rhythmic rocking and the chanting of karakia.[29]

Rather than causing the victim 'to dance', however, tohunga mesmerism seems to have more often induced catalepsy or paralysis of the body. In this condition, the patient sang or shouted while unconscious. At this point the patient could be humiliated, for the muscular rigidity allowed the limbs to remain in whatever position the tohunga chose to place them, though the condition generally passed off within a few minutes.[30] Sometimes the patient simply lay paralysed and, with no discernible breathing, appeared to the audience to be dead. Perhaps by the timely uttering of appropriate karakia as the catalepsy passed off, some tohunga appeared capable of bringing the dead to life.

My reputation as a *tohunga* was now fairly established, and I could afford now to increase my influence by marrying a few more wives. A number of wives was a very usual custom among the Maoris, and the chiefs and *tohungas* were estimated in a social sense by the number and dignity of their wives. The ladies were not treated like soul-less animals as in many more civilised lands, but they were allowed as much freedom and licence as the men. A chief by uniting himself to a goodly number of wives, if they were of rank, by this means greatly extended his hospitality, for each lady dwelt on her own land, which was cultivated by her slaves, and thus she was able to receive her husband and his friends with fitting honour when they came to see her, and to entertain them as became her station. There is a good Maori proverb regarding this, – 'a man with many wives never wants food, but with only one can never receive his friends according to their rank'. It was from this idea that I set about making alliances with the most influential ladies in the *kainga*, and there was little wooing required, for it was a matter of eager desire amongst the females to be united with a *tohunga* of so great a *mana.*

Marmon's tohunga reminiscences take the reader into the world of Māori myths, lore, social rituals and sacred ceremonies and while grossly embellished by Maning, they cannot be dismissed lightly. Steeped in maritime superstitions and the folklore of old Ireland, Marmon's own boundaries between the natural and the supernatural were never sharply defined. Perhaps like some of his Irish forebears, he, too, possessed the gift of second sight or matakite as it was known to Māori. Many nineteenth-century Irish and Māori shared similar beliefs: mana and luck were tangible commodities, breath symbolised life and 'the liquid of the soul', a bird flying into a house was a portent of death, defamation or cursing could cause sickness or death, and certain people had the gift of seeing and communicating with spirits.[31]

While deliberately seeking the more spontaneous and instinctual life of Māori in the pursuit of autonomy, Marmon underwent a complete psychological and spiritual transformation. Having fully absorbed the values and beliefs of Māori culture, he recalled distinctive Pākehā-Māori modes of experiencing, thinking, feeling, valuing and perceiving himself in the Māori world.

I was now to all intents and purposes a Maori. I discarded the European shirt and trousers for the more comfortable *kartaka* or blanket; I relinquished European cooked meats and acquired, not without difficulty, I confess, the fat oily fare of the natives, even to the length of rotten wheat, putrid whale, and raw tainted pork. I could subsist on raw eel and fern-root, the former being considered a dainty kinaki (relish) to the latter, though almost certain to bring on scrofula. I lost the use of knives and forks, preferring the utensils nature has granted us, and I did not complain more than the others during the grumbling months when our sole food was shell-fish and *nikau* pith.

Not long after marriage I found that I must exercise a little wholesome discipline with my spouses or else I would be a mere nothing in my own house. One of them had cherished a fondness for a young chief called Hakanui, before her marriage, and after it kept the tender regard up, so that I occupied but a second place in her affections. This might have

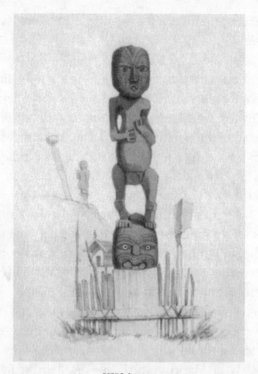

Wāhi tapu
This sacred site contained a tiki image and an elevated box for holding the bones of
a deceased child.
George French Angas, 1822–1886, 'Shows five different Maori tombs or mausolea' Hand-coloured
lithograph tinted 440 x 310 mm. From: The New Zealanders Illustrated *by G. F. Angas, London,*
1847, Plate 50, PUBL-0014-50, Alexander Turnbull Library.

been overlooked, but when I was convinced that the matter went further
and that her character was not spotless, it was time for man's self regard
to take arms and reassert itself. What did you do? I hear the gentle reader
ask; give her a writing of divorcement, or send her back, in disgrace, to
her friends? No such thing. I simply provided myself with a musket and
ammunition, summoned her, told her of her fault, and quietly blew her
brains out! I never found my wife unfaithful again, and it raised my *mana*
(reputation) vastly in the tribe. I was regarded as a man who would stand
no humbug and who must be implicitly obeyed. Take my advice, reader,
and when you have to act, act with promptitude and courage.

    While avoiding direct contact with Europeans, Marmon nevertheless
obtained several muskets, and powder canisters from the Pākehā-

Māori traders. As the Bay peoples prepared for Hongi's great campaign against the Ngāti Paoa and Ngāti Maru tribes, Jacky was subject to further challenges by a tohunga and an unidentified rangatira desperate to obtain muskets. In *Old New Zealand*, Maning noted the enormous stresses individual toa and entire hapū experienced in attempting to accumulate muskets for military campaigns. The exchange rate, he says, was typically one musket for a ton of flax, and a further half ton for powder and ammunition.

In consequence as every man in a native hapu, of say a hundred men, was absolutely forced on pain of death to procure a musket and ammunition at any cost . . . the effect was that this small hapu or clan had to manufacture . . . in the shortest possible time, one hundred tons of flax, scraped by hand with shell bit by bit.[32]

Around this time Marmon received a challenge from a rival tohunga.

It was at this time that I had a visit from a rival *tohunga*, Matoki of Urikipana, who came to have a *korero* with the man who had been to the fabled Te Reinga, and could evoke at will the spirits from thence. He was by no means a pleasant specimen of a man. Short, squat and deformed through an accident to his spine, he seemed fit for no work of any hardship; whilst his leering eyes, his distorted mouth and drawn cheeks, rendered more hideous by very intricate tattooing, made him as near an approach to the devil as it ever has been my fortune to see. His nature was cruel, crafty and suspicious, capable of any treachery to gain an object.

Although his avowed object was to visit the man who could raise the dead, his real one was to do a little swindling if he could possibly manage it. He could not take me in with his flax and his pigs; I saw through the snare at once; but when I was away at Tawitiwai's *whare* on business, he entered mine and carried away the musket I was cleaning for the expedition. Probably I would never have found out who the thief was had he not dropped one of the *kiwi* feathers from his cloak by which I was able to identify him. I did not go to him and upbraid him, demanding back my property. Nothing so undignified would accord with Maori etiquette. I simply light a fire without my *whare*, and prepared to offer up some of the incantations, as well as to practise the *maketu* or witchcraft.

Gradually a crowd collect anxious to see the ceremony. Asked what I was engaged in, I reply, 'Bewitching Matoki for stealing a gun of mine.' The news flies to the culprit at once. He rushes in a frantic state of dread towards me, vehemently denying all knowledge of my musket. I shake my head contemptuously, and proceed in silence. Then I begin the curses or *tuktukus*, which, as they become deeper, and more terrible, begin to bring out a strong perspiration on the thief. He trembles with apprehension, yet cannot bring himself to give up the musket.

I commence now to bewitch him with mesmerism. I fix my eye steadfastly on his, move my arms slowly through the passes. Ah, no more is needed – Matoki has fallen on his face and is entreating me to take the spell off him and he would restore the musket, which he asserts, was only taken to shoot some birds. I consent on the musket being brought to me, and after some ceremony, in which I thoroughly frightened the unfortunate *tohunga* by letting him hear supposed threats from the gods should he repeat his offence – threats that seemed to come from within a gigantic *kauri* tree – I released him, and let him go. He departed thoroughly scared, and ever after asserted that I was no human *tohunga*, but an incarnate devil.

Māori believed that a tohunga could bestow a curse on them with a malevolent look or stare (known in many cultures as the evil eye) that caused misfortune, wasting illness and eventually death. Kimball Bent believed that mākutu or death cursing was effected by a combination of three factors: projection of the will force, the malignant exercise of hypnotic influence and sheer imagination and fright on the part of the person who had been subject to mākutu.[33] Confronted with the tohunga Pākehā's formidable 'witchcraft', a combination of sacerdotal fire, the evil eye and an impressive display of ventriloquism, Matoki was defeated and humiliated. As Marmon's reputation grew, he began receiving generous payments for his services as seer, medium and healer and he prospered.

Riches, according to Maori estimate, were plentiful with me. I had my own eel-weir on the Kerikeri, my own *mahinga* (cultivation) round my *whare*, my own pigs in the bush. I had now many muskets in store that I used in the flax barter, besides several tons of flax to be disposed of when a trader should come up. I had several things *tapued* to me by devotion of the tribe, such as canoes, *meres*, fishing-nets, etc; etc; all of which were regarded by the natives as constituting wealth. These things were rendered *tapu* by making it red.

When a person died in a house, it was marked with red *kura* (ochre), shut up, and no one ever entered it again; if a chief wished to preserve a tree, a grove, a canoe, nay even a river, from use, he had only to tie a piece of red cloth round a post and it would be safe for all time. The *tapu*, though troublesome in many cases, and extremely intricate in its actions and restrictions, yet was of the utmost service in early times in preserving law and order, and giving some security to possession when the hand of lawlessness would have broken through everything.

Not long before joining Hongi on his 1821 campaign Marmon had to contend with a further challenge from an unidentified rangatira who visited Kerikeri, hoping to intimidate Marmon and seize his hard-earned cache of muskets and munitions.

Yet, if it is pleasant to have the consciousness that one is a wealthy man . . . yet it has its troubles also . . . some men imagine that another has wealth only to share it with them. Yet this was the case with a . . . *rangatira* amongst the Ngapuhis who came to Kerikeri and coolly demanded by the law of *tapu* . . . a half of the wealth I had laboriously collected. Of course I promptly told him to go to the devil (in English, reader, which he did not understand), remarking, in his own tongue, that he must grow a little wiser before he could make such a claim, whereupon he became most violent, began to storm and stamp, and to shower no end of threats on my devoted head.

Then he as suddenly reduced the dimensions of his demand to one musket, which he said he must and would have. I returned that when he brought me a ton of flax he should have the musket. He cried that he would not defile his fingers by handling the *pipi* shell, and unless his request was complied with *maketu* me so that I would not be alive in a fortnight. I told him to do his worst, and went inside my *whare* to finish my smoke. Even into this sacred retreat he penetrated with his clamour, until worn out and wearied by his row I fixed my eyes on him and mes-merised him. In an instant he was quiet, and for the next half-hour was punished by making a precious fool of himself before the crowd who were assembled at the entrance. I had no further trouble with him either. When he came out of his mesmerism he was as quiet as a lamb, and looked twice as foolish.

The psychological transformation made by some fully assimilated Pākehā-Māori also included a belief in the power of the tohunga mākutu or tohunga whaiwhaia (wizard) to fatally bewitch them. During the 1830s, two trader Pākehā-Māori, an Englishman named Taylor at the Bay of Plenty and a Hicks Bay flax trader known to Māori as Katete, were reported to have died after being subject to mākutu.[34] The tohunga Pākehā Kimball Bent told the journalist James Cowan that tohunga Māori possessed 'branches of knowledge that were unknown to the Pākehā and undoubtedly, one of the hidden powers was the ability to exercise a mysterious influence over people at a distance, an influence so great as to cause death'.[35]

Marmon's contemporary, the missionary Thomas Kendall, lived a completely Māori existence for a time, abandoning not only his European identity but his Anglican faith. Kendall later wrote that the 'apparent sublimity' of Māori religious ideas had almost turned him 'from a Christian into a savage'.[36] Marmon, a Catholic, may also have realised that the European world, while vastly superior in technology, was no more wealthy in spiritual concepts than the Māori world. For both men, the psychological transformation from European to Māori involved attaining knowledge of Māori cosmological beliefs and religious practices. Though their protection against Māori 'superstitions' had originally been their disbelief, Marmon underwent a spiritual re-adaptation that included a belief in the psychic mana of the Māori tohunga, for he fell prey to a powerful mākutu placed on him by one or more of his former challengers.

It was at this time that a strange melancholy seized upon me, threatening to drive me to take away my own life. Many a time I had the musket loaded to do the fatal deed, yet had not the courage to pull the trigger. What my low-spiritedness proceeded from I could not determine. All my affairs were going on well, yet I felt as if some calamity were hanging over me, and I was helplessly waiting for it to fall. I seemed to have no hope of ever enjoying happiness again. A wild desire seized me to see Sydney once more and . . . even had not pride of station restrained me I should have sent for the missionaries to talk with me. Yet how would it look for the great Ngapuhi *tohunga* to be consorting with parsons? The thing would never do, and accordingly, I had to bear my burden alone.

Not only was I troubled in mind, but I began to lose in body. I lost flesh daily. I became thin as a scarecrow, with no inclination either to eat or sleep, but only to brood over my own fancied troubles. I became so weak that I could not accompany Hongi on his expedition against the Ngatipous. I knew some envious ones with hearts as hard as stone have said that my illness was only feigned to escape going upon the journey, but I feel convinced the gentle reader, fully aware of my proven courage, will treat such a report as it deserves, with sovereign contempt.

When Hongi returned [from two local expeditions] he found me almost restored to health. My melancholy had left me, and I was ready to join him in the expedition he was planning against Hinaki of the Thames, whom he alleged to have eaten some Ngapuhis. There was of course, a grand feast of . . . captives, extending over many days. No other meat was

Scene at Hokianga
In this hauhunga or bone-scraping ceremony, six skeletons lie against the fence covered in red cloth. Part of the cloth has been pushed through the eye sockets by the tohunga in the headdress to give the deceased 'eyes of fire'.
Watercolour by John Webster. MAN 110, Auckland Public Library.

permitted to be brought within the settlement. Hongi's orders were that his warriors eat only human flesh that they might inherit the courage of those they devoured.

I also attained at this time to considerable proficiency in making bread from the *aruhe*, or the *hinau*, or finally from the *pua* or light dust on the *raupo* or New Zealand bulrush . . . Hongi would *tapu* a whole batch for his own use, so fond was he of it, to add a *konaki* or relish, to his cannibal repast. Also as a fisher I gained celebrity, my success being attributed to the power of the incantations I was supposed to use. All tried to get near me, so as, if possible, to come within the circle of my spell, which was supposed to extend a few yards around my *mangio kopapa* or canoe. To keep up the idea I was always particular in observing the religious rites peculiar to angling. I always disengaged from the hook 'the *mataika*', or first fish caught, placed in its mouth a hair plucked from my head, and repeated over it an incantation as I returned it to the water, directed it to drive its companions and relations towards my hook.

Marmon did not enjoy his secluded existence on the Kerikeri for long. Although just six London-based whaling ships were reported in New Zealand waters in 1814, 10 visited the Bay during 1820 and 14 the following year.[37] The consequence was an explosive growth in the number of firearms among Ngāpuhi from an estimated 500 muskets in 1820 to several thousand by 1822 (though some 500 of these had been imported from Sydney by Hongi Hika). The inflow of guns was accompanied by increasing numbers of ships' deserters who settled among the coastal tribes and became Pākehā-Māori. On the Kerikeri, Marmon encountered one of these runaways, Phillip (Hans) Tapsell, whom he had first met aboard the whaler *Catherine* in 1815.[38]

That night I was surprised, when lying in my house smoking, to see a European come into the settlement, and under the clear light of the moon make straight for my house. All sorts of dangers came to my mind, but these were set at rest by him asking, in broken Maori, when I opened the door, if I would grant him a night's lodging, as he had lost his way. He seemed surprised when I answered him in English, and still more so when he found out I also was a European. He told me his name was Tom Tapsell, and that he had deserted from a ship in the Bay. Little did I think that in after years I was to know him so intimately. I made him as comfortable as I could for the night, and in the morning he preceded on his journey to Whangaroa.

Marmon was increasingly held in high regard by Hongi and Ngāpuhi because of his supernatural connections with gods, taniwha and other familiar spirits and, later, the way he came to excel in prophecy and healing. Apart from challenges by rival tohunga and the covetous rangatira he seems to have been treated with great consideration by Hongi and his fellow rangatira, not so much from love, but from the very natural dread of his growing power. Having successfully trialled his newly imported guns in his two brief, local wars beyond the Bay, Hongi and his musketeers passed through Kawhitiwai's village on their return to the Bay of Islands, during which a great honour was bestowed on the tohunga Pākehā.

Whilst Hongi and his band were here I was called upon as *tohunga* to perform a most sacred and solemn duty, one invested by the Maoris with the greatest importance. This was the general hair cutting of the tribe, which could only be done by one made *tapu* for the purpose, or else by a tohunga. Many spells were repeated during the operation to avert thunder and lightning supposed to be occasioned by it, and I was not permitted to eat or to engage in any other occupation it will be seen that progress could not be very rapid, and that a man would feel precious hungry long before he was done. The first lock of hair clipped off was cast into the fire as an offering, accompanied by a potent *karakia* beginning 'Oe he pikanga he Rakenga'.

Marmon will not have found his subsequent duties as a war tohunga radically different from similar roles performed by the Catholic priests of his former faith. He blessed the warriors before battle and offered prayers on behalf of those setting forth. He blessed weapons prior to battle as a priest might bless regimental banners before a campaign and occasionally took part in the fighting. He had duties and karakia to perform for the wounded and dying as did the priests and, in the aftermath of battle, removed tapu from the victorious toa during the ceremony of whakanoa, the equivalent to a Western thanksgiving service for victory.

Scarcely were the bands of warriors rested when Hongi was impatient to be on the move again to see the effect his fire-arms would have on presumptuous Ngatipaoas who had dared eat one of his tribe. Therefore, having tangied abundantly over those who had fallen in the preceding campaign, we prepared to go to the Thames. Alas poor Hinaki, your doom is sealed.

CHAPTER FOUR

War tohunga, 1821

At dawn on a fine September morning in the year 1821, a flotilla of 60 war canoes propelled by chanting warriors swept out of Whangārei harbour and turned south, bound for the Hauraki Gulf. Between 50 and 70 feet in length, the prows, sides and tall stern posts of the waka were handsomely carved, painted red or black and ornamented for war with a profusion of feathers. Incorporated into the figureheads at the prows were grotesquely carved human heads with eyes of mother of pearl and protruding tongues in contempt and defiance of the enemy. The leading waka, powered by 80 paddlers and carrying the distinctive armour-clad figure of Hongi Hika, was most tastefully ornamented and richly carved. Nearby, crouching motionless on a thwart, cloaked in a fine flax mat and chanting karakia, was the white tohunga Jacky Marmon.

The six decades that Marmon lived among Ngāpuhi encompassed the turbulent years of the intertribal Musket Wars (1818–39). A time when tribal New Zealand was wracked by ferocious gun warfare, the numerous raids, battles and sieges are estimated to have killed between 20,000 and 30,000 Māori. Achieving an early and decisive lead in the intertribal race for flintlock guns, Ngāpuhi under Hongi Hika launched four devastating amphibious expeditions against tribes armed rākau

Māori (traditionally): Ngāti Paoa and Ngāti Maru (1821), Waikato (1822), Arawa (1823) and Ngāti Whātua in 1825.[1] Marmon participated in the first and last of these campaigns.

Māori military expeditions (taua) of 2000 warriors were not uncommon in the days of traditional Māori warfare, but a remarkable feature of the Musket Wars was the evolution of predatory armies, numbering between 3000 and 4000 warriors armed with flintlock guns. These formidable battle groups campaigned over longer distances and for longer periods than many previously recorded expeditions yet their movements, logistical arrangements and battle tactics have remained something of a mystery. Anglican missionaries at the Bay of Islands recorded the dramatic departure and return of several great Ngāpuhi musket taua but Marmon's *Star* reminiscences provide inside accounts of Hongi's 1821 and 1825 amphibious campaigns. They also cast light on the operations of Hongi's composite battle groups within enemy territories and the phases of two of the most fiercely contested and costly intertribal battles fought in New Zealand.

The ethnographer George Graham and biographer Charles Davis recorded several stories peripheral to Hongi's 1821 expedition.[2] Eyewitness accounts were also provided by Wharepoaka of Ngāpuhi and by Hongi himself.[3] In 1824, Tuai, another of Hongi's generals, described several key events in the campaign to Rene Lesson, ship's surgeon aboard the French frigate *La Coquille*.[4] Hoane Nahe of Ngāti Maru related a brief tribal account of the campaign to the ethnographer S. Percy Smith in the late nineteenth century.[5] By combining these accounts with Marmon's reminiscences and modern historical research, the scale and significance of this epic campaign can be recreated along with insights into Marmon's role as a warrior priest and the motivations and tactics of the predatory raider Hongi Hika.

According to Marmon, 'Hongi's ambition was to carry to the Thames the finest army ever seen in New Zealand', and witnessing the departure of the first contingent from the Bay on September 1821, the Anglican missionaries also recognised that Māori warfare in New Zealand had entered a new era.

There has never been anything like such an arrangement in New Zealand before. Tuai, Titore and all their friends are in the general onset, Shungee

[Hongi] and Waikato have returned from England with a great quantity of guns, swords, powder, balls, daggers etc etc. and thus they are fully armed to murder, kill and destroy without reserve, which is the highest pitch of glory to a savage in New Zealand.[6]

Determined to enhance his mana tangata (personal reputation), Marmon, now aged 23, prepared for war.

There were many arrangements also to be made before I went on the expedition with Hongi . . . I had to plan and make fitting attire for the occasion, so that the *tohunga* of so great a tribe as Ngapuhi might

Hongi Hika and Waikato
The return of these Ngāpuhi chiefs from London and Sydney with a large consignment of guns and munitions precipitated the great campaign to Hauraki and Thames in 1821.
Hongi Hika and Waikato, drawn in London at the time of their visit with Kendall in 1820, Hocken Library, Dunedin.

not shame his friends. Also, my weapons had to be got into order; my muskets, being mostly old and rusty, had to be scoured and repaired, my *mere* had to be polished and sharpened; my *taiaha* or wooden sword brought to an edge. Besides it was the season for planting the *kumara* and the *taro*, therefore I was anxious to get these completed before our departure took place.

Ngāpuhi Pākehā-Māori like Marmon and John Rutherford were trained to fight rākau Māori by their chiefs with the mere pounamu, a short thrusting weapon of jade, and the taiaha, a long, two-handed striking and stabbing weapon of hardwood. Lacking the trained Māori warrior's agility and quickness of hand and eye, Marmon established his reputation as a Pākehā toa (white warrior) by using European firearms in battle, fearing that his use of native weapons might 'injure my reputation, and have the taunt thrown in my teeth that I had *nga ringa ringa mahi kai*, the hands of a husbandman'. Trained by his father in the use of firearms from the age of six, it was Marmon's musket and marksmanship that ensured his inclusion in Hongi's elite band of armed retainers. During the grand rākau–musket battles, he and a scattering of fighting Pākehā-Māori, including Rutherford and James Burns, joined the ranks of the kai paura (powder eaters), an emerging warrior elite distinguished by their possession of, and proficiency with, the pū or flintlock musket.

Several visitors to the Bay of Islands during the early 1820s noted the presence of European adventurers like Marmon who accompanied their tribes to war.[7] As the tribes acquired flintlock arsenals and attacked their neighbours to settle old scores, the need for manpower and firepower escalated. Throughout tribal New Zealand Pākehā-Māori were obliged by kinship group obligations and the desperate nature of intertribal battles to join the ranks of musket armies as tribal fighting men. The missionary Richard Davis was to lament: 'supplied with firearms and ammunitions [they] fight army to army, and in some cases it is feared, white men join them'.[8]

Valued for their practical skills, men like Marmon were also in demand as gunsmiths, bullet casters and cartridge makers, for the first musket armies required a variety of miscellaneous military paraphernalia that were seen to include casks of gunpowder, cartridge belts and boxes, casks of prepared cartridges, spare flints, tools for the muskets, spare parts for the gunlocks, spare gunlocks, casks of lead bullets, sheets of lead and moulds for bullet making.[9]

I was ready to join him [Hongi] in the grand expedition he was planning against Hinaki of the Thames, whom he alleged to have killed and eaten some Ngapuhis. Of course, Hongi only wished an excuse for war, and although Hinaki when on board the vessel coming, [from Sydney] to New Zealand after spending some time with him at Parson Marsden's used every effort to dissuade him from attacking an innocent man . . . all the satisfaction he received was a remark from Hongi, 'Make haste to your *kainga*, fortify your *pah* as best you can for I shall attack you.'

Marmon vividly recalled the departure of Hongi's own division from Rangihoua. During the siege of the twin pā of Mokoia-Mauinaina near modern-day Panmure, Auckland, he participated in the largest and bloodiest intertribal battle of the Musket Wars. Marmon joined Hongi's taua when it departed the Bay on 5 September 1821. One of several war tohunga performing ceremonial duties for this chief, Marmon, always the opportunist, determined to obtain as much loot as possible without risking his life unnecessarily.

[A]midst furious war dances, shouts and firing of muskets, the fleet bore out . . . having been confirmed in their confidence of victory by consulting the gods through me. There was a chance here of getting spoils and wealth, and although I did not intend to fight, yet I intended always to be present at the division of the booty.
    Under this Maori Napoleon, thoroughly disciplined and equipped in every way, there sailed in great war canoes, four thousand warriors, of whom, one thousand were armed with muskets. Hongi had besides numerous *tohungas* and camp followers to swell the train.

The 'thoroughly disciplined' warrior force admired by Marmon was the outcome of Hongi's relentless training of the Ngāpuhi musketeers and his fusing of European tactics he had studied in England with familiar Māori ones. Hongi understood that fighting independently with slow-loading muskets the toa were little more than a rabble, likely to

War canoe, Bay of Islands

As Hongi's only white tohunga Marmon was given a place aboard the great war
canoe (waka taua) of his patron during the campaign against Ngāti Paoa and Ngāti
Maru in 1821.

*Louis-Auguste de Sainson, War Canoe, c. 1827. Sketch. Reproduced from an engraving in Dumont
D'Urville's* Voyage Pittoresque Autour du Monde, *1839, vol. 2, p. opp. 366. Auckland Museum
and Institute.*

cause significant casualties among their own side and, after their initial
volley, to break and run when charged by their enemies. Only when
the warriors were drawn up into organised tactical units where each
man supported his comrade could Ngāpuhi deliver controlled volley
fire and achieve victory. Thereafter, in battle, Hongi was dependent
on the loyalty and discipline of an elite force of trained musketeers,
comprising men of the Ngāi Tawake, Ngāti Tuatahi, Ngāti Rahiri and
Ngāti Rehia hapū to which he was closely related and to which he gifted
most of his imported guns.

The missionaries Samuel Butler and Samuel Leigh calculated the
departing taua at between 2000 and 3000 toa armed with 1000 guns.[10]
Marmon confirmed the 1000 muskets, but his recollection of 4000
toa was founded on the taua's final numbers. Believing they had just
cause (take), for attacking Ngāti Paoa and Ngāti Maru, the Ngāpuhi
army left the Bay of Islands for the general rendezvous at Whangārei
in several divisions under their own chiefs but were later reinforced
by a large, unidentified contingent possibly from either Whangaroa
or Hokianga harbours or both. According to Marsden, 60 war canoes
eventually departed the Bay, and with most waka taua carrying

between 50 and 60 men, Marmon's final estimate of 4000 toa is the more reliable.[11]

A vast fleet we were as we passed Pataua, on the coast near Whangarei, where Hongi was strongly inclined to land and take *utu* from the Ngatiwhatua for their murder of [the Ngāpuhi chief] Te Raharaha and we were increased [in numbers] as we approached Mahurangi and Whangaparaoa.

Voyaging slowly southwards the waka taua stopped periodically, to await more settled sea conditions, to gather supplies and for military exercises. Marmon continued to manipulate Māori superstitions to maintain their belief in his powers.

I was in daily request by the chiefs in Hongi's army to give them exhibitions of second speaking and mesmerism, but I declared that I would not profane holy things by performing them to satisfy idle curiosity. There was policy in this; for as familiarity breeds contempt so constant association with the mysteries of the unseen world would only lessen the estimation in which it was held.

On Whangaparāoa Peninsula, Hongi repeatedly put his musketeers, the expedition's shock troops, through their drills, before staging military exercises that co-ordinated the movements of the entire army. By combining coercion with the distribution of muskets and munitions in lavish gift-giving ceremonies, Hongi had persuaded the hapū chiefs to unanimously accept his leadership in battle. Marmon, recognising in Hongi a fellow schemer who possessed a similar flair for bending others to his will, was clearly impressed by the chief's abilities. 'His men were thoroughly under his control now, and he could move and work them as easily as one could a machine . . . had he been a white man he might have eclipsed Buonaparte himself in the rapidity and originality of his tactics.'

At the Weiti (Wade) River south of Whangaparāoa, the taua surprised and captured a number of Ngāti Whātua. Before the final voyage into Ngāti Paoa territory the musketeers practised firing at moving targets, freeing their prisoners to run across open ground. The less fleet of foot and the unlucky became meat for the ovens.[12]

I was in Hongi's own canoe, seated near him, and occasionally varied the weary miles by singing some stirring Maori song or repeating some powerful incantation to put spirit into the weak hearted. We rounded long North Head and passed rugged Rangitoto, and viewed the placid stretch of the Waitamata, reaching away to the dark Waitakerei ranges on the horizon. We passed the island of Waiheke and bore down the gulf.

The waka taua entered Te Wai Mokoia (the Tamaki River) on a rising tide. 'It was a lovely morning when our fleet moved down the river on its mission of slaughter. . . . How soon was all the peaceful beauty to be disturbed by the din of war and the shriek of the dying!' The taua paddled some five miles down the broad estuary, then bordered by flax swamps and dense forests of mānuka. From the twin pā of Mokoia-Mauinaina looming high above the surrounding countryside came the sullen braying of native trumpets and the hollow gong of the pahū as keen-eyed watchmen beat insistent warnings on canoe-shaped beams of resonant wood. With their progress paralleled by columns of smoke from Ngāti Paoa signal fires and running messengers, Marmon remarked drily, 'Already we were within hostile country.'

'At length we landed' near-present day Panmure wharf. The fleet's advance guard was dispatched upriver to assess the strength of Ngāti Paoa's fortifications and kiore (scouts) were sent to view them from the landward side. Foragers dispersed among the vast cultivations described by Rev. John Butler, who had visited Ngāti Paoa with Samuel Marsden in 1820, as the 'largest portion of cultivated land in one place . . . in New Zealand'.[13] Armed contingents meanwhile scoured the district 'to cut off stragglers', for information and for meat.

Reconnoitring the Tamaki district from the heights of Maungarei (Mount Wellington), a few miles to the west, Marmon joined Hongi and his generals Rewa, Pomare, Tuai, Titore and Patuone in studying Ngāti Paoa's defences through a spyglass. The twin hilltop pā of Mokoia-Mauinaina were located on a broad peninsula protected by the Tamaki River on one side and Kaiahiku Lagoon (Panmure Basin) on the other. To the north and directly below the twin pā was an immense village, some one and a half miles in length and a half mile in width, laid out in streets and divided into neatly fenced allotments containing many 'fine

Armed Māori warriors
As the Ngāpuhi subtribes assembled for war the Bay area took on the appearance of
a vast armed camp with warriors increasingly armed with flintlock guns and cutting
and stabbing weapons of iron and steel.
Wood engraving 170 x 270 mm, Illustrated London News, 'Group of Maories', 1847,
PUBL-0033-1847-040-btm, Alexander Turnbull Library.

houses'. With a normal population of 3000 inhabitants, the kāinga now
seethed with 4000 additional refugees from the 20 outlying villages in
the district.

Ngāti Paoa had protected the previously unfortified landward side
of the peninsula with an outer earthen rampart, topped by a wooden
palisade and fronted by a deep fosse or defensive ditch. Encompassing
the village and both pā, this extraordinary wall curved one and a half
miles in length from the cliffed edge of the Tamaki River to the steep
escarpment above the Panmure lagoon. Walking its ruins in the early
twentieth century the ethnographer Elsdon Best described the great
crescent-shaped outer ditch and bastion as a 'demi lune'.[14] Now hazy
with smoke from countless hāngi fires, the enemy position boomed
and echoed ominously to the roar of successive haka as the ranks of the
defending toa leaped and stamped the trembling earth.

Built directly above the northern side of the Panmure Basin's outlet
with the Tamaki River, was Mokoia, the pā of the chief Rauroha. A
headland or promontory fort, it was a daunting prospect. Protected on
two sides by water and steep cliffs, the approach was barred by two

massive excavated ditches, still evident in late nineteenth-century photographs. Between the base and summit citadel (tihi), now crowned by St Mathias' Church, were three steeply scarped faces, topped with strong palisading to protect level terraces with many houses. Marmon's reference to the unusual number of 'ghastly heads' carved into the tops of the main posts 'to represent sentinels' suggests a particularly heavy outer stockade. Other posts incorporated elaborately carved life-sized human figures, representing named male ancestors who grinned defiance at the invaders.

Nearby but further inland and with more powerful defences still was the larger and higher pā, Mauinaina, home of the senior Ngāti Paoa chief Te Hinaki. Its citadel, now occupied by St Patrick's Catholic Church, stood some 50 metres above Mokoia Pā. Directly below Mauinaina and to the north-east of the village's outer defences lay the only possible battlefield suited to Hongi's new tactics. A broad expanse

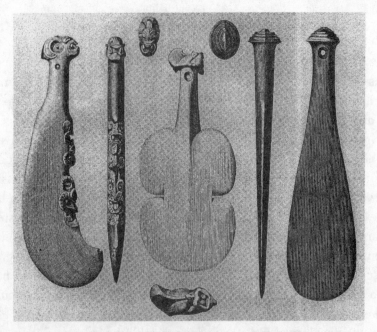

Patu Māori
During the great rākau–musket battle chiefs on both sides continued to carry their favourite short weapon (patu or mere) alongside their flintlock pistols and double-barrelled guns.
John Miller, 'Bludgeons used as weapons by the New Zealanders', PUBL-0095-3-46, Alexander Turnbull Library.

of flat, cultivated ground near the estuary, over a mile in width, Panmure market gardeners would extract musket balls by the hundred from its rich soils during the twentieth century.[15]

Marmon considered Māori 'natural strategists and engineers' and noted that Ngāti Paoa 'had not been idle', using the final days before battle to 'put the finishing touches to defences of the *pah*'. Becoming tactical innovators by necessity, Te Hinaki and Rauroha had constructed a high earthen rampart fronting the citadel on Mokoia's summit, which proved unassailable by conventional means and impervious to Ngāpuhi musket fire.

While contingents under Pomare and Tuai advanced overland to make diversionary attacks on the outer wall, Hongi's fleet attempted to gain access to the lagoon behind Mokoia-Mauinaina. This manoeuvre would deny Ngāti Paoa any reinforcements, cut off their retreat by water and allow the invaders to seize the intricately carved Ngāti Paoa canoe fleet and carving workshops (wharewaka) located there. Forty of these prized waka were later taken back to the Bay of Islands as booty. According to Tuai, Ngāti Paoa blocked access to the lagoon by driving tree trunks vertically into the riverbed.[16] For two days Marmon's luck held and he emerged unscathed as the Ngāpuhi fleet, under a hail of lethal missiles from the pā above, repeatedly attempted to force this blockade without success.

Hongi then launched a war of nerves against Ngāti Paoa. Avoiding any direct and costly assault on their prepared positions, Ngāpuhi remained encamped beside the river for several weeks. Having almost consumed their carefully stored water and provisions, some 3000 Ngāti Paoa fighting men and allied contingents assembled at first light one morning to give battle outside their great iwi fortress. Marmon recalled how the defenders, 'leaving only a chosen band within the *pah*, posted themselves near the bank of the river to dispute the passage with Hongi'. Meanwhile, in their encampment beside the river, the Ngāpuhi army prepared for battle.

It was an animated scene . . . and every warrior was making preparation for the coming strife. The war-paint on their faces and bodies was renewed, arms were inspected and tried, adornments placed most conspicuously, everything, in fact to evince to the Ngatipoas how great a tribe was Ngapuhi.

The arms 'inspected and tried' by the Ngāpuhi hapū and allied tribes who had limited access to the shipping were mainly traditional long and short rākau Māori weapons of stone, bone and wood. Providing the auxiliary contingents for Hongi's musketeers, these forces engaged Ngāti Paoa in the melees outside Mokoia-Mauinaina and in the final pursuit when their ranks had been broken with gunfire. By 1821 and the Tamaki campaign, however, the auxiliaries were seen to have replaced many of their rākau Māori weapons with a bizarre collection of European cutting and stabbing blades of iron and steel: specifically, swords, daggers, bayonets, whaling harpoons and lances, boarding pikes, long and short-handled tomahawks and a variety of modified agricultural implements.[17]

The guns 'inspected and tried' by Ngāpuhi's musketeers were mainly cheap and shoddy weapons of 'plain iron', bartered directly from the shipping for provisions and flax or through trader go-betweens like Marmon. Specifically, these trade guns took the form of single and double-barrelled trade muskets of large calibre which were 'snapped' or fired to ensure that they were still functional. European visitors to the Bay during the early 1820s also describe single and double-barrelled shotguns, blunderbusses, muskatoons, flintlock pistols and a variety of antiquated military muskets.[18] In this period the musketeers generally carried one or two wooden cartridge boxes, each drilled with holes to contain 14–18 cartridges. Attached to their waist belt, one before, the other behind, many of the boxes were leathered with the tattooed skin of vanquished enemies. Meanwhile, Marmon joined the tohunga Māori who moved among the army reciting karakia over all weapons to make them more effective.

We were a goodly company and, when marching twenty abreast, presented a most imposing and martial appearance though the [haka] indulged in by the braves to express their impatience [for] battle and the havoc they would make of all enemies of Hongi, would not exactly have seemed in accordance with the stricter discipline of a European army. A heavy bush and scrub covered the entire country growing heavier in the gullies. Accordingly, we selected the shore as the best road to march not knowing that some ambuscade might lurk in the undergrowth.

Musket haka

At the great Tamaki battle Marmon witnessed the earth-shaking massed haka that
preceded kōkiri or reckless charges by both sides over open ground.
John Williams, 'The war dance', 1859. Wood engraving 150 x 230 mm, PUBL-0144-1-front,
Alexander Turnbull Library.

Part of the advance guard, Marmon 'could not but look at [Hongi] as
he marched in front with his musket ready primed, anxious to be the
first to draw blood [the honour of mataika].' The hoarse roar of the puha
(war song), braying shell and wooden trumpets and calls from European
military bugles heralded the approach of Hongi's army. Emerging from
the scrublands along the shore, the taua deployed in a unique formation,
waka toru (in three divisions) among the cultivations.

Marmon's descriptions of battle formations, offensive and defensive
tactics and appalling mortality rate dramatically illustrate the
devastating impact of the musket on traditional Māori tactics and tribes
armed rākau Māori.

The two armies were somewhat differently arranged. Hongi had drawn
his men up in the form of a T, with orders [for the tail] to open out if there
was any chance of being surrounded. Hinaki, on the other hand, had
simply massed his in a double line, relying apparently on hand-to-hand
combat to decide the day. . . . I retired very much to the rear, in order to

be out of the way of the bullets and . . . to repeat my most powerful spells for the success of my tribe. I retired to a spot also where I could see all that went on.

Motivated by material gain and the need for self-preservation, Marmon's personal disquiet and strategic withdrawal challenges the myth that Ngāti Paoa owned few muskets by 1821 (four and six are the oft quoted numbers), while adding credibility to Tuai's estimate of 100.[19] The Ngāti Paoa chiefs wielding these guns easily identified Hongi by the shimmer and flash of his armour and his comprehensive personal array of flintlock weaponry. Among these was his famous tūpara or double-barrelled gun Patu Iwi (killer of tribes), a personal gift from King George IV. They were also familiar with his reputation for invincibility and divinity, Hongi being widely known among his traditionally armed enemies by such titles as 'the New Zealand god' and, according to Marmon, 'the demon of war'.

Marmon's observation that Hongi 'was accompanied by four gunbearers whose task it was to load his muskets', agrees with the writings of Charles Davis, who settled in the Hokianga during the early 1830s. In later years, Davis interviewed Marmon's patrons Patuone and Muriwai and other elderly veterans of the Tamaki campaign for his book *The Life and Times of Patuone*.

Hongi was not only formidable in regard to his personal prowess but the accoutrements he wore. He was generally dressed in an ornamental mat over which he wore his coat of mail, six pistols and a dagger were fastened to his belt and he carried two guns and to add to the singularity of his appearance, his black face was buried in a large mass of glittering metal in the form of a helmet. Four attendants were always at his side, whose particular business it was to load his guns and pistols.[20]

For Ngāti Paoa, the peculiar battle formation adopted by Ngāpuhi and the strange appearance of Hongi's army that November morning must have been a fantastic and perplexing sight. Though tattooed, barefoot, and with faces and bodies traditionally painted with red ochre, to the modern military historian, in armaments, dress and paraphernalia Hongi's first musket taua had more in common with the colourful exuberance of late medieval armies of the steel and powder model than with the grim uniformity of subsequent Māori musket armies.

The various Ngāpuhi contingents had assembled beneath giant 'battle' flags, generally signal flags bartered from the shipping. Caught up in the craze for European military dress that swept the north, the chiefs told Marsden how they appeared on the battlefield at Tamaki wearing the uniforms and accoutrements of British and foreign military officers.[21] At a time when all metal was highly prized, the chests of the toa were bedecked with discs of polished iron or copper, their earlobes hung with slivers of metal, silver shillings or gold sovereigns. The musketeers and many of the rākau-armed auxiliaries were attired in red trade blankets, or red and scarlet military cloaks. It was by these distinctive flags, their red 'military dress', the glitter of steel blades and highly polished gun barrels that advancing Ngāpuhi musket armies were recognised at a distance by their enemies throughout the early 1820s.

'At last Hinaki and Hongi met face to face on flat ground. A great battle was imminent; both could not live. Each leader recognised this and encouraged his men in his own way.' Hongi and Te Hinaki strode up and down in front of their respective armies, blowing challenges on their European military bugles. Hongi, studying the enemy ranks through his telescope, easily identified Te Hinaki. Standing under Ngāti Paoa's only battle flag, this chief was dressed in British 'regimentals', armed with a mere pounamu, a musket with a fixed bayonet and two holstered pistols, the last being gifts from Hongi when the two had met in Sydney. Marsden had described Te Hinaki as 'a great warrior, a very fine, tall, handsome man, apparently about thirty-six years of age and has been in many actions'.[22] Assessing the generalship of both chiefs, Marmon concluded that while Hinaki did not have the tactical genius of Hongi, '[he] was an infinitely braver and finer man, rejoicing to rush into the thickest of the fight with only his *mere* in his hand'.

Heeding the advice of several leading chiefs intimidated by Ngāti Paoa's numbers and their thunderous haka which shuddered the earth beneath the invaders, Hongi did not immediately attack. For the next three days the armies assembled at dawn and remained in position while the leading chiefs parlayed. Ngāti Paoa tried to buy off the invaders with their most precious treasure, a collection of greenstone and fine cloaks. Hongi simply took the treasure and kept his army in the field.

On the morning of the fourth day, following their own ferocious haka, the Ngāpuhi army advanced. 'The battle commenced with a furious volley from the Ngapuhis which did very little damage, replied to by a more effective shower of [missiles] from the Ngatipoas.' During the initial volley, many Ngāpuhi muskets misfired due to the use of poor-quality flints and powder. The rate of controlled or free fire thereafter varied according to the warriors' familiarity and confidence in their weapons, the type of flintlock gun, and the quality of flint and powder used. The trade guns were notorious for misfiring and the few quality Brown Bess military muskets then in the Ngāpuhi armament generally misfired three times out of 10.[23] Nevertheless, during the first rolling volley from 1000 guns on the Tamaki battlefield, Hongi could still count on a minimum of 600 to 700 shots for tactical purposes, but beyond 50 yards, the range was too great to inflict significant casualties.

A major advantage of muzzle loaders in early Māori battles was that they could be loaded and fired repeatedly and with increasing effect as the musketeers advanced steadily towards a stationary enemy force. Flintlock guns, however, were extraordinarily difficult weapons to fight with and a high degree of co-operation from the enemy was needed to be defeated by them. Familiar with the sound and effects of musket fire, Ngāti Paoa did not co-operate by breaking and running at the flash and thunder of the first volley, nor did they stand bewildered to be slain or enslaved as had some tribes previously attacked by Ngāpuhi.

Then Hinaki flung his left wing against Hongi's right, while with his own right he strove to attack his opponents in the flank. It was a cleverly executed manoeuvre, and seemed for a time to confuse Hongi, especially as immediately after this Hinaki with his centre hurled himself against the centre of the Ngapuhis. The chief of the Ngatipoas was a man of splendid form and indomitable courage, and perseverance; he fought like a tiger, and pressed the Ngapuhis step by step back despite their most determined exertions. I feared much for my friends, the battle seemed most doubtful; if it were lost farewell to my reputation as a *tohunga*.

Marmon indicates that by boldly charging the Ngāpuhi advance, Ngāti Paoa neutralised the firepower of the musketeers by close and skilled infighting with mere, patu, taiaha and tewhatewha. Compelled

Crouching warrior
Hongi compensated for the limited range of the trade guns and their tendency to
misfire by massing his musketeers before destroying enemy formations with close-
range gunfire.
E. H. McCormick (ed.), Markham, Edward, New Zealand, or Recollections of It,
Wellington, 1963.

to use their muskets as unwieldy clubs or resort to rākau weapons, the
musketeers were easy prey for veteran fighters like Te Hinaki, who
thrust his mere under the ribs of his adversaries, under their jaws and
through their temples as opportunity offered. Ngāti Paoa broke the
ranks of the kai paura, forcing them off the battlefield and the entire
Ngāpuhi force into retreat.

Arthur Thomson, a British army officer and historian who interviewed
many Musket War veterans during the 1840s and 1850s, concluded
that rallying retreating Māori warriors was an impossible manoeuvre.
'Repulses were defeats and defeats were frequently destruction.'[24] One of
Hongi's fiercest rivals, Tuai, however, informed Rene Lesson that Hongi,
'roaring', was able to rally his panic-stricken men and 'return to the
charge'.[25] Hongi's singular ability to rally his shattered forces at Tamaki
and again at Rotorua in 1823 attests to the extent of his mana as a war
leader, the discipline of his warriors and their belief in his invincibility.

Pitched battles featuring kōkiri or headlong charges by taua over open ground were uncommon in rākau Māori warfare where tribal tacticians preferred less costly stratagems to achieve victory. Here, the greatest casualties generally followed the fall of a fortified position and the massacre of its inhabitants. At Tamaki, Marmon witnessed the most distinctive feature of rākau–musket warfare. Pitched battles were now fought on open ground outside central iwi fortifications as the traditionally armed defenders tried to disperse the enemy musketeers before they reached the civilian population behind the palisades. In these pivotal battles, both sides resorted to reckless charges that endangered their entire warrior force.

Accounts of when and how Te Hinaki was killed vary, but Marmon's and Wharepoaka's versions are similar. When Hongi and Te Hinaki, with their respective lieutenants, found each other in battle, Hongi was struck on the helmet with a mere and knocked down, while Wharepoaka was speared through the arm. Hongi was then shot twice, at least once by Te Hinaki, now armed with his musket and bayonet. The ball was turned by Hongi's coat of mail though some of the links were broken. Te Hinaki fired again, this time with one of his flintlock pistols but without effect. Hongi's brother Rewa and the chief Iwi then fired at Te Hinaki who already bore several gunshot wounds.[26]

Again and again had [Hongi] striven to bring down Hinaki, but although successful in wounding him twice it seemed to have no effect in staying the prowess of the chief. At last a bullet shattered the brave Ngatipoan's thigh, and brought him to the ground. Instantly the bloodthirsty Ngapuhi rushed forward with a fiendish yell of triumph, and scooped out with his knife the eyes of his enemy, and swallowed them to give him the courage of the fallen foe. Not content also with this, he buried his *mere* in the dying chief's neck and lapped Hinaki's warm blood as it spouted from the gash.

Marmon considered Hongi 'one of the best [Māori strategists] having the art of turning to account circumstances the most trivial or accidental'. In Māori battles, the death of a leading chief generally signalled the defeat of his tribe but Ngāti Paoa, resolute and well led, continued to fight on under their rangatira Kohirangatira, Te Kanawa and Koinaki. As the fighting became more frenzied, and 'hundreds fell on either side', the leading chiefs on both sides, seeking a decisive advantage, committed the last of their reinforcements.

At this critical phase of the Tamaki battle, Marmon ran forward with the tohunga Māori to reinforce and inspire the ranks of their kinsmen. In such crises elderly and infirm tohunga were excused combat to continue uttering karakia from afar, but never the able-bodied priests, some being famous fighting men in their own right.

After repeated volleys, the barrels of the muzzle loaders became increasingly clogged with burnt powder. As it was impractical for Ngāpuhi and their Pākehā-Māori to stop and clean their muskets in a battle characterised by swift advances and withdrawals, the toa were compelled to use smaller shot to seat the musket ball on the powder charge. While this did not generally kill the enemy outright, the lead balls, flattening on impact, inflicted terrible disabling wounds. The musketeers were also able to maintain momentum of fire by 'the distinctive Maori method' of placing three spare cartridges between the fingers of the left hand and by speed loading.

In loading the musket they rarely use the ramrod. Some powder from the cartridge was used to prime the pan which was then shut. The remaining powder was dropped into the barrel and the butt end struck upon the ground. The ball then followed with another blow given to set the piece, the musket being ready to fire.[27]

The flintlock guns soon became unbearably hot to handle and Marmon and his fellow musketeers, half blind with sparks and smoke, saw their Ngāti Paoa opponents as hazy, fleeting targets through a thick smoke screen. Suffering a raging thirst, the effects of saltpetre in the mouth from biting open their cartridges, the hands, faces and bodies of Ngāpuhi became blackened with burnt powder, hence the emergence of the title borne with pride by these men, kai paura (powder eaters).[28]

The battle was by no means over. The Ngatipoas were so far from giving way that they had entirely defeated Hongi's right wing and were advancing to assist the centre. This Hongi saw must at any cost be avoided as it would cut his army into two, therefore, giving his men the order to form themselves into a vast wedge, at the point of which he placed himself, he drove through the Ngatipoa lines, divided them in two and after a few minutes of sharp fighting completely defeated his opponents.

Contrary to the view held by some historians, the kawau maro (flying wedge) described by Marmon at Tamaki was not a borrowed European military tactic founded on the ancient Roman cuneus. Nor did Hongi learn of the tactic while studying European military history in London. Originating in the wars of the classical Māori period the kawau maro was a proven Māori offensive tactic and there are references to it in early waiata.[29] The tactic was only used on desperate occasions where a tribe suffering heavy losses or inspired 'by the fiery eloquence of their chiefs' would devote themselves to death or victory 'and forming themselves into a solid wedge, would hurl themselves on their enemy that defeat of one or other of the parties was inevitable'.[30]

Given the inaccuracy and unreliability of Ngāpuhi's trade guns, the composite nature of musket taua and the sheer weight of enemy numbers, Hongi was compelled to originate greater variety and flexibility in group tactics. The kawau maro remained a ploy founded in desperation, but during the great rākau–musket battles at Tamaki, and later against Arawa at Rotorua, it became a shock tactic, a Māori blitzkrieg, whereby the charging wedge, spitting fire, split the opposing army and killed many of their chiefs before devastating the enemy ranks with close-range gunfire. Heedless of their losses, Ngāti Paoa continued to fight on before Hongi employed the kawau maro in a well-rehearsed secondary manoeuvre.

At length Hongi, who had the greatest number of muskets, and who had arranged his men in a form called in Roman tactics the 'cuneus', or wedge, placing himself in the apex and directing those behind him to wheel round upon the enemy from right and left, or to fall back into their original positions as opportunity offered . . . defeated [Te Hinaki's] army with great slaughter.[31]

Thus following the initial onslaught, Hongi's men retained their core wedge formation before the left and right wings of the wedge swung outwards to envelop Ngāti Paoa. The kai paura then advanced through the ranks of their reloading comrades to deliver volley fire, before withdrawing back into the formation when counter-attacked, protected by supporting fire. This enabled the kai paura to maximise the destructive potential of the iron trade guns without compromising their preference for close-quarters fighting and without recourse to traditional hand-to-hand combat.

In Māori warfare as in the Napoleonic battles of the period, most casualties were inflicted on enemy combatants not during the shock of the charge, but in its aftermath, the pursuit. Unable to improvise tactics to counter the relentless rolling volleys, a dilemma exacerbated by the loss of Te Hinaki, their leading chief and tactician, and in the absence of the usual close pursuit, Ngāti Paoa now inadvertently co-operated with Ngāpuhi by repeatedly regrouping and charging into the mouths of the guns.

Meanwhile the women and older children of Ngāti Paoa watched apprehensively through the palisades of the great defensive wall as the tide of battle turned decisively against them. This civilian population began to stream back into the twin pā above, carrying their remaining food supplies and most important treasures as Ngāpuhi broke and destroyed their formations of fighting men.

Marmon states that, finally breaking, Ngāti Paoa 'fled in all directions . . . pursued by the victorious Ngapuhi's who shot them down without pity'. Some survivors swam the Tamaki River and fled south to the Waikato, hotly pursued by the Ngāpuhi auxiliaries. Others recrossed the great outer ditch on the log bridges and ladders before slipping back into the kāinga through ngutu (sally ports) in the outer fence. Closely pressed by Ngāpuhi, however, these survivors were forced to conduct a fighting retreat through the great village before fleeing through its narrow streets and enclosures, deliberately designed as a maze to assist in defence, to join the garrison and civilians within the twin pā.

The defenders closed and barred the kūwaha or gates, withdrew their log bridges over the outer ditches, drew up the access ladders from the ditches and grimly awaited attack. Ngāpuhi looted what remained in the finely carved houses and storehouses and, on Hongi's orders, set the entire village ablaze before returning to the battlefield. Fifty-five years after the event the scale of carnage on the battlefield and its gruesome aftermath remained indelibly printed on Marmon's memory.

Cannibal feast
Marmon's appetite for human flesh raised his standing among the leading chiefs at the Bay of Islands and Hokianga.
Masson after Rouargue, 'Sauvages de la Nouvelle Zélande', GoAR852-725, Hocken Library, Dunedin.

The battle . . . had been fought and won, and although dearly bought was the greatest triumph of Hongi's career. He always referred to it as the most fairly fought field he had been engaged in, and longed always to find foes who would fight as determinedly as did the Ngatipoas. But the scene on the battlefield was not over . . . parties of *rangatiras* were busily engaged in gouging out and swallowing the eyes of the fallen [to prevent them becoming stars in the heavens] . . . while imparting to themselves the courage of the possessor . . . hoping therefore to rival Hongi in his great deeds.

The Ngatipoa loss had been very heavy, about seven hundred men being killed, amongst whom were the two brothers of Hinaki, who fell striving to avenge his death. Such a quantity of good food must not be permitted to be devoured by the birds and beetles. Accordingly, the ovens were instantly prepared, over three hundred dead bodies were roasted, and a splendid feast celebrated in honour of the victory, from which a portion was set apart for the gods.

All night long that feast was kept up . . . which the defenders of the . . . *pah* could overlook and burn with indignation to avenge. All night long the fires blazed, round which bands of warriors discussed the events of the day, boasted how many they had slain with their own hand, foretold how great their prowess would be on the morrow, when the *Pah* would be attacked, or sang songs of old heroes and *rangatiras*. Little sleep was enjoyed by either party that night. Our mutual fear [of attack] then kept us awake, my fear chiefly being that any one should acquire the share of goods falling to me, on the stripping of the remaining bodies tomorrow.

After several days of feasting, the stench of putrefaction drove Ngāpuhi from the battlefield and preparations were made to storm the twin pā. Advancing in two divisions downriver by canoe, and overland through the blackened ruins of the great village, the attackers skirted Mauinaina's powerful outer defences to first attack Mokoia, according to Marmon, 'at dawn'. It was, he says, 'a really wonderful work of engineering . . . defended by four hundred of the bravest Ngatipoas [who had] retreated to it after the battle'.

Rushing the outer defences in the half light, Hongi, at the head of the attacking force, tripped on a vine and fell. He rose only to have his helmet knocked from his head by a musket ball fired by a defender. Considering these incidents bad omens, Hongi withdrew his forces and considered returning to the Bay. However, Patuone of Hokianga and other chiefs wanting further utu and not wishing to return home in shame persuaded their shaken war leader to resume the attack.[32]

The Ngāpuhi auxiliaries descended the first great outer ditch (approximately 20 feet in depth) on crude ladders and long notched poles before using them to ascend the higher, inner face. Meanwhile, Marmon joined the kai paura, who, standing shoulder to shoulder on the outer edge of the ditch, shot down the exposed defenders gathered atop the earthen bastions opposite, to roll down stacks of prepared logs and boulders weighing one to five pounds on the besiegers. Ascending the scarp and attacking the first lines of palisades with ladders, axes and ropes, the Ngāpuhi auxiliaries suffered heavy losses. Many were impaled on huata or long spears thrust repeatedly through gaps in the stockade by the defending women. Others were maimed or killed by the defenders crowding the extended fighting platforms (taumaihi) projecting outwards over the top of the palisades. Partly protected from musket fire by wooden parapets, these warriors rained down stockpiled stones on the heads of the besiegers and hurled 'darts', or short spears (tao), of mānuka wood, about four feet in length, sharpened at both ends and frequently barbed.

Using flax ropes attached to wooden bars, Ngāpuhi eventually pulled down a section of the first stockade and crossed the second ditch, but their ascent of the precipitous cone was fiercely contested at every step. 'The defenders fought with desperate and heroic courage. Again and again they succeeded in driving back the assailants. . . . In warfare, a man will rather die a horrible lingering death than fall into the hands of his enemies, because he knows slavery will be the result.' The first attackers to surmount each new line of palisades and drop to the ground were invariably killed by the defenders who struck fiercely with taiaha, tewhatewha and pouwhenua. Some five feet in length, and made of hardwood, these long clubs had sharpened edges for striking and proximal points for stabbing.

Practically impregnable in pre-musket days, the defences of Mokoia fell in stages to Hongi's kai paura who systematically shot down the rākau-armed defenders as they gathered atop the bastions and taumaihi or swarmed behind the palisades. Clambering over the final stockade at the head of the Ngāpuhi advance, Hongi jammed his foot between the palisading and became trapped. Armed with a toki or adze the Ngāti Paoa chief Kaea and several warriors closed in for the kill. Hongi, however, was able to hold them at bay with empty pistols until rescued by his men.[33]

Finally reaching the summit, Ngāpuhi found the defenders and civilians within the stockaded citadel protected from their muskets by the high earthen rampart. Hongi ordered a wooden pūwhara or fighting tower to be constructed which overlooked the obstacle. Ngāpuhi passed a stream of loaded muskets up to their marksmen, who, firing volley after volley, killed all those guarding the entrance. The position which had served Ngāti Paoa as an important tribal citadel for many generations was stormed. Pākehā-Māori were expected to seek out and fight each other during intertribal battles, and among the last defenders to fall in the furious clash within the tihi were three Ngāti Paoa fighting Pākehā-Māori.[34] These men were killed by their Ngāpuhi counterparts including Marmon, whose 'courage' was subsequently well rewarded by Hongi.

A fearful slaughter of the women, children and wounded warriors commenced until the attackers' blood lust was sated. Ngāpuhi spared the remainder, who were bound and led in columns back to their beachside encampment. Singing songs of derision, Ngāpuhi dragged the dead defenders into heaps beside their own ovens before burning their dead comrades on huge pyres built from the palisading. The decapitated heads of the common toa were piled up and disfigured by stones or by other heads being flung against them. Māori accounts state that 300 of the 400 toa defending Mokoia Pā were killed during the attack and that again Ngāpuhi feasted on the slain for several days. Marmon recalled that very few of the garrison escaped and that Hongi honoured their heroic resistance by eating all the fallen. 'Hongi held here his greatest *hakari* [feast], when four hundred human beings were served up cooked.'

Building twin pā like Mokoia-Mauinaina was not unusual in pre-musket times. This arrangement allowed the defenders of one to come to the aid of the other when attacked. Deterred by the strength of Ngāpuhi firepower, the defenders of Mauinaina remained within their pā, watching the terrible scenes unfolding below on Mokoia. According to Hoane Nahi, an unspecified disagreement among the leading Ngāpuhi chiefs on how Mauinaina should be attacked saw 'four or five of the *hapus*' sit out this siege.[35] In recalling how Hongi's 'craft prevailed where force was unavailing', Marmon completed the picture of Mauinaina's fall by subterfuge but intermixed events from the fall of Te Tōtara Pā also taken by trickery shortly thereafter.

Few Ngāpuhi or Ngāti Paoa rangatira had foreseen that concentrated musket volleys from imported firearms would produce slaughter on so grand a scale. The chief Waikato who had accompanied Hongi to England was so appalled by the numbers who fell on both sides and the subsequent orgy of rape, blood drinking and cannibalism that he was unable to eat for four days, determined never to go to war again and refused to accompany Hongi on his campaign against the Arawa people at Rotorua in 1823.[36]

Also witnessing the horror of modern warfare founded on mechanical innovation, Mauinaina's shocked and demoralised garrison readily accepted Hongi's offer of peace. Having allowed Ngāpuhi to enter the pā, however, they were attacked by their guests and massacred. Māori accounts state that over a thousand were killed within Mauinaina. Succeeding this 'was the customary feast upon our foes', each toa carefully laying his weapon aside lest human flesh should pass over it and destroy its effectiveness.

Marmon states that Hongi was so impressed with his efforts during the battle 'that taking off his own *heitaki* he put it round my neck saying Success and the favour of the gods go with the brave hearted'. Subsequent gifts from Hongi included 'many valuable presents, especially two finely tattooed heads embalmed, for which in subsequent days of poverty I realised a very good sum from the captain of an English frigate'.

Missionary reports claim that most Ngāti Paoa were killed at Tamaki including the majority of rangatira and that 2000 captives were taken back to the Bay of Islands as slaves. Those who escaped the carnage scattered to hide in the cave country surrounding Mount Wellington, or raced their pursuers westwards across the pumice country towards the distant Waitakere Ranges. Others, including the chiefs Rauroha, Kohirangatira and Koinaki, fled south, seeking refuge among the Waikato tribes.[37]

The rise of powerful musket armies set in train 40 major heke or tribal migrations that emptied vast reaches of New Zealand by 1840, paving the way for European settlement that proceeded largely unopposed until the 1860s. As the Tamaki River became a main route for Ngāpuhi's annual amphibious campaigns after 1821, the remnants of Ngāti Paoa resettled within Waikato territory. Small parties of refugees occasionally returned to the isthmus to catch fish and birds, but the tribe never returned to reoccupy Mokoia-Mauinaina. The laboriously constructed bastions and stockades crumbled away, the vast cultivations reverted to fern and mānuka and the once populous Tamaki district became a wasteland. A European traveller visiting the main battlefield in 1844, recorded that it remained a scene of desolation. Cooked human remains were still visible in the ovens and the bones of 2000 men lay whitening on the plain.[38]

The facts of the battle and siege of Mokoia-Mauinaina as reported by Marmon are substantially correct. Of the four eyewitness accounts Marmon's is the most detailed. His description of the initial Ngāpuhi

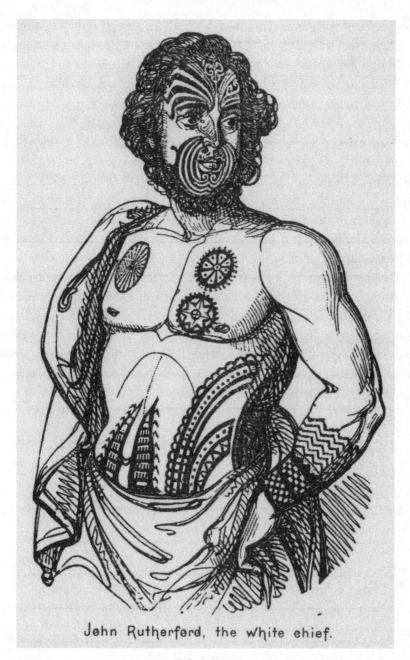

John Rutherford, the white chief.

Pākehā toa

A fighting Pākehā-Māori from Otuihu Pā near Kororareka, Rutherford was among the
Pākehā toa who accompanied their chiefs on the grand 1821 campaign to Tamaki.

*R. A. A. Sherrin and J. H. Wallace, 'John Rutherford, the white chief', Early History of
New Zealand: From Earliest Times to 1840, Auckland, 1890, p. 229.*

advance in T formation, their use of the flying wedge and a siege tower confirms the effectiveness of Hongi's synthesis of traditional and new military tactics. Nor does Marmon exaggerate battlefield casualties as did many later writers; indeed, he understates them, perhaps from a belated sense of guilt and remorse. Marmon's reminiscences emphasise his duties as Hongi's war tohunga, while suppressing his role as a fighting man.

The Rev. John Butler, as previously noted, made several references in his journal to 'the notorious John' during the early 1820s. Interestingly, Butler's references to this character cease in the second half of 1821, when Hongi mobilised every able-bodied Ngāpuhi, including their Pākehā-Māori, for his first great musket campaign, but resume following the expedition's return.

Despite the passing of years, Marmon's recall of local geographical features, fortifications, personalities and phases of battle carry the detail and directness of an actual participant. Several Tainui contingents from the Waikato fought alongside their Ngāti Paoa kinsfolk at Tamaki and Jacky's account is given credence by the Tainui tradition that 'a white man named Marmon' was present in the ranks of Hongi's army during the attacks of Mokoia-Mauinaina.[39]

CHAPTER FIVE

Eyewitness and convict, 1821–23

It was late October 1821 before the Ngāpuhi army boarded their battle fleet at Tamaki, according to Marmon, 'after interring the bones of our friends and holding a great tangi over them'. The victors carried with them the preserved and packaged heads of their own fallen rangatira to be presented to the families of the deceased to grieve over. The white tohunga again travelled in Hongi's leading waka as the great armada, now escorting a fleet of captured Ngāti Paoa canoes, laden with captives, slowly exited the Tamaki River on the ebb tide. At the entrance to the estuary, the Ngāti Paoa prisoners were permitted to turn and gaze in sorrow for the last time upon their ancestral lands. The twin pā of Mokoia-Mauinaina had been torched and two columns of dark smoke rose vertically to merge with the clouds. The waka taua progressed eastwards across the Hauraki Gulf, before turning south into the Firth of Thames to seek utu for past defeats at the hands of the Ngāti Maru people.

The prisoners whom we had taken in battle were conveyed along with us, and we were moreover laden with the spoils of the Ngatipaoa, highly polished *pounamu meres* and ornaments, beautifully wrought mats, carved weapons, and tattooed heads. These were the property of the chief to reward as he chose the bravery of his followers.

Te Tōtara Pā was the central stronghold of the Maru Tuahu branch of Ngāti Maru, who were Hauraki members of the Tainui confederation. Their great fortress stood on a bluff terminating in a steep 90-degree escarpment above the entrance to the Waihou or Thames River where it joins the Hauraki Gulf. The landward side was protected by a massive ditch and bank, beyond which lay the large kāinga or village and surrounding plantations. Marmon refers to the siege and fall of Te Tōtara as the 'kauaeranga battle', from the pā's location near the Waiwhakauranga sidestream.

Ngāti Maru were planting their main crop of potatoes when the Ngāpuhi fleet swept into view. While anticipating Hongi's attack, the sheer size and speed of the approaching armada, and its cacophony of war trumpets, sent the defenders rushing from the cultivations to the pā. Warned by the watchmen's constant gonging of the pahū, audible to a distance of 20 miles, the residents of outlying Ngāti Maru villages on the Hauraki Plains scattered towards the mountains of the Coromandel Range. Despite its strong defences, Te Tōtara's garrison was seriously under-strength as many rangatira and warriors had joined the 1821 Amiowhenua, an intertribal expedition of exploration and killing to Cook Strait. The defence of Te Tōtara fell mainly to the warriors of two Ngāti Maru hapū led by the rangatira Te Puhi and Te Aka te Rangikapeke and to visiting fighting men belonging to Waikato, Arawa, Ngāti Awa, Ngāti Pukenga and Te Whānau-a-Apanui.[1]

Marmon remembered Te Tōtara as 'a really wonderful work of engineering, as it had been strengthened by wooden piles in every imaginable way, and rendered more impregnable'. Before the rise of intertribal musket armies such strongholds had generally been bypassed by conventionally armed expeditions. Large musket taua not only enabled Hongi to destroy the rākau-armed tribesmen who massed to give battle outside centralised iwi fortifications like Mokoia-Mauinaina, but to surround and besiege great fortresses like Te Tōtara. During these sieges the Ngāpuhi army sustained itself primarily on local fern root and shellfish, and crops foraged from the extensive plantations of their enemies. As these food sources were depleted, the invaders

Beach gathering

According to Marmon, Hongi's forces always established strategic encampments on beaches a few miles from the great iwi fortifications they planned to besiege. *Hand-coloured lithograph, 238 x 377 mm. Augustus Earle, 'War speech previous to a naval expedition', D-PP0015-09-CT, Alexander Turnbull Library.*

became increasingly reliant on the flesh of the defenders to sustain them, following the capture or capitulation of Te Tōtara.

Ngāpuhi disembarked near the pā and established their camp on the beach at Te Amo o te rangi. Ngāti Paoa prisoners were killed and 'another great feast was commenced upon the dead'. Small, fast-moving contingents meanwhile scoured the Hauraki Plains for Ngāti Maru stragglers, and part of the fleet paddled swiftly upriver, to catch the occupants of several smaller pā by surprise. Marmon states that, 'When day broke we prepared to commence our attack upon the *pah*. . . . It was a most formidable task to attempt its capture.' Using their rākau Māori weapons, the defenders held off Ngāpuhi for two days and one night, during which a Ngāti Maru marksman, employing the only musket in their possession, managed to shoot many of the besiegers before running out of powder. The combined firepower of the Northerners meanwhile, caused few casualties among the besieged, who, shrewdly hidden from view, rained down darts and stones from atop the massive ramparts of their pā.

[Hongi] desired to see if he could not effect a possession by an easier method than another battle. His own loss though he tried to conceal it had been very severe and he could ill throw away men when he was in the very heart of the enemy's country. If he could get by stratagem what he might not get by force all would be well, therefore pretending friendship . . . he offered them their liberty if they would conclude a treaty of peace with him.

Though there were many opposing [Ngäti Maru] voices to an arrangement full of such danger, and though further warned by their *tohunga* who pronounced the single word *kiatupato* [or] caution, the majority were determined to take Hongi at his word and conclude a treaty of peace with them, admitting him at the same time within the *pah*. This was done and the Ngapuhis to the number of two hundred and their leader were received into a place which they would never have entered by force.

Taking enemy pā by subterfuge was not a common strategy, but Hongi had been advised on this course of action by his blind wife Turitatuku, who accompanied him on military expeditions as a valued seer and advisor.[2]

Outwardly there seemed perfect reconciliation between the two tribes. Dances and wrestling matches were indulged in; the young females of the tribe were sent as a present *for the time* to the warriors of the Ngapuhis, and there seemed a possibility of lasting peace. But I noticed Hongi was absent-minded and silent . . . for he called me away from the others to walk with him round the pah . . . he had determined this night when the inmates of the pah were asleep to put [them] to the sword.

The key to the successful operations of the large composite musket armies was the custom by which the different divisions journeyed independently to a rendezvous near the battle zone and fought under the direction of their own factional leaders. These allies, however, reserved the right to sit out a battle if they disagreed with the main tactical plan. Hongi's main ally and rival during the campaign was the ruthless predatory raider Pomare. When this famous rangatira and his Ngāti Manu hapū heard of Hongi's plan to take Te Tōtara by subterfuge, so soon after taking Mauinaina Pā by treachery, they returned to the Bay of Islands in disgust.[3]

Meanwhile, pretending to return home, the remaining force launched their canoes from the beach below the pā, only to land according to Marmon 'at a place called Tararu' located about five miles along the coast. Travelling during the night, the northern army lay quietly before the unguarded pā to await the first signs of daylight. An enterprising scout located an unbarred gate and, soon after, the invaders had stealthily assembled within the palisades.

That night when a universal stillness reigned over the pah, when the Thames river glided peacefully along in the moonlight, when the only sound breaking the hush was the cry of the *hui* or *morepork* in the bush, a great cry broke on the night like the despairing yell of all the damned, and a scene of wild confusion succeeded to one of perfect peace. Hongi and his men were carrying out the project of slaughter. Men, women, and children were mercilessly killed; fugitives in trying to escape only dashed against an outer circle of savage Ngapuhis thirsting for their blood. Bravery was of no avail against an unseen foe that poured a fatal leaden hail into any band of warriors inclined to rally and make a stand. In an hour's time not [one] was left alive.

Ngāpuhi lost several men during the confusion including two young chiefs, Pū and his brother Tete, who were related to Hongi. The latter was killed by Ahurei of Ngāti Maru, whose weapon was a toki panehe, an adze with a blade made from hoop iron. In revenge, Hongi ordered the slaughter of all prisoners including the children of Te Aka. Ngāti Maru survivors put the number of their people killed at Te Tōtara at 1000, with only 200 prisoners surviving the massacre. Like Ngāti Paoa, the shattered remnants of Ngāti Maru abandoned their ancestral lands to settle further south among their Waikato relatives. Marmon observed that 'Hongi had taken a most effectual way of avoiding further trouble with them. From that day to this Totara *pah* has been without inmate and the name of Ngati Maru [and Ngatipaoa] and was wiped out from the Hauraki territory.'

Having successfully defeated and dispersed Ngāti Paoa and Ngāti Maru, Hongi concluded his Thames campaign, and began the voyage home, 'the success of our expedition render[ing] Hongi's name celebrated and dreaded throughout the North Island'.

Our return to the Bay of Islands was celebrated with great pomp and ceremony. The canoes moved slowly up the Keri-Keri in procession, many of them adorned at prow and stern with the heads of the slaughtered. [The] Ngapuhi warriors were singing their songs of triumph and were decked with triumphal ornaments, their countenances also being streaked with charcoal, and their heads and bodies with red ochre. As we neared the settlement the women, children and old men who alone inhabited it came out with songs to greet us. Again as we approached the landing-place they joined in a universal chorus of '*Haere-mai, haere-mai*'.

Mobilising all able-bodied tribesmen including their Pākehā-Māori and modernising their expeditions of war subjected Ngāpuhi society

Field workers, Bay of Islands
Slaves captured during Ngāpuhi's early musket raids helped produce vast quantities of potatoes. These were bartered with the shipping for additional muskets which made possible even greater slave-taking expeditions.
Lithograph. Louis Auguste de Saison, 'Defrichement d'un champ de patates', F-251-1/4-MNZ, Alexander Turnbull Library.

to economic and social pressures comparable in magnitude to, if not greater than, those experienced in Europe with the rise of mass armies during the Napoleonic Wars. This new Māori militarisation entailed enormous costs that had been unforeseen by tribal leaders.[4] Contrary to the popular view, there were few easy victories for the Ngāpuhi musket armies and their heavy losses during the battles and sieges at Tamaki and Thames, and during subsequent campaigns, had fatal consequences for many captives.

It was at this stage that the ferocity of the Maori nature, even in the females, came out. Hongi's daughter, married to a very promising young Ngapuhi chief who had fallen at Kauaeranga, after anxiously scanning all the canoes for her husband, when she perceived he was absent, with a cry like a wounded boar she dashed at the captives, and seizing the sword presented by King George IV, in England, to Hongi, cut off the heads of sixteen of the unfortunate prisoners, who laid their heads down over the side of the vessel to receive the blow. Conceiving even this to be insufficient company for her husband to Te Reinga, she afterwards strangled herself that she might not be separated from him. This was a common custom in Maoriland, either to kill all the slaves belonging to a deceased chief, or that some or all his wives should make away with themselves, so that the soul of the departed might not be lonely in the great, dim spirit land.

Of course there were the usual feasts and *tangis* when all the warriors were safely on land; these I omit as only tiresome to describe, as the reader is already acquainted with the course of such things, and pass on to note some facts on my own career.

Marmon is silent about his own fighting role during the siege and fall of Te Tōtara Pā but during the post-battle cleansing ceremony he was given the honoured role of chief tohunga for Hongi's three related hapū which again suggests another particularly effective performance as a war tohunga.

All the warriors assembled round me in ranks three deep, each headed by a *tohunga* . . . they came to thank the gods for victory and ask help for the future. I was standing in the *wahi tapu* or sacred grove to receive

the offerings of the warriors. At this time, being quite naked, they struck
the palms of their hands together, and then rubbed them on their thighs
to remove the defilement of human blood. As [each] band came nearer
to me each warrior gave the . . . hair of the slain to his *tohunga* . . . which
I offered up to Te Mara with many prayers. The ceremony concluded by
my taking off them the *pureinga* or sacredness of fight so they could now
eat, weep over their relations, and sleep. After this came the invariable
tupeke or war dance whilst the slaves prepared another feast.

Because Māori had such strong faith in signs, omens and mani-
festations of nature, Marmon was able to commence his priestly career
as an imposter, a mere trickster who set out to deceive his hosts and
exploit their superstitions. Over time, however, he came to believe
implicitly in his own powers as a tohunga. Jacky's recollections of the
Thames campaign confirm in clear and unambiguous language the
depth of his assimilation and spiritual conversion that are startling
in their forthrightness. Equally interesting is how Marmon came to
perceive himself as a Māori rather than a Pākehā-Māori.

Some readers may think it a peculiar thing that I a Pakeha and a stranger
should be raised to such a high honour as chief tohunga of the Ngapuhi
tribe. It must be recollected that although lineage was greatly regarded
amongst the Maoris it was not by any means the sole requisite in rank
and reputation. A slave or a common native could inspire to the rank of
Ariki or *Tohunga*, if his abilities were of sufficient order to entitle him to
it as was proved in the case of Te Heuheu of Taupo; also if he seemed to
be the special favourite with the gods or spirits of Te Reinga, as evinced
by his success in evocation and prophecy, he might claim the coveted
honour.

I had become a Maori as far as I could possibly do so. I had renounced
the religion of the pakehas, and had embraced that of the Maori, this
alone would have entitled me to consideration, but when I had returned
from Te Reinga to leave which even Maori had failed, as runs the legend,
when I could call up the spirits, and be so filled with the power of the
gods as to subdue people to my will as I chose, I was truly a *tohunga* to
be propitiated at any cost lest I should turn the force of my curses against
my friends.

A priestess removing the tapu from a house
On the Kerikeri River from 1822, Marmon completely immersed himself in Māori
religious beliefs and practices.
*Pen and wash drawing. Joseph Merrett, 'A priestess performing her incantations in taking the tapu
from a house which had been sacred', British Library.*

In contrast to reminiscences by more respectable culture-crossing traders like Maning, Richard, Barrett and Charles Marshall, Marmon's is an unconventional Pākehā-Māori narrative. Like these traders, Jacky initially joined Māori for material gain and adventure, but his *Star* narrative develops into something else – a spiritual journey that takes him deep into the heart of the Māori world where he finds mana, peace and meaning. Marmon's second sojourn was largely a journey back to the essence of Maoridom. Pākehā-Māori narratives generally reflect the Māori cosmos through European eyes but Marmon offers perspectives of a fully assimilated Pākehā-Māori. Whereas in *Old New Zealand* Maning transcends or remains detached from his Māori experiences, Marmon is more at ease with the alien events that surround him and the social structures that impact upon him. Marmon's *Star* account defines the outer boundary of the savage Pākehā-Māori, a being who dressed, spoke and came to think and believe as a Māori.

Though he became convinced of his own ability to mākutu or to place a death curse on others, Marmon was not the only tohunga Pākehā to have possessed this power. Ngāti Ruanui's white tohunga Kimball Bent came to believe in the power of death curses.[5] Bent claimed only to have used his skills for healing purposes, but the Ngāti Ruanui tohunga Hupini stated that Bent had killed men with his mākutu, a combination of witchcraft and the power of the evil eye.[6] Marmon never claimed to have killed men by mākutu, but recalled that soon after returning from the Waitemata and Thames campaign, his powers and personal tapu were so great that all he owned could not be touched by any lower-ranked person without serious consequences for them.

I found all my affairs just as they were left, since I had affixed a stringent *tapu* to everything. Also I found my *mana* or reputation as a *tohunga* very strong, independent of the increase it had received during the Thames campaign. I had unwittingly left outside my house a *calabash* which a slave finding drank from and threw away. On being told to whom it had belonged, he instantly threw up his hands saying 'Oh I am doomed then,' and fell back a corpse. This was a striking instance of the force of the imagination and the effect of the tapu. . . . All that a chief or *tohunga* possessed was supposed to be rendered so sacred by their use that any individual of lesser rank was exposed to the risk of death by employing what [the tohunga] had employed previously.

Marmon was indeed an insightful observer with an excellent memory and the *Herald* and core *Star* narratives are simple yet powerful records that fix more than just his many adventures. Simple early 'inside' accounts chronicling the everyday features of Māori and Pākehā-Māori life are rare. Both *Herald* and *Star* 'autobiographies' bring together a wealth of information on everyday life in the kāinga, including Māori food-gathering practices.

It was now the season for hunting the rat, always amongst the Maori an undertaking of some importance, requiring several people to assist in it, as not only were many traps needed but roads had to be formed with great care as any obstacle would have ruined the success. When this happened it was a most serious affair. The New Zealand rat is considerably smaller than the imported one, but is now nearly extinct, owing to the persistent snaring indulged in. It was caught in ingenious *tawiti* (traps), the *poa* (bait) used being *Miro* or *Kahikatea* berries. This year our supply snared was very large, owing it was alleged to my new incantation whilst they were cutting the roads to the traps.

I remember seeing my first wife catch one on top of the water. When it was caught it looked something like our rat, with a pretty soft fur. When cooked it was like rabbit or fowl. I have often seen women and slaves hunting for them among the cultivations . . . they must have been something like what game is among the gentry in England, for there would be hunting parties got up to find rats; and places where they

Māori canoes loading with provisions
Avoiding Hongi's 1822 and 1823 campaigns, Marmon traded actively with hapū at
Kerikeri and the Bay of Islands.
*Calvert, Samuel, 'Maori canoes loading for market', PIC-AN10328768, National Library
of Australia.*

were plentiful were considered very valuable, and there were dreadful rows and fights about poaching in those days. I have often [transported] convicts to Hobart Town who told me they had got sent out for poaching the game belonging to the swells in England – and here they would kill one another about rats.[7]

People think that in old times the natives lived on fern root only . . . but they had lots of good food . . . fish in any quantities fresh from the river in the fine weather; in winter they had stores of dried fish to fall back on. The bush, too, was full of birds, everywhere. I have often seen koroi [kōwhai] trees quite black with tuis; mocking birds [bellbirds] were plentiful enough. Why, the natives would go into the bush and snare them by the hundreds, fill large kits full. They would make a low roof of flax leaves or nikau to hide under, they had a long stick bent a bit at the top to form a sort of perch, then a flower that had honey inside; one of their favourites was placed on the top, a piece of flax was made into a noose and placed near the flower. [T]he native would creep into his shelter, put up his stick, and imitate the bird's note. Then the birds would settle on the perch-like end of the stick, taste the flower. The noose caught their feet, was drawn tight, the string pulled the bird down the stick, the head squeezed, and into the kit in less than no time.

It was a fine thing in the morning to hear the birds, their notes were beautiful; some did not sing, but still they made pretty noises. I cannot make out what's become of all those birds, though they did catch such heaps for kai, they seemed as plentiful as the leaves on the trees. Now the bush seems as still as never a bird had lived in it. 'Quiet as the grave' is a saying; but I am sure here where we live you might say 'as quiet as the bush'. The natives need and do still eat the owl, and if they are fat are not at all bad, though I have a dislike to them myself.[8]

On the Kerikeri, Marmon lived a life of quiet monotony with his fishing and gardening activities, punctuated periodically by trading and tohunga duties and by the excitement of war. He inhabited a timeless world, marked only by singular, memorable events and the passing of the seasons. In a pattern that became common among later Pākehā-Māori, Marmon broke the monotony of village life by briefly visiting the Australian colonies in 1819 and later in 1822 and, when opportunity permitted, by 'spreeing' on rum.

I was very nearly bringing myself into disgrace at this time by a return to my old habits. For months I had been dying for a 'spree', and when at last a vessel was lying in the Bay I went down, procured a small keg of rum, and brought it up with me to the *kainga*. In the secrecy of my own *whare* I went in for a right royal booze, until I was as the saying goes blind drunk.

Unfortunately at this time Tangiwhare, Hongi's chief wife, had a dream she wished explained to her, and sent for me to come. This at present I did not feel inclined to do, and told the messenger, without delay to go to —. This was a most serious offence, as the lady was a chieftainess in her own right, though as ugly as sin, and was followed by an angry message the next day to come to her at once. Being then comparatively sober I went, and explained away the remark of the preceding day by saying that as I was under the influence of the gods, I did not know what fell from my lips. This was satisfactory to her and we became again fast friends.

Considered to have slipped back down the scale of civilisation and to have become white savages motivated by their basest instincts, Pākehā-Māori were also frequently portrayed in the contemporary literature as drunken, licentious men. As a young man Marmon was promiscuous, but, in the *Star* account, Maning spun an elaborate fantasy about Marmon managing, single-handedly, to persuade Hongi Hika to embark on further military conquests so that he could conduct an affair with Tangiwhare, the chief's senior wife.

About this time I had another visit from Tom Tapsell, who gave me the latest news from Sydney; How colonial wool was now run after at home to such a degree that the supply was utterly unequal to the demand; how twenty-five men were executed at Sydney and ten at Hobart Town for bushranging; how St. Mary's Cathedral, the first Roman Catholic church in Australia, was in the course of erection; and finally, how Governor Macquarrie, who had done so much substantial good to the colony, and was regarded with universal respect, was to be succeeded by Sir Thomas Brisbane; also, he told me, what interested me more, that the liquor traffic was to be extended in New South Wales so that there was now liberty to distil drink in certain quantities. Tom Tapsell seemed to

Titore Takiri and Patuone

These sketches show two of Hongi's musket generals in formal dress, though they also had armour of their own. Patuone eventually became Marmon's protector at Hokianga.

R. A. A. Sherrin and J. H. Wallace, Early History of New Zealand: From Earliest Times to 1840, *Auckland, 1890, p. 342.*

consider my life a perfect heaven upon earth, and was hot on becoming a *Pakeha-Maori* at once, but I dissuaded him from it at present, partly because I did not want any other *pakeha* to share the influence I held.

Marmon's *Star* narrative outlines Hongi's preparations for and the progress of his grand expedition against the Waikato tribes in 1822. Unusually, Marmon did not join this powerful taua, 3000 strong and fully armed with muskets, his skills as interpreter of dreams and healer being much in demand by the women of the tribe. Nevertheless, the progress and events of the campaign, conveyed to Marmon by returned veterans from among his own kin, provides further useful information on Hongi's 1822 Waikato campaign which, like the Tamaki and Thames expeditions, was remarkably successful.

But the restless spirit of Hongi could not relish the peace we were now enjoying. He burned to be once more on the battlefield, for the clash of weapons seemed his natural element. . . . Thus were the Ngapuhi's again plunged into the bustle of preparation for another war, and one that promised to be more tedious and uncertain than that waged against the Ngatipaoa. One thing I resolved was that, if I possibly could, I would avoid going . . . because I hoped to do a good trade in flax when everything was quiet, also because I never at any time had much affection for powder and shot.

Danger had menaced the settlement in my absence before; many of the women had died in child-birth, a very rare thing amongst the Maoris; Hongi's wives had been troubled with strange dreams of danger to their lord and master, and there was no one at hand to explain these dreams; therefore to my extreme satisfaction, I was permitted to remain at Keri-keri and pursue in quietness my existence.

At many points during the *Star* account, Marmon is cast as an opportunistic, self-serving rogue, an evasive slippery chancer who preferred whenever possible to avoid accompanying dangerous military expeditions. While not given to recklessness, the primary evidence indicates that Marmon was a tough, combative character who, once committed to battle, fought ferociously to preserve his own life and those of his kinsmen. Like his Pākehā-Māori peers, Jacky continued to prime his musket and stand shoulder to shoulder with his kinsmen during intertribal battles throughout the 1820s and 1830s.

Before he left, however, Hongi sustained a great loss in the death of his youngest daughter, Manaia, to whom he was greatly attached. That she might be preserved to him, he gave orders to embalm the head – an operation devolving on me and an old chief, Tamore. . . . The Maori process of curing heads may be of interest to those who have a weakness for relics of their relations.

They made a small hole, put in some stones and then wood, the same as making a hangi. When the stones were hot – the hole was made funnel-shaped – they would take out the brains of the head, then the eyes (which they eat), sew the eyelids together, and then the lips, put little sticks up the nostrils, to keep them from shrivelling up, take the bones out of the throat, and sew the skin tightly round a small hoop, Then the head was placed over the small hole, the hot stones being underneath, and there left to dry. The teeth they often pulled out, and if he were a very great chief they would be worn as earrings.[9]

This was the process of embalming, and it was pretty general all through New Zealand. In fact in these latter days, when the barter of heads may be regarded as a branch of trade, a man's head was not safe on his shoulders, since, if it happened to be highly ornamented with the *moko* or tattoo, even a friend, to secure the price set upon it, would *accidently* shoot the possessor of it and after a prolonged *tangi* quietly offer it for sale to the Pakeha.

Hongi expressed himself highly pleased with the work Tamore and I executed. After a *tangi* over it, and a solemn *hakari*, the ruling passion prevailed, and he prepared to set out on his expedition against the [Waikato]. In a week he [Hongi] had assembled one thousand men fully equipped ordering two thousand more to be levied and to follow him. This was no light strain upon the Ngapuhi tribe, since it would demand every young man above sixteen . . . but they rose to the occasion, and the stipulated number of men joined Hongi.

Marmon witnessed the rise of the grand Ngāpuhi musket armies at the Bay when musket chiefs like Hongi, promoting large-scale predatory campaigns founded on flintlock guns, mobilised the manpower and economic resources of their people on a much larger scale than previously. Ngāpuhi, despite their monopoly on the gun trade, did not invariably embark on their campaigns with great enthusiasm. As the great taua began to assemble, they became, in the hands of the leading chiefs, coercive instruments of considerable power, drawing into their ranks both willing and unwilling hapū. The war chiefs operated an ad hoc conscription system, meeting with the hapū to determine the number of warriors each would contribute to the campaign. Fear of retribution was a further means of compelling participation; as one of Marmon's trader contemporaries at the Bay reported, 'They told me that they got a great name by fighting, and should they refuse to go, others would come and fight against them and plunder them of all their things.'[10]

Kororareka (Russell)

Hapū from all parts of the Bay of Islands, including this vital trading port, were
obliged to contribute armed contingents for Hongi's grand musket campaigns.
R. A. A. Sherrin and J. H. Wallace, Early History of New Zealand: From Earliest Times
to 1840, *Auckland, 1890.*

Hongi again left the Bay with the same pomp and ceremony and we
relapsed . . . into our former quietness. We pursued our fishing and our
trade, and sometimes had visits from the Mission settlement that was
now established on the Keri-Keri.

Time passed with no news of Hongi's return and less about his movements and conflicting reports declared him defeated, killed and eaten
. . . or pursuing a career of conquest as brilliant as his Waitemata and
Thames campaigns. Such reports kept us in a state of great anxiety, as
we knew that if Hongi was killed numberless tribes would pounce on us
like vultures on their prey . . . Hongi, in the meantime, had a conquering
career before him which I shall merely briefly sketch.

He reached the Waitemata . . . and pushed on drawing his canoes
across the narrow neck of land at Otahuhu and Waiuku, and descended
the Awaroa. Nothing was permitted to check his victorious course. Even
Nature was compelled to alter her face to permit him to pass, as when

in the Awaroa one of his canoes was stopped by a narrow bend in the stream, he ordered a canal to be cut for her to proceed – a monument of his perseverance which remains to this day.

The terror inspired by the approach of a Ngapuhi musket army led many tribes to undertake a variety of measures to slow the advance of their enemies. Waikato felled so many trees into the Awaroa stream which had previously provided an easy route between the Manukau Harbour and the Waikato River that Ngapuhi took two months to clear these obstructions to their fleet.

Ascending the Waikato [at] last he reached the great Matakitaki Pa situated on the banks of the Waipa River, where a number of Waikatos and Ngatiwhatuas had fled for safety. The position was strong, the defenders were determined to hold out to the last, and even Hongi seemed to have doubts whether an attack would be successful. Yet there was always this in Hongi – an indomitable perseverance. Difficulties only spurred him on to fresh endeavour, and the attempt was made. The assailants were assisted by natural allies. A vast portion of the earthen rampart fell in on some of the defenders, and when the Ngapuhis, having driven back [the defenders under Te Wherowhero], who sought to hold the breach, were rushing in to secure any fugitives in attempting to escape over the mound, there was but a single log thrown across the great ditch at the rear of pa. Hundreds were pushed into the ditch and [were] crushed to death by the pressure of the crowd, until a suffocating mass of humanity was all that was remained within Matakitaki.

Marmon's is the only reference to the collapse of one of the great earthen bastions, but it resolved a question that had previously puzzled New Zealand military historians. Faced with the formidable defences of Matakitaki Pā and the large, disciplined defending force under Te Wherowhero, how had the Ngāpuhi army entered the position so quickly?

Such good fortune had never come to Ngapuhis before, and a week's feasting was utterly insufficient to consume the amount of *kai* (food) thus unexpectedly provided. The capture of Taurakohia, another great pah on the Waipa, followed immediately after, and the subjugation, if not the desolation of Waikato would have been complete had not peace been made between the two tribes through the endeavours of Wharerahi, a Ngapuhi chief, and Te Wherowhero of Waikato. Te Wherowhero's relative Kati, of Waikato, taking to wife Toa, daughter of Rewa, of Ngapuhi.

Hongi swept up the Bay with his canoes in war procession, with all the terrible accompaniments of native warfare. . . . We had our usual *tangis* over our dead relatives, ate our customary feasts, sometimes of human flesh, and engaged in the sports proper to such solemn occasions. At all of these I had to be present to take my share. . . . Thus ended this raid upon [Waikato], only to be followed by another [against Ngāti Whātua] in which I myself was engaged.

Marmon was one of three pre-annexation Pākehā-Māori known to have openly relished human flesh and participated in post-battle cannibal feasts, though there were probably many others. James Caddel of southern Ngāi Tahu, originally captured by Māori as a teenager, was described by the Europeans who interviewed him during the 1820s as a savage and a cannibal.[11] 'Smith', a Ngāti Toa fighting man, was Te Rauparaha's favourite Pākehā-Māori. Honoured by his chief at a feast on Kapiti Island in 1830, this Pākehā-Māori was presented with a portion of the heart of the Ngāi Tahu chief Tamaiharanui. Shortly thereafter, Smith was himself captured, killed, cooked and eaten by Ngāi Tahu during a disastrous Ngāti Toa raid into the South Island.[12]

Marmon did not admit to cannibalism in the *Herald* memoir and, not wishing to upset Alice Bennett, may have considered this type of information best forgotten. He hints instead that the white savages at the Bay of Islands indulged in this practice and worse.

You should understand that though the New Zealander did eat human flesh, they had plenty of things to eat besides. . . . Cannibalism mostly took place in times of war, and the flesh of a dead enemy they considered sweet. I am not defending what they did, but when I tell you things it is what I have seen and what I think about it. The greatest insult you could offer to a native now would be to call him a cannibal. He would be as much horrified as you would yourself. I am sure that some of the white men at the Bay of Islands in the early times were not a bit better than the natives and some not half as good, I can tell you. Why there were lots of things done by those chaps that would make a savage ashamed of himself. Any of the old hands knocking about could tell you some nice yarns if they liked.[13]

Marmon initially ate the flesh of a slave to ingratiate himself with Hongi Hika during the chief's 1821 recruiting tour, and for Pākehā toa of all ranks cannibalism became a necessity as the Musket Wars escalated. Without a permanent commissariat the great musket taua on their long-distance campaigns were dependent on the bodies of their enemies to sustain them on remote battlefields and at the conclusion of prolonged sieges. Confronted with a choice between cannibalism or death by starvation on far-flung battlefields during extended campaigns Pākehā-Māori could not afford to be precious regarding the origins of their meat. The similarity in smell, flavour and texture of cooked pork, dog and human flesh served up by slaves in flax baskets during evening feasts at their home villages ensured that many became involuntary cannibals, at least initially.

Convict labourers, Sydney
Having worked as a sailor aboard colonial convict transports, Marmon was himself imprisoned in 1823 and compelled to work in a convict road gang.
Augustus Earle, 'A government jail gang Sydney', NIA.PIC-AN6065451, National Library of Australia.

Again and again have I been asked if it is possible a man could acquire such a taste for human flesh as was reported. I reply most certainly. Serve up a leg of man the same as you would a leg of mutton, and ten to one you will not be able to tell the difference. An Englishman makes very funny faces when he hears of the 'Mounseers' eating frogs. Let them be served up as the Frenchmen serve them, and the beef eating Englishman, not knowing what they are, will eat as heartily of them as he would of young chicken. To a Maori nothing is more distasteful than lean pork, or as they say in Sydney, lean beef. They rejoice in everything oily, even when it becomes putrid.

Marmon's notoriety, too, was founded mainly on his cannibalism. The Hokianga settler John Nimmo recalled that during a Māori feast at the Hokianga in the early 1830s Marmon offered him a basket of human flesh 'cooked in their earth oven'. When his guest refused to take the basket, Marmon said that Nimmo had 'no idea how good it tasted'.[14] Smithyman's enquiries led him to conclude that Marmon was not the only Pākehā-Māori at Hokianga to relish human flesh but, rather, he was the district's 'last known white cannibal'.

After his return from the Waikato expedition, Hongi left Keri-Keri to live on his lands at the Whangaroa. Our *kainga*, therefore, relapsed once more into the quietness of old and Kawitiwai was once more lord and master. . . . I pursued my trade in flax and pigs, did a little interpreting work when required, discharged my duties as *tohunga* and engaged in the manufacture of grog from potatoes. The desire to rove again seized me and it was with difficulty that I repressed it. Great change, however, was pending, not only for me but for the whole Ngapuhi *iwi*.[15]

According to Rev. Butler's journal, grog making by the 'notorious John' continued to trouble the Kerikeri missionaries until October 1822, when references to the Pākehā-Māori cease before resuming in 1823.[16] Although Marmon had determined to live reclusively among Māori, by late 1822 the Kerikeri River had become a thoroughfare for Europeans visiting the Anglican Mission station. Marmon's decision to visit Sydney in late 1822 was prompted by increased European contact, including Tapsell's news about Sydney and by sheer boredom. 'I was beginning to weary of Keri-keri and to desire a change to some other part.'

Making his way downriver to the Bay in late 1822, Marmon found a ship and sailed to Sydney, but soon fell foul of the authorities. The record shows that he was arrested for the theft of a locket and imprisoned in January 1823 pending his trial. In both newspaper accounts Marmon claims to have been falsely accused and considered his imprisonment, 'the greatest misfortune that ever happened to me in all my life. . . . They were dreadfully hard on folks in those days, and people were severely punished for very slight offences'.[17] He recalled his loss of freedom and three brutal months of hard labour.

I was a convict, had my head shaven, donned the prison dress, lost my own name and passed current under the meaningless title of No. 356. I was set to road making. Day after day passed in the monotonous round of work until my very soul was sick, and I longed for death to free me from my misery. My arms ached with handling the spade; my feet were swollen and blistered with the coarse shoes and the heavy walking. Oh, it was a terrible time, with no chance of escape from the eagle-eyed sentinel standing over us with loaded musket. Heaven pity the wretched man that ever becomes a convict.

On 1 May 1823, the *Sydney Gazette* reported:

John Marmont was indicted for stealing a miniature, and found Guilty. In consideration of the prisoner being a native youth, and reared to the sea, the Court was leniently induced to dispose of him accordingly. He was sentenced to be kept at hard labour on board of the Government Colonial vessels, for the term of two years.[18]

Marmon considered his prison experience the greatest of all the injustices he suffered at the hands of Europeans and it drove his decision to permanently abandon colonial society. In the *Herald*, he recalled first being assigned to a ship which transported convicts from Newcastle to Fort Macquarie and coal to Port Jackson and, in the *Star*, how he resolved to take a ship to New Zealand and desert at the first opportunity.[19] Tracking Marmon's movements aboard the shipping of the period is difficult as he signed on under a variety of aliases including 'Bill Turner'. He was certainly aboard HMS *Elizabeth Henrietta* when she sailed for New Zealand in November 1823, for he is listed as a convict sailor on the ship's manifest.[20]

A locally built brig of about 2150 tons captained by John Rodolphus Kent, the *Henrietta* was dispatched by the New South Wales Government to collect a cargo of flax. Wigglesworth speculates that Marmon may have deserted as soon as the ship arrived in New Zealand before settling at the Hokianga under the protection of Muriwai.[21] It is also possible that Marmon was aboard the *Henrietta* when it ran aground at Ruapuke Island in Foveaux Strait and that he was reassigned aboard the rescue ship *Tees*, a government sloop of war. In the *Herald*, Marmon claims to have deserted the *Tees* when it anchored at Queen Charlotte Sound in Cook Strait and he may have subsequently worked his passage north to the Bay of Islands aboard an unidentified ship before deserting with a teenage sailor, 'Jim the Boy', in late 1823.[22]

Meeting his old friend Samuel Marsden at the Bay, Marmon and his companion accompanied the missionary to the Kerikeri, where the Rev. Butler's journal resumed, 'I have already hinted that Mr Marsden brought down again with him the notorious John.'[23] Marmon did not rejoin his hapū on the Kerikeri River. On visiting the kāinga he found his old protector Kawhitiwai had died, perhaps of natural causes or at the ferocious pitched battle on Mokoia Island fought between Ngāpuhi and the Arawa people at Lake Rotorua during Hongi's grand 1823 campaign. Marmon's contemporary, the Pākehā-Māori James Burns of Waitangi, accompanied this taua and attributed Ngāpuhi's loss of 300 toa 'to the enemies' considerable numbers'.[24] Regardless, Marmon realised that without Kawhitiwai's support he would not recover the considerable influence he had once wielded among Hikutu and, ever the pragmatist, elected to find another protector and hapū.

With his [Kawhitiwai's] death I knew my influence in the tribe was gone. I had many enemies whose jealousy would go to any extreme to rid themselves of my presence, therefore I determined to save them the trouble and make myself scarce at once [and was] on my way to Hokianga, which was to be my future home.

CHAPTER SIX

Pākehā-Māori, 1823–30

During the summer of 1825, a Ngāpuhi war party some 200 strong toiled slowly northwards, skirting the ocean's edge alongside the scorching iron-sand beaches of the North Island's west coast. Having recently helped crush their Ngāti Whātua enemies at the battle of Te Ika a Ranganui and laid waste their territories, the warriors drove before them two lines of naked male taurekareka (prisoners of war), their necks linked and hands bound behind their backs with flax cords. Several captive chieftainesses walked among the victorious toa, their hands unbound, but restrained by lengths of braided flax woven into their hair and tied to the wrists of their future husbands. As the taua neared their homes where the Hokianga River opens to the turbulent Tasman Sea, they were met and accompanied by a large babbling crowd of kinsfolk.

Among the welcoming throng were four newly arrived European sawyers, who observed with interest the progress of the expedition's baggage train. Some 60 women and older boys trudged by, the former bowed under booty in the shape of captive children, woven cloaks, carved jewellery boxes and greenstone ornaments, the latter laden with enemy muskets, rākau weapons, small casks of powder and a prized box of flintlocks. When the rearguard emerged from the heat haze it was seen to comprise a score of fierce fighting slaves. To the visitors' horror, they were pikauing (backpacking) the smoke-dried heads and the flesh of the conquered. To the visitors' astonishment, the contingent was led by a wild-haired white man in Māori dress, tattooed, heavily armed 'and a full kit of human flesh on his back'.[1]

Hokianga, the fiord-like inlet in the western coast of the Northland peninsula, was settled early by runaway convicts and ships' deserters. A poor harbour, the river mouth was swept by sea and blocked by a sand bar which deterred all but the most daring sea captains. Jacky Marmon and his companion Jim the Boy or Jim the Māori were the first known Pākehā to live on the Hokianga River.[2] From late 1823, they lived a completely Māori existence and were known by their transliterated names Hake Mamene and Hēmi Mowri. Re-establishing himself as a tohunga, Marmon joined Ngāpuhi on raids led by Hongi Hika, Muriwai and Patuone. Comments by the English visitor Edward Markham and colonial official William Hobson confirm Marmon's residence among Ngāpuhi during the 1810s, but from 1823 Marmon's life and adventures among Hokianga Ngāpuhi can be verified more consistently in historical records, and parts of the *Star* and *Herald* accounts begin to coincide.[3]

When Marmon settled permanently at the Hokianga at the age of 25, he had already spent nearly six years living among Māori. Life in New South Wales held little appeal, for on visiting Sydney in 1822 he found that his father had died, his mother had remarried and his brothers and sisters were too young for him to have formed any attachment to them. In later years Marmon claimed that it was the social disgrace of his conviction for theft (he maintained that he was innocent) that prompted his decision to settle permanently in New Zealand.[4]

In the *Herald* memoir, Marmon recalled that, having fled his ship and journeyed overland from the Bay to Hokianga with Jim the Boy, the people of Utakura, a settlement near the headwaters of the Hokianga River, attempted to induce him to become their Pākehā by offering him a wife. Marmon declined but Muriwai, one of their senior chiefs who was visiting the settlement with his retinue, was more successful.

There was an old chief here named Muriwai, of the Rarawa tribe, whose highest ambition had been to secure me as a *pakeha* [and] when I arrived

Pakanae village, 1827

Marmon spent his first weeks in Hokianga at this village which overlooked the dangerous harbour entrance.

Augustus Earle, 'Village of Parcuneigh [i.e. Pakanae] and the entrance of the E-o-ke-angha [i.e. Hokianga] River, New Zealand', PIC-AN2820785, National Library of Australia.

at his settlement I received a most flattering and cordial reception. So overjoyed was he that without any difficulty I obtained a large grant of valuable land [200 acres] for the price of my residence among them. I took the upper hand with Muriwai from the first, accordingly, I never had any trouble with him. I therefore began my trading in flax and pigs once more, certain that a good thing was to be made out of these commodities.

Marmon had allied himself with the powerful Te Popoto hapū led by Muriwai and his brother Makoare (Macquarie) Te Taonui, whose lands were mainly in the Utakura area. Marmon spent his first weeks at Pakenae 'shooting ducks and walking about. I was quite happy and comfortable; plenty of pigs, shell-fish and potatoes – besides the river down there was alive with fish'.[5] Though not required to work, he was expected to acquire guns for his chiefs as, in 1823, the northern inter-hapū arms race was at its height. The treacherous bar at the harbour entrance had only been crossed twice previously by Captain Kent's *Prince Regent* in 1820 and Captain Herd's *Providence* in 1822. Their return to Sydney with profitable cargoes of kauri timber encouraged other daring skippers to enter the river carrying the typical trader's cargo of muskets, powder, ammunition, general merchandise and liquor.

Jacky always found Hongi Hika, the most formidable of the chiefs, a benign despot, but like his Kawhitiwai, Muriwai was to prove just benignly devious. These chiefs did not give European fugitives refuge out of charity and Muriwai expected his Pākehā to prove himself as a resourceful trading intermediary, though the number of visiting ships was very small before 1826. That 'Muriwai was a great chief – next in rank to Hongi', and closely related to the powerful Hokianga chiefs Patuone and Waka Nene, gave Marmon a monopoly on the musket trade. 'Muriwais people built a house for us . . . and in that I kept my muskets – I was quite a man of property; wife, house, clothes, and enough [trade goods] to last a long time.'[6]

'It is not good for a man to be alone' is the maxim of the Maori, and I had not been long in Hokianga before Muriwai insisted upon my marrying . . . so as to bring myself into closer connection with himself.[7] . . . I took the daughter of John King [Hōne Kīngi Raumati]. Her name was Hawauru [Hauāuru] (westerly wind), a very pretty girl, with beautiful long black hair. . . . I paid for the wife one musket. Jim the boy was too poor to buy one for himself, so the natives made him a present of one.[8] . . . Although some of my wives were living at the Bay of Islands and I had four or five children by them there, I . . . settled down again as a domestic man to taste the sweets of matrimonial life.[9]

While living among Hikutu on the Kerikeri River from 1817, Marmon had derived considerable mana from his marriage to a chief's daughter, his association with a powerful chief and success as a trading intermediary. With his black hair, blue eyes and fair skin, Jacky once again became an exotic curiosity, a figure of wonder, admiration and the subject of endless speculation. Able to obtain muskets from the Pākehā and repair these strange and murderous devices, Marmon was exempted from punishment by muru. Granted full freedom of movement by Muriwai, he periodically accompanied trading parties of Popoto to the Bay of Islands, generally making the crossing on foot and by canoe in one day, along well-established bush paths and waterways.

Never satisfied with the dependent status of a trader Pākehā-Māori, Marmon, well versed in the arts of the Māori priesthood, worked diligently to re-establish his reputation as a tohunga Pākehā. In isolated

Hokianga it was very easy for Māori to imbue Marmon with superior powers for he was tangata tipua (foreign), exempt from the diseases destroying Māori and, astonishingly, he could violate a tapu and suffer no retribution from the atua.

Profound respect was inspired in the minds of the Hokianga natives by my powers in mesmerism and ventriloquism. They considered those accomplishments as showing a peculiar nearness of relation to the gods, and when I made answers to their questions proceed as it were from the sea or some towering *kauri*, an awe stole over all as if they felt they were in the presence of something more than human. . . . I demanded a tithe both of the fish caught and produce of the ground, also of the spoils taken in war, which, after some hesitation, was granted to me. I was on the fair way to become a rich man. . . .

Muriwai was the greatest dreamer I ever knew; each morning he had some new dream to be explained to him, and my wits were kept pretty busy devising explanations of them for him. He was, perhaps, the most superstitious Maori I ever met. . . . The Maoris generally are great believers in dreams which they consider to be sent by the gods to forewarn men of coming events. Anyone who had a *moe hewa*, or dream, must never rest until he had a satisfactory explanation of it. Whenever a man had a bad dream he repeated a *karakia* called *uriuri*, to prevent the fulfilment of it, because it was considered impossible for a dream to be false in the forewarning it gave.

For in dreams it was thought that the spirit leaves the mortal clay and betakes itself to Te Reinga where it has intercourse with the spirits of its friends. In fact it is a very important part of the office of a *tohunga* to be a skilful interpreter of dreams – that is, to deliver the answers in such ambiguous manner that they may be read either way, or at least a loophole left for escape. Muriwai had all sorts of dreams and sometimes it was most puzzling to get an explanation that would exactly suit his cause, but generally a little tact in finding out his own inclinations was sufficient to furnish an answer agreeable to him.

A challenger to Marmon soon appeared. Influenced perhaps by missionary teachings at the Bay of Islands, this young chief had begun to question the validity of Māori religious beliefs and the sanctions

Te Waenga, high priest of the Hokianga Harbour entrance
Marmon could only practise as a tohunga Pākehā with the approval of senior
tohunga Māori.
R. A. A. Sherrin and J. H. Wallace, Early History of New Zealand: From Earliest Times to 1840,
Auckland, 1890, p. 364.

underlying traditional customs. In a bizarre reversal of roles, Marmon, a former Roman Catholic, found himself defending Māori religion and used the opportunity to both confound the doubter and impress the chiefs.

I had some trouble about this time with a most unbelieving young Maori who considered himself as wise beyond his fellows, and therefore entitled to express his opinions on every point. He asserted that the gods were a mere trumped up set of unrealities, that all communications with such was a fraud – in a word, that I was little better than an imposter. Being the son of Pakatariti, a great *rangatira*, his words were listened to with attention and seemed to be exercising some influence upon the younger natives. I knew that if the evil were not nipped in the bud it would cause me great and serious annoyance.

Accordingly I asked him to meet me in the guest house when, before Muriwai and his chiefs, I would prove him to be in the wrong. On the evening stated, the entire settlement of Tahitaira was assembled to witness the contest as it involved issues important to everyone. . . . I first permitted them to ask any questions through me to deceased relatives, which, by the help of ventriloquism, I answered in the usual low whistling tone . . . [and] having mesmerised him and caused him, while under the influence, to declare his entire conversion from his former views to the faith of his fathers, the enthusiasm of the crowd knew no bounds and they would have worshipped me on the spot had I so desired it. My triumph was complete, and henceforth I was never troubled with enquiring spirits seeking the *how*, the *whether* and the *why* of our existence.

At Hokianga, Marmon again completely immersed himself in the world of Māori and assumed full kinship obligations. During the early 1830s the Jewish trader Joel Polack described tattooing as a key element in the 'naturalisation' of European culture-crossers and the tā moko or face tattoo marked several fully assimilated Pākehā-Māori including James Caddell, John Rutherford and Barnet Burns. Polack encountered a number of tattooed Pākehā-Māori at Hokianga during Marmon's residency, but he does not identify them by name.[10]

The sketch of Marmon that appeared in the *Auckland Weekly News* 12 years after his death does not show moko lines.[11] Several modern researchers, however, believe that Marmon may have had a tā moko.[12] Kendrick Smithyman, the Northland-born academic, poet and literary archaeologist who did much research on Marmon at Hokianga during the 1950s and 1960s, for instance, described him as 'a heavy-headed horse-faced tattooed man'.[13]

Some Pākehā-Māori including Caddell and Burns bore both tā moko and tikihope, the elaborate scroll patterns that covered hips, buttocks and thighs. The trader Pākehā-Māori John Cowell (junior) bore a tikihope only, which could be covered by trousers or a kilt when among European company.[14] Others like Maning and Webster found it convenient to have just their upper and lower arms tattooed.[15]

If Marmon was tattooed, his tā moko will have been completed in stages over several weeks to allow the finished sections to heal. The process, described by Pākehā-Māori as 'agonising' and by Smithyman as 'where your cutting edge of experience runs out', required the systematic incising of the face with distinctive patterns by the tohunga moko or priest specialising in tattooing. Tā moko was an important form of identification. Emerging as blue lines on his white skin, such patterns would have indicated Jacky's tribal connections, and rank as tohunga and toa.[16] Having taken the tā moko, Pākehā-Māori were expected to distinguish themselves in expeditions of war and Marmon acknowledged or was observed by European witnesses, participating in at least nine intertribal battles between Hongi Hika's 1821 campaign and the end of the 1845 Flagstaff War.

Rather than having to take 'the upper hand' with his chief, Marmon would have found Muriwai a pragmatic and magnanimous host who protected many later settlers, including the Wesleyan missionaries. Rev. John Hobbs reported that, by 1827, Muriwai was 'looked up to by almost every person on the River as a sort of father'.[17] Free to visit the Bay of Islands when he chose, Marmon also moved about the Hokianga living with his wife's relatives at Omananai, Paekanae and Waihou and practising his tohunga skills for a time at Wiria, near Hokianga Heads, where he was known as Te Manene, 'the stranger'.[18]

I should remark, however . . . that for nearly eight years I lived with Muriwai, treated by him with unvarying kindness. They were stormy years those too, for Pomare, emulating the example shown him by Hongi, was carrying death and war throughout all north New Zealand. But we were not troubled by these commotions: our kainga was too remote to be included in any summons to come to fight, so we lived on in peace and quietness.

Marmon's peaceful existence ended in the year 1825, when contingents of Hokianga Ngāpuhi under Muriwai, Patuone and Waka Nene joined Hongi Hika's last amphibious campaign, against the Ngāti Whātua people. Ably led by their great tactician, the chief Murupaenga, who had previously inflicted severe defeats on Ngāpuhi, the iwi lived in numerous pā and kāinga scattered around the shores of the Kaipara Harbour south of the Hokianga. The fighting men of a hapū were a close-knit, interdependent fighting unit and though he now lived among Hokianga Ngāpuhi under Muriwai's protection, Marmon was again recruited by Hongi Hika because of his proven reputation as a war tohunga and fighting man. Having narrowly escaped arrest by a ship's captain while visiting one of Hongi's pā at the Bay, Marmon was keen to join the campaign and remove himself from the region for a time.

Rather than give up [a] tohunga who was so useful to him both in peace and war . . . Hongi seemed determined to take me along with him on his next expedition. This was against the Ngatiwhatua at Kaipara to avenge the slaughter of the Ngapuhis in the expedition led by Pokaia. . . . Again I accompanied Hongi both as *tohunga* and friend . . .

Both *Star* and *Herald* accounts contain Marmon's detailed descriptions of the Kaipara campaign but, interestingly, it is the more conservative *Herald* account which details the incidents of cannibalism. The 1825 expedition had been instigated by Te Whareumu of Ngāpuhi who

John Rutherford
Marmon met this fighting Pākehā-Māori from Otuihu Pā in the Bay of Islands on the
Te Ika a Ranganui battlefield, near Kaiwaka, in 1825.
A-090-028, Alexander Turnbull Library.

sought utu for the killing of his relative by Ngāti Whātua in 1820. Hongi, similarly, saw the campaign as an opportunity to remove dangerous neighbours and avenge the loss of kin at the battle of Moremonui on the Kaipara coast around 1808. Here, many Ngāpuhi chiefs were killed including Pokaia and two of Hongi's brothers. Hongi escaped through flight and concealment, and the battle's name, Te Kai a te Karoro (the seagull's feast) recalled the vast number of gulls that gathered to feed on the slain.[19]

The details of the epic battle of Te Ika a Ranganui were first recorded by the ethnographer S. Percy Smith in his *Maori Wars of the Nineteenth Century*. Smith drew on accounts left by the participating warriors Paikea, Te Toko and Pūriri of Ngāti Whātua and the rangatira Hongi Hika and Hoera of Ngāpuhi.[20] Both Marmon and the chief Pomare's fighting Pākehā-Māori John Rutherford dictated their own accounts of the battle. In his text, Smith firstly and incorrectly cast doubt on Rutherford's presence, stating that the Pākehā-Māori 'must have heard the account from others, and that very imperfectly'. Secondly, Smith plagiarised Marmon's *Herald* description and cited a fictitious Māori informant.[21]

Hongi's last campaign commenced in February 1825, when the first Ngāpuhi contingent of 170 toa under Te Whareumu set off by canoe down the east coast from the Bay of Islands followed soon after by Hongi's force of 300. Each division was accompanied by their Pākehā-Māori and a commissariat of women, boys and trusted slaves. The missionary George Clarke estimated the overall number of departing waka at 50 and noted, 'muskets are the New Zealander's idols, he will part from everything he possess for one of these instruments of destruction'.[22] James Kemp, the mission blacksmith at Kerikeri, said of Hongi's contingent, as they departed the Kerikeri basin, 'as many as four hundred left . . . and a great many more would join as they went down the river, and that a large party from the Hokianga also departed the Bay for the general rendezvous on the coast at Mangawhai'.[23]

Meanwhile most Ngāti Whātua clans had gathered under their rangatira at the head of the Kaiwaka River south of Whangārei to discuss the impending invasion. Murupaenga suggested launching a surprise attack as Ngāpuhi disembarked at Mangawhai. His fellow

a monument to the memory of Rawiti at Tarawera
Nov 22. 1845

Memorial to a chief
Distinctive wooden monuments or totems were often constructed to commemorate
deceased Māori and Pākeha-Māori. This practice continued into the twentieth
century.
*Pencil and watercolour, 90 x 150 mm. Richard Taylor, 'A monument to the Memory of Rawhiti at
Tarawera', E-296-q-013-2, Alexander Turnbull Library.*

chiefs, believing Hongi Hika could never be caught in a trap, overruled
the plan and the Kaipara chiefs prepared to confront and defeat their
old foes in a pitched battle.

Whareumu went by water to Mangawai, then dragged his canoes across
to Kaipara, his force amounting to two hundred men. Hongi, alleging that
as chief of the Ngapuhis his presence was required wherever members
of his tribe were, prepared another expedition of three hundred men, and
came up with Whareumu at Mangawai engaged portaging his canoes
across.[24]

The combined Ngāpuhi force then hauled their fleet across the ancient
portage, about 10 kilometres in length, which terminated in the shallow
tidal Kaiwaka inlet on the Kaipara Harbour. They camped on the first
night beside their canoes on the Waimako Stream which flows into the
Kaiwaka River. The Pākehā-Māori John Rutherford also accompanied
Hongi's taua. With face and body tattooed, armed with a greenstone

mere, a brace of flintlock pistols and a double-barrelled gun, Rutherford later claimed to have accompanied his hapū to the battlefield as a mere spectator. Moving among the various hapū, Rutherford found Marmon seated among Hongi's contingent. Rutherford, who eventually returned to England, dictated an account of the battle that was published in 1830 in George Craik's *The New Zealanders*.

I afterwards was seated in the midst of them by the side of the white man, who told me his name was John Mawman, that he was a native of Port Jackson, [Sydney], and that he had run away from the Tees sloop of war while she lay at this island. He had since joined the natives, and was now living with a chief named Rawmatty [Raumati] whose daughter he had married, and whose residence was at a place called Sukyanna [Hokianga] on the West coast within fifty miles of the Bay of Islands. He said that he had been at the Bay of Islands a short time before, and had seen several of the English missionaries. He also said that he had heard that the natives had lately taken a vessel [the whaler *Mercury*] at a place called Wangalore [Whangaroa] which they had plundered and then turned adrift.[25]

While the two Pākehā-Māori were exchanging news, Hongi, who was seated among the senior chiefs, suddenly rose up and, with his mere of polished steel, struck and killed a slave who had been brought before him. Having stolen Hongi's precious armour, the slave had been seized by the Ngāpuhi sentries while attempting to cross to the enemy. Both Pākehā-Māori watched as Hongi immediately cut out and devoured the heart of his victim.

For three days the two tribes negotiated without success and Wharepoaka was wounded when Ngāti Whātua began firing indiscriminately. That night the Ngāpuhi camp was attacked by two contingents of picked men led by Murupaenga. As one party spread confusion, attacking and killing some of the invaders, the other burned and holed many of the canoes. Ngāpuhi worked at repairing their fleet over several days but ceased when the entire Ngāti Whātua army, 1000 strong, was observed advancing in column, at pace, through the fernlands towards the right bank of the Waimako Stream. In *Old New Zealand*, Frederick Maning paints a dramatic picture of the advance of a taua of identical size.

The whole taua has emerged upon the plain. 'Here they come! Here they come!' is heard in all directions. The men of the outpost cross the line of march in pretended resistance; they present their guns, make horrid grimaces, dance about like mad baboons, then fall back with headlong speed to the next advantageous position for making a stand. The taua however comes on steadily; they are formed in a solid oblong mass. The chief at the left of the column leads them on. The men are all equipped for immediate action. . . . Every man, almost without exception, is covered in tattooing from the knees to the waist; the face is also covered with dark spiral lines. On they come, a set of tall, athletic, heavy-made men . . . but they do not keep in step; this causes a very singular appearance at a distance. Instead of the regular marching step of civilized soldiers . . . this mass seems to progress towards you with the creeping motion of some great reptile, at a distance, and when coming down sloping ground this effect is quite remarkable.[26]

The 500 Ngāpuhi kai paura who rushed from their camp to take up a strategic position on the left bank of the Kaiwaka Stream were superbly equipped veterans of numerous rākau–musket battles. By 1825, the exuberance and colour of the early Ngāpuhi musket taua had given way to a grim uniformity of arms and equipment that made for easy logistics. Some kai paura now wore a third cartridge box attached to a shoulder belt. Others had replaced their shoddy trade guns with the Brown Bess, a more robust and reliable black-powder military musket that was being bartered on the coasts in increasing numbers. George Clarke had observed that every warrior departing the Bay carried a musket with an attached bayonet.[27] Each toa had thrust into their belts, at the small of their backs, patiti (steel tomahawks) or patu for close-in fighting and for finishing the wounded.

Comprising fighting men drawn from nearly all their major hapū and reinforced with contingents of their Te Roroa and Te Uro o Hau allies, Ngāti Whātua deployed into two ranks while still on the run. Though few trading ships had visited the Kaipara, before 1825, most rangatira and leading toa had obtained muskets through intertribal trading and gift-giving practices. The common toa were generally armed rākau Māori, with traditional long, two-handed weapons like the wooden sword (taiaha), battle axe (tewhatewha) or spear (huata) and a short, one-handed weapon such as the steel tomahawk or flat-bladed patu of stone, bone or wood like the mere, kotiate and wahaika. The long weapons were carried in the right hand, never in the left, which was the tapu or female side. Among the leading rangatira supporting Murupaenga were Te Ahumua, Rewarewha, Tieke, Te Toko, Pūriri and Paikea. The veteran chiefs accompanying Hongi included Te Whareumu, Te Morenga, Taiwhanga and Tirarau from the Bay and Muriwai, and the brothers Patuone and Waka Nene from the Hokianga.[28]

'On a long flat were posted the Ngatiwhatuas determined to give battle', their right flank protected by dense forest, their left directly barring the passage of Ngāpuhi. Chosen by Murupaenga as the battle site, this flat straddled the Waimako Stream about a mile from its junction with the Otamatea [Kaiwaka River]. The surrounding country known as Te Ika a Ranganui was undulating, covered in stunted fern and mānuka and bordered to the north and south by forested ranges. In the vicinity were the two 'strong *pahs* of Te Ikaranganui and Makiri about a mile distant from each other. The former was defended on one side by a precipitous cliff descending sheer into the river, on the other by strong ditches and rampart.' Marmon states that Ngāti Whātua planned to take refuge within, and continue the fight from, these positions if defeated in the field.

Advancing ahead of Hongi's larger contingent, Te Whareumu's own force began deploying into two lines when Ngāti Whātua suddenly charged across the stream. Taken by surprise, Te Whareumu was unable to complete the manoeuvre and maximise the firepower of his musketeers. Compelled to fight hand to hand while encumbered by heavy muskets and their accoutrements, Te Whareumu's men were quickly disadvantaged by the more lightly armed Ngāti Whātua who easily dodged or parried the clubbed musket blows and bayonet thrusts of the invaders.

The conflict at first was entirely between Whareumu's men and the Ngatiwhatuas. He had originated the expedition and it was but fair he should have a chance of distinguishing himself in it. Hongi therefore held aloof. But Whareumu had not the reputation of Hongi to give terror to his onset, gradually his men were forced back and defeat was imminent when Hongi, who considered such an event would be a disgrace not only on Whareumu's *hapu* but the entire tribe, charged at the head of his men.

Whareumu rallied his retreating warriors who, turning, joined Hongi's charge and drove back Murupaenga's forces. The combined Ngāpuhi contingents commenced continuous rolling volleys which killed many Ngāti Whātua, who were compelled to retreat across the Waimako. Regrouping under their rangatira, Ngāti Whātua launched a second charge through the drifting gun smoke only to be halted at the stream edge by the concentrated gunfire of the invaders as every musket was brought to bear. Armed only with a mere pounamu, Murupaenga remained unscathed, while his personal retinue of rangatira and leading toa was thinned by each volley. A few hapū forced a crossing and closed with Te Whareumu's contingents at several places along the stream edge.

Rutherford reported that during these chaotic melees both sides threw their empty muskets behind them before 'drawing their meres and tomahawks out of their belts', and fighting traditionally.[29] Thunderous volleys from Hongi's supporting kai paura again forced back the attackers and those who stood their ground to haka were shot down in scores as they roared defiance. At one fiercely contested spot where

Mokomokai, or tattooed heads
The preserved heads of enemy chiefs were sometimes mounted on short cross sticks which were covered by cloaks, giving the impression that a group of seated chiefs were engaged in conversation.
E. H. McCormick (ed.), Markham, Edward, New Zealand, or Recollections of It,
Wellington, 1963, p. 72.

120 Ngāti Whātua 'fell in one heap', Hongi Hika's eldest son Hare fell, mortally wounded by a musket ball.

Both tribes performed haka during a lull in the battle, before the depleted forces of Ngāti Whātua launched a final desperate charge which only carried them within arm's length of the gun muzzles. Hongi, sensing the battle's critical moment, led his men in a counter charge 'and in spite of the desperate courage of the Ngatiwhatuas, [Ngāpuhi] gained a complete victory'. The shouts of the combatants and the noise of the guns was so great at the site where the two sides clashed that it was known thereafter as Te Ra Reo Reo (Day of Voices). The victorious invaders dragged the slain to the ovens which the slaves had been heating even before the battle had commenced.

Marmon does not describe his role as fighting man at Te Ika a Ranganui or at any other intertribal clashes until the siege at Mangonui in 1838 and the battle of Te Ahuahu during the Northern War of 1845. Suggestions by some writers that Pākehā-Māori were permitted to stand aloof during desperate intertribal battles while their kinsfolk fought and died are not supported by the contemporary evidence. Modern historians have calculated that Ngāpuhi suffered 3000 casualties during the Musket Wars when every musket and foreign fighting man was valued and recruited for intertribal battles.

Marmon's acquisition of several captives at this time certainly suggests a combatant role. Not surprisingly, and in keeping with his intransigent nature, he chose to retain these taurekareka into the late 1840s, long after most northern chiefs had converted to Christianity and freed their own slaves. One *Herald* statement does hint at his behaviour in the battle's aftermath when Jacky states: 'the New Zealand chiefs cared so little for human life, particularly if it was a slave or tutua (nobody), that, I suppose, almost unknown to myself, I must have in a measure, got to think as they did'. Descriptions of the uninhibited cannibalism following the battle of Te Ika a Ranganui are detailed and graphic, and reflect the preoccupation of both *Star* and *Herald* editors with the sensational and the need to sell copy.

Ngapuhi did not escape scatheless in this expedition. Many of their best and bravest chiefs were slain. In fact, although victorious it was the most disastrous campaign Hongi had as yet engaged in. Te Puhi,

Hare Hongi, son of Hongi Hika and Te Ahu were all killed. . . . Besides these there were numerous lesser *rangatiras* all of whose deaths would be liable at any time to be made an excuse for attack.

During several hours of heavy fighting some 70 Ngāpuhi were killed and a similar number wounded. Ngāti Whātua, who suffered terrible casualties, were defeated and forced to flee the battlefield, leaving their muskets in the hands of the victors.[30] Under fire from the pursuing invaders, one group of survivors led by Murupaenga fled down the Kaiwaka River. Others commenced the long retreat 'south to the Waikato, where they received shelter from Te Waharoa'. Marmon recalled how another band attempted to flee overland to Te Ika a Ranganui Pā.

[A] band of Ngapuhis intercepted them and drove them into the river. Many fled to Makiri and a smaller pah called Waikoukou in the very heart of a dense bush, but in vain. Here their relentless pursuer tracked them, stormed the pahs and made great slaughter.

Meanwhile, with the battle won, Ngāpuhi commenced burning their own dead and there was a 'grand feast on the dead bodies and fern roots' in honour of the victory. Rutherford watched as 20 heads were placed on long spears around his own camp with 'dancing and singing all night'. Hongi, still clad in his armour and working by firelight, managed to extract the musket ball from Hare's chest but failed to save his son's life. To avenge this loss, Hongi had most of the prisoners taken by his hapū executed and some hundred of their heads were presented to him. Rejoining Muriwai and his Popoto kinsfolk, Marmon saw the heads of four senior enemy chiefs staked on poles around his own camp.

They had been dried and feathered – that is, feathers were stuck in their hair. Charlie Hongi, the great Hongi's son, had been killed and his body lay in a canoe alongside. Muruwai's mob, to which I belonged, camped about a mile from the main body.[31]

Having repaired their damaged canoes, Ngāpuhi completed their portage to the Kaipara inlet where the two divisions went in search of booty, slaves, further human flesh and their arch enemy Murupaenga.

Motiti Island, Hokianga River
Fortified island and trading vessel on the Hokianga Harbour, 1827. As the number
of visiting ships increased after 1826, Marmon began to interact more frequently
with Europeans.
Augustus Earle, 'A fortified Island in E.O. Ke-ahanga [i.e. Hokianga] River, New Zealand',
PIC-AN2820797, National Library of Australia.

We went on together, sailing down the Otamatea with its banks fringed
with heavy undergrowth into the broad Kaipara Gulf. Here as usual with
the unwieldy canoes we hugged the shore, past the Komokiriki and
Makarau creeks until at length we entered the Kaipara river. This was
once a densely populated district one time, but repeated raids cut off
most of the natives who lived around the shores. We held on up the river
seeing not a curl of smoke to guide us, passing the Kaukapakapa and
Awaroa rivers, following the windings of the most serpentine river in
New Zealand the Kaipara.

Elements of the fleet scoured the many tidal creeks and inlets of
the Kaipara Harbour pursuing and killing or enslaving Ngāti Whātua
wherever they found them. The Kaipara and parts of the Tamaki
Isthmus were largely abandoned by the tribe. A small band of fugitives
under the chiefs Paikea and Te Otene, however, continued to live
secretly in south Kaipara, but most of the tribe eventually scattered in

small parties to the Waikato, to the Tangihou and Waitakere ranges and to Mahurangi. Here they lived in constant fear of attack. Murupaenga and some of his tribe found refuge on the east coast north of Auckland but, within a year of the battle, they were surprised near Puhoi by a small amphibious expedition of Hokianga Ngāpuhi and Murupaenga was killed. The Hokianga chiefs did not accompany Hongi's fleet back to the Bay, choosing instead to return in several contingents north to the Hokianga along the black beaches of the west coast.[32]

We were now bound for home and went by Horihori. There found that a cannibal feast had taken place. Everywhere round about were the remains of the dead, such parts as they had not dared to eat. . . . Next morning we went on, passing heads stuck on stumps – they belonged to those who had been eaten. When we got to the beach, we had a great feast upon shell-fish and fern-root. Further on, we passed some more heads stuck on poles. My wife was very ill, and a few of us hurried on ahead. After we had passed, a woman belonging to the Kaipara, who had been hidden in the bush, came out. She thought the main body had passed, and went along the beach toward her home. Nene and Patuone's mob came upon her, and, finding she was an enemy, killed and ate her. Tamati Waka Nene told me long afterwards that this was the last time he tasted human flesh. Marched on.[33]

Marmon's return to the Hokianga with his backpack of human flesh, as described in the *Northern Luminary*, was witnessed by four 'Scotch' carpenters from Captain Herd's expedition. His ships, the *Rosanna* and *Lambton*, carrying 60 prospective English settlers, visited the Hokianga but, terrified by a welcoming haka of 1000 warriors, the vessels promptly sailed for Australia. The four carpenters, Gillies, Nimmo, Nesbitt and McLean, returned to New Zealand to become Hokianga's first respectable settlers.

No sooner were we returned home and had divided the spoils taken as far as division existed among the Maoris, Hongi whose thirst for blood was insatiable, planned an expedition to Waikato to follow up the Ngatiwhat-ua who had fled to Waikato, and to avenge the death of his son Hare. . . . This can scarcely be called a tribal raid, it being more carried on by

Hongi and his immediate friends to satisfy private quarrels. Accordingly no more than one hundred and eighty men were engaged in it, and of these but few from our *kainga*.

In [Hongi's] expedition I did not take part, I was more inclined for the enjoyment of domestic peace than follow the war-trail any more. Besides my trade with the vessels coming into the [Hokianga] was gradually falling away, for when they did not find me at my post they transferred their custom to other traders. And this I objected to, since I wished to be the sole medium of exchange between the pakehas and the natives and thereby keep up the prices.

During his first Pākehā-Māori interlude on the Kerikeri River, Hikutu had attempted to pressure Marmon into adopting many conventions of Māori society by applying social sanctions. By hoarding rather than sharing his muskets, however, Marmon violated Māori custom. Subjected to the law of muru, he was plundered and driven away. By 1825, as a fully acculturated Pākehā-Māori among the Te Popoto hapū, Marmon was motivated by Māori concepts of utu (vengeance) and whanaungatanga (caring for and sharing with the wider community) and his behaviour, which was now tika or consistently appropriate according to circumstance and occasion, won him widespread approval.

I employed myself making fish-hooks from the bones of the Ngatiwhatuas, slain at Kaipara, this being considered the greatest indignity that could be paid to a fallen foe. First eat him, then convert his bones to fish-hooks. It was at this time also that the entire *kainga* got drunk upon a keg of rum that had drifted ashore and was seized upon as the grandest prize that could be conceived. We had two days of pretty stiff spreeing . . .

Upon his return to Keri-Keri, Hongi disbanded all his forces for awhile and prepared to enter upon a career of peace. I, for my part, was glad of this. . . . For two or three months – in fact until the end of 1826 – I pursued trade in flax and pigs, doing a little interpreting work when required, discharged my duties as *tohunga*, engaged also in the manufacture of grog from potatoes . . .

The sudden influx of shipping from 1826 required Marmon to do more than 'a little interpreting'. He translated for the four main Hokianga chiefs in the sale of land to Raine, Ramsay and Browne at Horeke where they established a shipyard under Captain David Clarke. In November 1826, he translated for Muriwai who sold additional land near Horeke to Captains Deloitte and Stewart (of Stewart Island), and was a witness to the deed of purchase and interpreted for the four 'Scotch' sawyers who settled at Waihou under the protection of Patuone.

In 1827, Marmon visited the Bay of Islands where he met Captain Dillon who was provisioning his ship *Research* before embarking on the long voyage to the New Hebrides in search of the La Perouse's Pacific expedition which had vanished in 1788. Marmon, who was given temporary employment as ship's interpreter, recalled: 'Captain Dillon called in at the Bay of Islands for wood and water. I was interpreter aboard while the vessel lay in the Bay of Islands. I got 10s a-day and lots of grog.'[34] Dillon eventually recovered relics from La Perouse's ship, proving that the navigator was killed or lost in the New Hebrides, and was subsequently knighted by the French Government.

Returning to the Hokianga, Marmon found the brig *Glory* anchored off Taumatawiwi. When the skipper, Captain Swindle, went to visit Captain Clarke at Horeke, local Māori discovered that their enemies, the Ngāti Toa chiefs Te Rauparaha and Te Hiko, were passengers and swarmed aboard intent on killing them. Marmon hurried off and informed Captain Swindle who returned to find that Muriwai had ordered his warriors from the vessel, though they had obeyed reluctantly. Nevertheless, Swindle had to pay Muriwai one cask of powder as compensation when the chief accidentally hit his head on a cleat.

In 1827, Marmon's trading monopoly was challenged by Captain John Kent, a former New South Wales Government skipper, who established his trading station near Hokianga heads under the protection of Moetara of Ngāti Korokoro. Kent, however, soon departed for less competitive climes. Joining the Waikato people and their paramount chief Te Potatau Te Wherowhero at Ngāruawāhia, he became their leading trader Pākehā-Māori. Though Marmon now had more regular contact with Europeans, his loyalties remained unchanged. While visiting his old Hikutu kinsfolk on the Kerikeri River in July 1827, some women boarded Captain Brind's ship *Emily* to conduct trade but were badly treated by the crew. The Rev. Henry Williams' Paihia journal records the extent of Marmon's fury and the nature of his utu.

Tuesday 24 . . . Late this evening I received a note from Captain Brind to state that an English man, named Mahamai of notorious bad character, had been firing on his men; and that he had, moreover, threatened to fetch the tribe, amongst whom he lives, from Hokianga, and take possession of the ship.[35]

The mid-1820s were also a significant period in Marmon's domestic life. In 1826, his wife Hauāuru gave birth to Mere (Mary), his only identified child. Hauāuru, however, became ill, believing that she had been bewitched when a slave woman used her tapu comb. Unable to reverse the mākutu, Jacky watched his wife slowly waste away. Preparing for her funeral, he received assistance from George Nimmo, an excellent coffin maker and a man of some forethought who always had a coffin ready for his own demise. His first coffin was donated to Marmon's wife, the second, to a former trading friend, but many years were to pass before Nimmo came to occupy the third.[36]

Soon after this [1827] I lost my wife. She died and I was very sorry . . . I was very fond of her. Besides being handsome, she was very quiet, and honest; and her death made me very miserable. Her little girl was only nine months old at the time. George Nimmo made the coffin [but] they would not let me bury her in the ground but built a house to put her in (whare tapu) . . . they did not bury their dead but kept them above ground . . . [in] the whare tapu sometimes between two canoes standing on end . . . and when they did not take the trouble to do that, put them in the trees covered with munga-munga. The body would be put in [the whare tapu] upright with hands joined together. . . . Later, after the bones had been scraped, they carried them to a secret place in the mountains.[37]

The Wesleyan missionary James Stack later reported an unusual, additional rite during Hauāuru's burial. 'He [Marmon] has buried one wife and interred her native fashion plastering her tomb with quarterly papers on which figures are. Some of those the natives got at Wesleydale.'[38]

We were free at Hokianga as yet from missionaries, and I hoped they never would come, as with them are always certain people who under

Rev. Henry Williams (afterwards Archdeacon of Waimate).

Rev. Henry Williams
In an 1827 journal entry, Williams described Marmon's prolonged solo attack on the
vessel *Emily* on the Kerikeri River.
R. A. A. *Sherrin and J. H. Wallace*, Early History of New Zealand: From Earliest Times to 1840,
Auckland, 1890, p. 263.

any conditions must be constantly riding over the necks of their fellows. Muriwai was a staunch upholder of the Maori gods, and the parsons were shown little favour by him. He had seen and heard of their doings at the Bay of Islands and did not approve of their presence.

Unbeknown to Marmon, 'the joint stock preaching company' in the form of James Stack and John Hobbs were already on their way to Hokianga. Driven from their mission station at Whangaroa in 1828 by harassment and intertribal fighting, the Wesleyans established a new Methodist mission at Mangungu a few miles downstream from the Horeke shipyard and Marmon's eventual lands at Rawhia. The newcomers were protected by his chiefs Patuone and Muriwai, though the latter regarded their sermons on death and eternity with amusement. Ironically, the task of translating for both parties fell to

Marmon. With Hokianga Māori still confident in their culture and religion, the Wesleyans had limited success, achieving only 250 to 300 converts by 1834. Nonetheless, the Māori who did attend their services greatly enjoyed the chants, responses and hymns.

The new settlers found Jacky a highly competent mediator, but irascible, and with a deep-seated contempt for European authority figures and the Wesleyan missionaries who constantly slandered him. Increasingly embittered by repeated mistreatment at the hands of his former countrymen and resentful of the Wesleyan intrusion into his world, Marmon's disdain for the missionaries frequently manifested itself in insulting or violent behaviour. Often fuelled by liquor, this was later reflected in print, in his *Star* autobiography.

The natives took very little notice of them, they used to go and trade for blankets, spades, or anything they had, for which they used to pay in potatoes. Mr Stack would wander about among them, and when he saw a few sitting together would talk about their souls . . . I never knew one Maori who was what they call converted. They would say they believed in what they were told on purpose to get into favour with the missionaries, or to get something out of them that they wanted, and then have a good laugh behind the parson's back for his being such a fool as to believe what they said.[39]

About this time Marmon was attacked, robbed and injured by three felons who had fled the pirated convict transport *Wellington* at the Bay of Islands before crossing to Hokianga. Eventually captured by local Māori, the fugitives were ransomed to Captain Clarke at the Horeke shipyard for a musket and a cask of powder apiece. Placed in chains aboard Clarke's ship *Enterprise* they were transported to Sydney where the authorities paid Clarke a reward of £20 the lot. Fearing for the life of his wounded Pākehā-Māori, Muriwai, who had always indulged Marmon, confided in Stack, 'I am distressed on account of my white man. He has been twice killed, twice his gun had been taken from him, presently he'll die.'[40] Jacky did not die, recovering instead to fall in love with Hawea, a granddaughter of Muriwai who became his second Māori wife at Hokianga. The *Herald* account states simply that Marmon 'fell in with a red haired girl'.[41] The *Star* memoir, however, contains

the only recorded account of a Pākehā-Māori love affair and glimpses of a love-struck Marmon (incorrectly referring to Hawea as Muriwai's 'grand-niece').

I was coming in one afternoon from fishing after a pretty successful day when my *karakias* had been peculiarly powerful, for at the bottom of my canoe lay a heap of *kahawai*, *schnapper*, and eels, altogether a good day's work. As I neared the landing-place I saw standing the grand-daughters of Muriwai a very pretty girl, rather lighter in hue than the usual run of Maoris. Her features were regular and pleasing, her limbs supple and exquisitely moulded, her whole bearing graceful and elegant, whilst a mixture of neatness with fitness in her attire proclaimed her to be of higher blood than many at Tahitaira. The bright-sunlight brought out a glossy tint in her wavy hair, and as she stood against the back-ground of some flax bushes and ti-tree she formed altogether a very pretty picture.

Her eyes were fixed on me with an enquiring look, as if surprised to see a *pakeha* in the settlement, and I heard one of her companions whisper that I was the great tohunga who had only to speak to bring the spirits at will from Te Reinga. Her image haunted me. I could not forget the light in her lustrous eye, the gleam of her little teeth beneath the slightly smiling lips. . . . On inquiry I found she was Muriwai's grand-niece, the daughter of a chief near Korarareka, in the Bay of Islands. He had died, and she had been sent to her grand-uncle to be taken care of.

Hawea, for such was her name, had in her train another suitor [Kariti], who was in the same state of languishment as I felt myself but was a younger and handsomer man. . . . Accordingly I away to Muriwai I went, and entered into a *korero* with him about it. I told him . . . that I had made up my mind to take another wife, and that I saw no one who would suit me better than his grand-niece Hawea.

Muriwai looked troubled. He had wished to secure the other young suitor in his tribe, and my wish seemed to put an end to his scheme. However, I was too powerful a man to be refused, and he gave his consent to her becoming my wife. But I was anxious to gain her own goodwill as well, and therefore told Muriwai that I would wait a little and bring her to consent to it of her own free will. Accordingly, I met Hawea and spoke to her for the first time. Without the least confusion she answered me, and I found her mind as interesting as her face.

This was the beginning of my *aru aru* or courtship. By every means in my power I strove to gain her regard and then made my *ropa* or declaration of love by pinching the fingers. All my endeavours were in vain, she had loved the other suitor before she came to Hokianga, therefore it was almost impossible to supersede him in her regard. But lose her I could not, therefore I told her I must and would have her. She said that she did not wish to be my wife, but would live with me accordingly to Maori custom for a year, after which she would be *tapu* (sacred) to her husband, but nothing would satisfy me.

So at the end of our year of courtship . . . I went to Muriwai and told him I now wished Hawea as my wife. He seemed very much troubled, he gave his consent, and accordingly she was made *tau mau* or betrothed to me, though difficulties yet lay in the way of making her my wife. As Hawea was living with Muriwai, it was according to Maori etiquette that I should go with a strong party and as it were remove her by force, though this latter often was necessary when another suitor offered opposition. I therefore summoned several of my friends; we armed ourselves and proceeded to Muriwai's *whare* having previously warned him that we would be there that day. Muriwai was on watch with his friends as well as the unsuccessful suitor and his party. . . . At length Hawea came out of the *whare*, and each side seized hold of her and commenced a struggle for her possession, in which her screams of agony at the outrages she received went unheeded amidst the tumult. Every stitch of clothing was torn from her, and at length when we did succeed in carrying her off, she was streaming with blood, and in a senseless condition. Such is a *puna rua* or fight for a bride.

Hawea, however, was not seriously injured. A day or two of rest put her all right again, and from that day [was] a most faithful and loveable wife. Her former suitor, in place of evincing spleen at my success, became a firm friend, and was killed in the war springing out of the destruction of the Kororareka flagstaff (1845). Singularly enough [Hawea] is the only one of my wives I consider as such . . . perhaps because she was the only one for whom I made a formal marriage *taua*.

Hongi Hika, meanwhile, had relentlessly pursued the remnants of Ngāti Whātua into Waikato and, having killed many of them, returned to the Bay. He soon moved north to settle at Whangaroa, this shift being

Tomb of a chieftainess
As the daughter of Hōne Raumati, Marmon's first wife at the Hokianga, Hauāuru,
was placed in a similar mausoleum after her death in 1827.
*Hand-coloured lithograph tinted 440 x 310 mm. George French Angas, 'Mausoleum of E. Tohi, the
mother of Rauparaha, on the island of Mana', PUBL-0014-50, Alexander Turnbull Library.*

partly motivated by his desire to punish the local tribes Ngāti Uru and
Ngāti Pou for plundering the brig *Mercury*. The plunderers had also
harassed and driven out the Wesleyan missionaries, angering Hongi
who welcomed the presence of European ships and missionaries for the
trade they attracted. During skirmishing with Ngāti Uru,

Hongi stepping out from the shelter of a tree to take aim, received a
bullet in the breast which shattered his collar bone and penetrated the
backbone. He fell at once and his men fell back, carrying with them
the body of their chief. Hongi was not dead but his fighting days were
done.

For a full year he lingered on in great agony, the wound never healing,
yet to the very last exhibiting the terrible spirit of ferocity. . . . He showed
no fear of death, but with savage merriment jested about the hissing
sound that came from the opening of his [chest] wound. He sent for me
to go to him, and with considerable fear I did so, for I imagined he might
have something against me, and would wreak his vengeance before his
death. But nothing of the kind, he merely wished me to be near him, al-

though he obstinately refused to have any karakias said over him or any prayers by the missionaries.

Jacky's special association with Hongi saw him precede the large contingent of Hokianga people who, led by Patuone and Muriwai, crossed to the Bay of Islands for Hongi's tangihanga. Marmon knew Hongi Hika better than most Pākehā including the missionaries and his account of the great chief's death concurs with contemporary descriptions.

He was terribly thin and fainted away more than once when I saw him (the day he died). He distributed his meres, muskets and other weapons amongst his sons, exhorted them to be bold and courageous, saying, 'Ka ora *Koutou*' (You will yet be well). Adding, when someone hinted the possibility of his tribe being cut off after his death, '*Kowai ma te hiakai mai kia koutou kaore.*' (Who will dare to desire to eat you – none). Unceasing were his advices to his sons to be as indefatigable in warfare as he had been, above all to be brave, his last words being '*Kia toa – kia toa*' (be courageous, be courageous). And so he passed away to the resting-place from which no pilgrim returns. Hongi was carried to the *wahi tapu* (burying ground) attended by the entire Ngapuhi tribe, amidst the sullen noise of the *maemae* (funeral dance), the dreary *tangi*, and the thunder of musketry.

Hongi died on 3 March 1828 but, fearing a retaliatory military expedition, his people tried to keep the death a secret. When the Hokianga people arrived, Patuone reassured them, and Hongi was honoured for many days before being buried.[42] Within a month of Hongi's death, Te Whareumu was killed and Muriwai was mortally wounded during an intertribal clash at Waimea. Some 1000 fighting men attended the funeral of Marmon's patron after the old chief succumbed to his wounds. Muriwai's body was placed in a sitting position with his weapons on his right side and, on the left, the body of his youngest wife, who had strangled herself.[43] With his death, Popoto leadership passed to his brother Te Taonui who shared Muriwai's indifference to the missionaries.

The death of Marmon's patron Muriwai coincided with the emergence of Pākehā-Māori rivals among several hapū at Hokianga. As the local arms race intensified and the possession of a Pākehā by the hapū became paramount, several rangatira offered Jacky their patronage and by 1829 he had joined the Ngāti Hao people and become the chief Patuone's Pākehā-Māori.[44] Anticipating the European rush for strategically located land, in 1827 Marmon had purchased a block of 200 acres at Pukeaitanga on the upper Waihou River from Hōne Raumati in exchange for two muskets, 300 musket balls and assorted trade goods to the value of £45.[45] '[T]hough I had a whare I wanted a proper house and got one too. I had got the boy Jim to help me saw some boards to build a wooden house.' From 1829, Marmon was able to live a semi-autonomous existence as a trader Pākehā-Māori, dwelling apart from Māori in the first of three European-style houses he built at Hokianga.

CHAPTER SEVEN

Landowner, hotelier and renegade, 1830–40

One fine morning during the summer of 1835, the little bell atop the white-painted Wesleyan chapel at Mangungu, tolled out across the blue waters of the Hokianga River. Soon after, the district's more tardy self-professed Christian Māori began drifting downriver on waka, or straggling along the riverside paths from nearby pā and kāinga. Bound for the last service of the morning, the extended families, attired in their finest native dress and with a pipe in every mouth, carried bibles translated into Māori. As the last of the parishioners filed into the cool, shadowed interior of the chapel, a small dugout shot out from the mangroves at Rawhia on the opposite shore, its single occupant paddling swiftly against the rush of the incoming tide.

The gathered flock had barely commenced the second hymn of the service when the chapel door opened. Rev. Stack, the officiating minister, stared aghast, the singing faded, but none in the Māori congregation dared turn to stare for they had sensed *his* presence. Beyond the hallowed doorway stood a figure, reviled by the brethren for his lawlessness, but admired by Māori for his intransigence. Of medium height, with a long distinctive face and dark hair flowing loose beneath a battered black top hat, there *was* something sinister about the stranger's

Patuone's village, upper Waihou River
Between 1828 and 1830 Marmon lived among Patuone's Ngāti Hao people as their
principal Pākehā-Māori trader.
*Hand-coloured lithograph 240 x 374 mm. Augustus Earle, 'Native Village and cowdie forest',
PUBL-0015-08, Alexander Turnbull Library.*

watchful stillness. A collective gasp accompanied his step across the
threshold and they audibly tracked his footsteps to the end of the far
right back pew where no Māori sat thereafter. By nightfall, the incident
was a topic of discussion in every pā and kāinga from Hokianga to the
Bay of Islands. Hake Mamene, a noted Pākehā toa and eater of men, Te
Manene, famed tohunga Pākehā and conduit to the spirit world of Te
Reinga, had turned mihinare (missionary).

The influx of shipwrights, sawyers and missionaries into the Hokianga
from the late 1820s inexorably drew Marmon back into the European
orbit and compelled him to re-adopt European ways out of necessity.
Despite reassuming his original Pākehā-Māori identity as advisor,
translator and trader and his increasing interaction with Europeans,
Marmon did not lose his deep psychological commitment to Māori
customs and beliefs. He continued to support Patuone and Ngāti Hao in
their skirmishes and raids within and beyond the Hokianga, maintained
his practice as a tohunga Pākehā and worked his extensive gardens with
the assistance of slaves taken in war.

Hokianga during the 1830s remained a Māori-dominated world

where Europeans lived on Māori terms and honoured important Māori customs if they wished to remain and succeed commercially. Their dependence on Māori for land, labour, women and protection placed Marmon in an advantageous position. As the dominant Pākehā-Māori he continued to be called upon to mediate Māori–Pākehā interaction and commerce. The flax boom was under way and 38 Sydney vessels loaded this commodity at New Zealand harbours during 1830, including Hokianga.[1] As the shipwrights at Horeke and the Wesleyan missionaries at Mangungu were joined by new traders in flax, squared timber and spars, Marmon, too, diversified into flax, pork and vegetable trading and prospered.

I employed myself chiefly in trading. I gave the natives so much a week to prepare the flax for me, and then disposed of it when the vessels came. Then I began to do a little in the cultivation of land. My maize crops had been successes, and I did not see why I should not try wheat and barley. They, too, repaid me, so that with my potatoes and my pigs I accounted myself a farmer on a small scale.

By the early 1830s Hokianga was attracting a steady stream of colonial Australian ships that increasingly exchanged muskets, liquor and general trade goods for sawn kauri planks, spars, pork and potatoes. These vessels contributed to the general glut of imported firearms that coincided with the peak years of the Musket Wars (1831–32). At the Bay and Hokianga leading rangatira and tohunga began lining the interior walls of their houses with racks of surplus muskets. Henry Williams reported that as far away as Tauranga, 'men owned ten muskets and boys three'.[2] Hake Mamene the gun-trader and advisor became indispensable at the Hokianga, the captain of one American whaler reported in 1833: 'muskets are now used altogether as war instruments by the Natives on the North Island, & they are now as good judges & keep them in as good order as the Europeans'.[3]

By 1830 Marmon was one of 50 trader Pākehā-Māori scattered along New Zealand's coasts. With the absence of his patron, Patuone, who was visiting New South Wales, the appearance of Pākehā-Māori rivals and dealings with a fraudulent skipper undermined Jacky's monopoly and devastated his finances.

It was now 1830. I had . . . hitherto got on well with [Patuone's people], but when I attempted to get all the trade between the savages and the traders in my own hands, as I had done at Keri-keri, I found that the system would not work, and that I must just pull my own boat independent of anyone else. Therefore I had no one to back me up when chaffering with the skippers for pigs, flax, or vegetables, and was fain frequently to be content with much lower prices than otherwise I would have had if there had been no competition.

I was rather taken in at this time in my trade transactions by a black-guardly thief. . . . There was a captain of a schooner running between Sydney and Hokianga who was known as Black Bill, and who always came to me for his cargo. Once, not having any convenient articles on board such as I wished to accept as barter, he agreed to bring me over goods from Sydney to the amount of the cargo. For instance, I wanted a keg of rum and some tobacco as I longed for a 'spree' once more, and was utterly sick of smoking *korimako* leaves. When he returned and I went on board to receive my goods, as I thought, he utterly denied all claim, and would give me no compensation, transferring, besides, his trade to one of the Maoris. It was rather a severe loss to me, but in the long run it hurt himself more than it did me, since, on his character becoming known, none of the natives would trust him or permit him to land without my permission, which I persistently withheld.

Black Bill's dishonesty reinforced Marmon's belief in the inherent untrustworthiness of Europeans and rekindled an antipathy founded on their past abuses and injustices. Ever resilient, Marmon set out to recover his financial position and in 1831 sold to Thomas McDonnell, a new settler, the 200-acre block at Pukeaitanga he had acquired in 1827.[4] Thereafter, Jacky embarked on a series of strategic marriages to women of rank and obtained more land, justifying his successive wives with the claim, 'The Maoris . . . have no marriage ceremony, not even a *karakia*, nor any rite so that I considered myself as not bound to stick to any woman to whom I was bound by no legal tie.' In 1832 he married a third wife, Ngāti Wai, 'a chief's daughter belonging to Mangamuka', though there is no record of her dowry.

By 1833 Marmon was living on land at Rawhia, provided by his former father-in-law, Hōne Raumati, located at the mouth of the

Waihou River, opposite the Horeke shipyard and several miles upstream from the Wesleyan chapel at Mangungu. Rawhia, soon known locally as Marmon's Point, became his permanent home. Australian vessels anchored nearby to load his pork and potatoes and Jacky soon recovered his financial position. By this time he had become something of a New Zealand identity. When Edward Markham, an English gentleman rover, toured Hokianga in 1834, he specifically sought out Jacky as his guide, translator and mentor, noting, 'he is mentioned by Rutherford's Memoirs published in the Entertaining Library'. Markham also noted the changes brought about by trader Pākehā-Māori like Marmon, particularly the enthusiasm of local Māori for guns, blankets and liquor.

It used to be called Why Pirah [waipiro] or Stinking Water. They like now to get Showrangi [haurangi] or drunk if they can. . . . They wear now English blankets, both men and women . . . Ki tuck-er [kaitaka] or Mat Cacahow [with] ornamented borders is rarely to be seen in the present day. . . . They barter for most things now. The Natives give Potatoes even for bars of Soap and ten Kits of Potatoes for a spade and five for a hoe.

Vessels come to Hokianga and buy and Salt all the Pork they can, say

Women dancing at Hokianga, 1834
As Edward Markham sketched this scene, Marmon, his guide and translator explained the significance of the women's dance.
Pencil and watercolour 225 x 374 mm. Edward Markham, 'A dance called Karne Karne or Cune Cune', MS-1550-006, Alexander Turnbull Library.

20 Tons at a time and take it up to Hobart Town and Sydney, and have got 60 [pounds sterling] a ton . . . in the same way they have bought Potatoes at 12/- a Ton and sold them for 12 [pounds], They give 5 large Pigs up the Whyhoe [Waihou] River for an old double-barrelled gun.[5]

Marmon reinvested his trading and land sales profits by constructing the largest house in the district and reinvented himself as a hotelier. 'As a matter of fact, he'd built it himself – out of solid kauri,' one old settler recalled. 'It was beautifully built . . . He was a wonderful craftsman, with various clever tricks of his own in building.'[6] Edward Markham recorded seeing 'Jacky Marmont's fine house', in 1834 but did not stop by for a drink.[7] Anecdotal accounts describe a smaller tavern Marmon later constructed on the end of his wharf. Visiting ships' crews would ascend a ladder from their boats beneath the wharf directly into the bar room through a trap door.[8] For drunken sailors, the return journey must have been fraught with risk.

I had a fine big house on the same spot as the home I have now, only it was much larger, two storeys high, and lots of room for everybody, and I had plenty of visitors, as I told you before, sailors and captains of vessels that came for spars.[9]

[I] put a bar into it, and made it as like a Sydney public-house as I could. . . . Then I had grown an adept in the manufacture of grog. Who can do without the cheerful glass that raises the spirits and makes a man look on the ills of life as of no account? I made a lot of wealth out of grog by this manufacture. Sailors would come to my place for a 'spree', and spend their money there like princes, which was much needed, as we had no currency except muskets and flax. I professed to sell different kinds of drinks, which was managed by seasoning with different types of native spices.

Though he never sought influence or status in the European world, Jacky Marmon became a man of property and importance at the Hokianga during the 1830s, and by 1834 was also operating as a sawyer on a small scale. In 1835 he married Ihipera (Isabella), another daughter of Raumati's daughters and later that year formally purchased 550 acres at Rawhia from his father-in-law and related chiefs in exchange for trade goods to the value of £41. In that year, Marmon also received from the chieftainess Taminauru 250 acres for Mary, Marmon's child and her grandchild, for a token payment of £2.[10]

In contrast to the increasing numbers of Europeans settling at the Bay of Islands, the number settling at Hokianga increased from just 52 to 70 between 1832 and 1834. Beyond the shipwrights' settlement at Horeke and the Mangungu mission station, a diverse population of sawyers, kauri traders, runaway convicts and sailors lived individually among Māori communities with their Māori wives. Yet they would congregate for war expeditions, parties, church services and at the funerals of their fellows and important rangatira. Pragmatic men who judged others by their actions rather than gossip, many had benefited from Marmon's hospitality, building and translating abilities and contacts among Māori.

In the Māori tradition of welcoming strangers, Marmon continued to keep open house for all comers including runaway sailors and convicts. When Thomas McDonnell, a disputatious retired naval lieutenant first arrived to take over ownership of the Horeke shipyard in 1831, he at once sent a letter to Marmon, in an attempt to exercise an authority that he did not possess. 'I am informed that you have two men living in your house supposed to be prisoners of the Crown. . . . Unless these men are delivered up to me instantly, I shall be compelled to make the same known to the Governor.'[11] Incensed that Marmon did not take him seriously, McDonnell persistently criticised the Pākehā-Māori in his reports. In a letter to James Busby, the British Resident at the Bay of Islands, McDonnell claimed, 'I believe that Marmon – in fact I know him to be a dangerous character – is quite capable of poisoning the minds of the natives. I have my eye on him, and will render him powerless to commit mischief if possible. He has been tampering with some of the minor chiefs.'[12]

Marmon was equally welcoming of his Māori relatives.

My wife's relations were something in the way of numbers. Why, on one occasion when they paid us a visit, how many do you think there were? Above forty. They did not just make a morning call as the swells do, I am told, but came to stay. They would bring a small quantity of kai as a present, but would not leave til they had eaten much flour and sugar. . . . A week or ten days the visit would last; they would sit inside the house

Kohukohu timber station, Hokianga River, 1830s
Local Pākehā-Māori including Marmon and Maning became involved in, and profited
from, the kauri timber boom.
*Charles Heaphy, 'View of the Kahu-Kahu-Hokianga River', C-025-020,
Alexander Turnbull Library.*

if wet, outside if fine, and there yarn by the day for the stories they often
told would last a day or a night.[13]

A number of pre-Treaty Pākehā-Māori, including Dicky Barrett,
Charles Marshall and Captain Harris, established 'bush hotels' and
were widely known for their generosity and congeniality. European
latecomers did find Marmon reticent and dour in old age, but his recall
of several amusing incidents from his seafaring and Pākehā-Māori years
suggest a keen sense of humour. In a world of oral language where
storytelling was important, Marmon was expected to 'perform' for
his tribe and for European listeners, alternately explaining the world
of Europe or Aotearoa to spellbound listeners. As one Kāwhia-based
Pākehā-Māori put it, 'we talk constantly [with Māori] the whole night
through', and few Pākehā-Māori were inarticulate or subarticulate.[14]
James Caddell of Ngāi Tahu was described as 'very conversive', and an
eyewitness described Dicky Barrett of Te Āti Awa as 'mystifying a whole
audience of gaping immigrants' with a tale from 'his Maori campaigns'.[15]
Dr Hocken described Maning as 'a great, almost incessant talker'.[16] For
Pākehā-Māori, their narratives became the drama of their lives and

were theatres for descriptions of self in New Zealand, and Marmon was no exception.

Mrs Bennett will have found Jacky an enthusiastic and loquacious narrator; the quality and length of their interviews influenced, however, by his state of sobriety, for in old age he was often drunk on gin or his favourite tipple, rum laced with tutu juice. A likely guess is that he greatly enjoyed relating his life story and Jacky's reminiscences are the most comprehensive left by any Pākehā-Māori.

Edward Markham described Frederick Maning as 'a double faced sneaking thief' when the latter thwarted his attempts to buy land locally.[17] Tellingly, Marmon, a runaway convict, while often accused of manipulating the chiefs for his own ends, was never accused of dishonesty at Hokianga. Indeed, local Europeans acknowledged his competence in Māori and his reliability as a translator. Markham reported in 1834, 'But no one in the place knew enough of the Language to keep up a Conversation so we had recourse to Jacky Marmont, a noted character who had been on the island fourteen years, and speaks better than even the Missionaries do'.[18]

Ironically, when Thomas McDonnell was appointed honorary British resident at the Hokianga in 1835, he chose to employ Marmon over other bilingual Pākehā and Pākehā-Māori for the 1836 committee of inquiry into allegations of adultery made against the missionary William White by Māori women.[19] White was declared guilty and later left for England when his Wesleyan colleagues began providing affidavits confirming his misconduct.

Marmon also had other accomplishments to sustain him. A competent carpenter and joiner, he was hired by Captain Clarke to build some of the houses, offices and store rooms at the Horeke settlement and shipyard. Marmon also completed much of the joinery at the old Horeke Hotel where he used kauri in his distinctive style and built houses for the merchant J. R. Clendon and another at Onoke Point for Frederick Maning who was then trading kauri.[20] Of Irish descent, Marmon and Maning knew each other well and, never men to avoid a fight, joined in the Irish settlers' fist fighting contests during the 1830s. The contests according to Markham would continue over two days.[21] Both supported their hapū during intertribal battles and proved to be great storytellers. There is no evidence that their relationship, while both men lived, was anything less than congenial with Marmon still a regular visitor to Maning's house as late as 1869.[22]

All Pākehā-Māori were engaged to some degree in rebelling against the constraints of European society, but Marmon was the consummate Pākehā-Māori renegade. His notoriety was founded in his self-confessed cannibalism, tohunga practices and participation in Māori battles and skirmishes. It was also founded upon his attack upon the vessel *Emily*, his shooting of Bill Styles, a fellow Pākehā-Māori, and his readiness to go to war in support of Māori and the Pākehā he favoured.

Before the arrival of Catholic missionaries at Hokianga, Marmon recognised no European authority and treated the Wesleyan missionaries and the British Residents James Busby and Thomas McDonnell with equal contempt. While dependent on his translating skills and standing among Māori, these officials never wholly accepted or trusted Marmon. Markham, who spent some months with Marmon during 1834, summed up the character of his translator and guide as 'a lawless kind of animal'.[23] Soon after the arrival of the Frenchman Baron de Thierry in 1837, Busby and McDonnell called a meeting of European residents and advised them to stay close to the crown for protection. McDonnell set out to identify possible Irish Catholic sympathisers and soon wrote to Busby, warning him that Marmon was 'quite capable of poisoning the minds of the natives'.[24]

Jacky's reason for living at Hokianga was obvious. Having escaped imprisonment aboard his majesty's ships, he knew that the British Residents, Busby and McDonnell, always hoped to arrest him without provoking the tribes. Meanwhile the chiefs kept their favourite Pākehā-Māori well informed of local news and any official European activity in their areas. They gave proof of their regard for Marmon in 1833, when Governor Bourke wrote to James Busby instructing him to arrest and transport the Hokianga's fugitive convicts to New South Wales. When Busby crossed from the Bay to Hokianga with a list of offenders, he met with the leading chiefs and offered rewards for any convicts surrendered to him. Eventually relenting, the chiefs agreed in principle and for a sufficient price to surrender their convict Pākehā-Māori but not Jacky Marmon. The chiefs told Busby that 'Hake Mamene' could not be surrendered as he had become one of them.[25]

The Wesleyans, on the other hand, considered Marmon an evil

influence on Māori. They seem to have been infuriated by his refusal to acknowledge them on their terms as well as by his influence on the leading rangatira. (The chiefs listened to their Pākehā-Māori advisors but invariably made up their own minds.) William Woon described Marmon as 'the terror of the river'.[26] Eliza White in 1832 recorded: 'Marmon, one of the vilest characters in New Zealand, a man who had adopted the worst of the native customs, and from his long residency among them, has acquired a great proficiency in their language, was drunk at Moses Tawhai's burial.'[27] Eliza offended Marmon when she invited his wife Ngāti Wai to join her literacy class at the mission. When Jacky arrived with a loaded pistol, he attempted to break into the school to forcibly remove his wife, but 'after firing ten shots, went away cursing'.[28]

The Rev. Stack recorded, 'This is perhaps one of the most dangerous characters an Englishman can meet with in this land.' Stack's warning was well founded as in a previous argument with the missionary the Pākehā-Māori had threatened to 'knock out his eyes'.[29] These descriptions were founded on Marmon's record of violence, cannibalism, drunkenness and cursing and on his status as Pākehā-Māori, fugitive convict, Catholic, Irishman and, later, opponent of the Treaty of Waitangi. A fierce, short-tempered man, when he or his clan were threatened or crossed, Marmon invariably responded with threats of violence and, too often, actual violence.

When James Clendon's schooner *Fortitude* became stranded at Motukauri in 1833 it was boarded and looted by the Rarawa and Hikutu people. The chief Moetara and his Ngāti Korokoro hapū, who had close trading ties with the Europeans, attacked the offenders and 22 combatants were killed in the clash. Marmon accompanied Patuone, Nene and 300 warriors who went to Moetara's assistance. According to Davis, 'Marmon and about thirty of Waka Nene's army crossed the river from one tree point, and began firing into Orongotea Pa', occupied by a section of the Rarawa.[30] The fighting concluded when Rarawa returned the ship's papers and the schooner was refloated. Soon after, Marmon clashed with Bill Styles, a Pākehā-Māori who owned lands adjacent to Rawhia.

About this time [1834] I had a row of my own. A man named Bill Styles stole a pig belonging to me. I was told of it and went to get payment or knock him down. We had a scrimmage in a canoe, and my gun going off accidently wounded him in the thigh. Taken to the mission at Mangungu where the missionaries attended to the wound. 'Styles got well, so no harm came of it, but I was very much frightened at the time, for I was known to be a man of violent temper.'[31]

When Jacky Marmon first appeared among Rev. Stack's Māori congregation at Mangungu from the mid-1830s, the missionary remained suspicious of the Pākehā-Māori's motives, describing him as 'a European who has suffered his hair to grow quite long like a native and of whom the natives speak in high terms for his assimilation of their abominable habits'.[32] Marmon's motives for attending the Wesleyan chapel are uncertain. At this time Hokianga Māori were still confident in their culture, the four Wesleyan ministers having made only 250 to 300 Māori converts by 1834, but Marmon was no longer essential to the chiefs as an intermediary. Consequently, he may have been hoping to use the Wesleyan faith as a bridge between his life as a white savage and his new position as a man of substance at Hokianga. Perhaps he believed that a return to Christianity might help expunge the memories and the guilt arising from the terrible deeds he had participated in and the need to save his mortal soul.

Stack was justified in his reservations because the Pākehā-Māori's attendance proved to be short-lived, Marmon recalling in the *Herald* memoir, 'being a [?] Catholic I did not attend the mission chapel'.[33] Far from going mihinare, Jacky seemed to relish his notoriety. He did not cease his tohunga and cannibal practices, close his grog shop or moderate his drunken and uncouth behaviour until the arrival of the Catholic mission. These malignant practices, combined with Marmon's varied commercial interests, numerous contacts, roles in both worlds and prickly disposition, may have well been the basis for Smithyman's poetic image of the Pākehā-Māori as 'a horse headed weta'.

In a world dominated by 5000 Māori and a scattering of European settlers, Marmon was secure in his status as a protected Pākehā-Māori and had little patience with European notions of respectability. Yet, his fellow settlers considered him important enough to seek the signature of 'John Mawman' for their 1837 petition to William IV of England.[34] It was eventually signed by 192 respectable settlers at the Bay and

Night gathering
Despite the arrival of British officials, traders and sawyers, during the 1830s,
Hokianga remained a Māori-dominated world.
E. H. McCormick (ed.), Markham, Edward, New Zealand, or Recollections of It,
Wellington, 1963, p. opp. 57.

Hokianga, including merchants, sawyers and Anglican and Wesleyan missionaries. The petition requested that the British government protect trade, thereby ending 'murders, robberies and every kind of evil' in northern New Zealand.[35] Marmon may well have signed out of concern for the continued success of his grog-distilling business and tavern at Rawhia but his landholdings (he had acquired two additional blocks by 1837) and translating and negotiating skills gave him a certain prestige in the eyes of respectable settlers at Hokianga and the Bay of Islands.

I have never told you what the Bay was like in those days. A lot of people have written about it, and there is one who has called it by an awful long name, but it meant 'hell' in English. Well, that's just what it was. Grog-shops kept by convicts – Well, I cant say ought what it was, but just fancy all and everything that's downright bad, and you would have a good idea of the Bay of Islands at the time I speak of. . . . There were fellows there who used to entice the men belonging to the vessels to stay ashore, keep them on the quiet, drunk most likely, til the ship sailed; then when a whaler or some other ship came in wanting hands, the men would be sent aboard, the crimps getting so much from the captain for the men, and the men had to pay out of their advance for their keep ashore.[36]

The missionaries did what they could, but what were their blankets

and Bibles against the rum and muskets of the whalers and trading vessels? I have often wondered about the things done in those old days.
There was no law: it was a strange sort of time when you come to think it
over like. There were the New Zealanders wanting muskets and powder
– rum too; then there was the missionaries telling them it was wrong to
get muskets and powder to kill one another with. Then the natives said,
'These men, the traders come here in ships like you did, and believe the
stories you tell us: they are your brothers. We don't understand, if it is
wrong, why do the white men do it?'[37]

By September 1837, some Hokianga chiefs had become so concerned
about the alcohol-induced havoc in Māori communities that they began
to meet with the Mangungu missionaries with the aim of prohibiting
the sale of liquor. The outcome was New Zealand's first temperance
society, with Thomas McDonnell as its president. McDonnell's zealously
appointed officials attempted unsuccessfully to confiscate the rum
stocks of incoming vessels. The society soon collapsed but not before
Marmon, whose establishment was in full view of the missionaries,
and many settlers for whom alcohol was a vital source of escape and
entertainment, gathered at Mangungu. During the protest, which soon
degenerated into a drunken brawl, Marmon fatally injured Thomas
Styles. According to Charles Davis:

Some of the settlers in defiance of the wishes of both Missionaries and
Maori chiefs, renewed their excesses, and some few went so far as to visit
the Mission Chapel at Mangungu, dancing round it with cheers, holding
bottles of rum in their hands. In a drunken brawl, one of them named
Thomas Styles, received a blow, which together with the poisonous
effect of his excesses, brought him to the margin of that great precipice
that divides time from eternity.[38]

In 1838 the French Catholics under Bishop Pompallier arrived at
the Hokianga and established a mission station at Tōtara Point near
Marmon's home. From this time references to his tohunga activities
cease in the Star, which strongly suggests a spiritual reconversion to
Catholicism. Becoming the Bishop's interpreter, one of Jacky's most
important tasks was to translate the Ten Commandments into Māori,

but not that accurately, claimed the Wesleyans.[39] The Catholic presence irritated the Wesleyans and in January 1838 a group of their converts, 'twenty savages led by chiefs', appeared at Tōtara Point 'with the intention we later learnt, of destroying religious vessels and hurling the Bishop and his priest into the river'. Several local Irish Pākehā-Māori witnessed the confrontation and, by intervening, 'were able to dissuade the natives from carrying out their wicked intention'.[40]

By 1838, Marmon had married another wife, Tauro, the daughter of a newly converted chief, with the approval of the Wesleyans, though her name is recorded as Pungi. They were not pleased when, soon after, Marmon had the marriage reconsecrated by a Catholic priest. The sawyer John Webster recalled with amusement just how anxious Jacky was to convince the Catholic priests of his piety.

Marmon was a Catholic and was absolved regularly by the priest. One day a boat appeared coming towards Rawhia (where he resided). He had noticed one of the men in the boat wore a broad brim black hat and he was sure it was a priest. He went into his whare and began praying aloud so that they could hear him. He was awfully disgusted when he found it was Henry Williams of Pakariaka [Pakaraka] and not a priest.[41]

Marmon's *Star* memoir is a particularly rich source, containing a wealth of anecdotes about local Hokianga personalities and events. Some of the stories Marmon shared with Mrs Bennett also confirm a rapid exchange of news throughout tribal New Zealand, some of it light-hearted, some tragic, but all of it important to the historical record.

Towards the end of 1837, some excitement was occasioned by the arrival of Baron de Thierry with a party of settlers. He proclaimed himself Governor of New Zealand, said he had been invited by the great chiefs, and had purchased a great part of the North Island. The natives laughed at his heroism, whereupon he struck his breast, said 'Look at me, me Governor of New Zealand, me one great chief,' and with a great deal of talking tried to persuade them that Hongi and their own chiefs had invited him to New Zealand; but they only laughed and said, 'Yes, all right, Kawana Pokenou (Governor green vegetable).'

Before his arrival aboard the *Nimrod* with 93 settlers, de Thierry had startled Busby by sending a message claiming rights of sovereignty in New Zealand. At the Hokianga he announced that he would establish a stable government with free trade and no taxation.

However, the Baron's purse was not deep enough to keep up appearances for long. His large silken banner faded; his followers deserted him; many returned to Sydney. He was evidently a gentleman and a scholar. He ultimately succeeded in obtaining some three hundred acres of bush land from the chief Tiro of Waimea.

In the *Herald* and *Star* memoirs, Marmon recalled several violent clashes that were widely known throughout tribal New Zealand including the *Elizabeth* affair, a bloody massacre of South Island Ngāi Tahu in 1830 by Te Rauparaha and 100 Ngāti Toa warriors. With the connivance of the *Elizabeth*'s skipper John Stewart and his Pākehā-Māori interpreter John Cowell, this taua was transported from Kapiti

After the battle

Despite the presence of missionaries and colonial officials, Hokianga continued to be rent by bloody inter-hapū musket warfare.

A. S. Thomson, The Story of New Zealand, *London, 1859, p. 129.*

Island on a mission of vengeance against the chief Tamaiharanui and his people at Banks Peninsula. Marmon's account, received first hand at the Bay of Islands from Stewart, Cowell and from Benjamin Turner, an eyewitness to subsequent events on Kapiti Island, has been cycled and recycled many times by nineteenth- and twentieth-century writers.

About this time I fell in with Captain John Stewart who came for spars. [In] 1830, Captain Stewart's brig the Elizabeth [which] went to Kapiti for flax . . . had a white man aboard to interpret – his name was John Cowell, and he lived with the natives. [John Cowell died a few weeks ago at Awhitu]. The chief Rauparaha went on board, and told Cowell to tell Captain Stewart he would give him 50 tons of flax if he would take him and 50 of his tribe to Bank's Peninsula to get [capture] the chief Maranui. . . . While Rauparaha and Captain Stewart were below talking, natives had been coming on board, and instead of 50 there were more than 100 in the hold. They sailed at once for Bank's Peninsula, and made it in two days.

When Maranui came on board . . . with his wife, and child . . . the chief was taken below. While he was talking to Cowell, Rauparaha came out and handcuffed the chief. As soon as this was done, the hatched were taken off, and the natives rushed on deck and were at once in the ship's boats pulling for the pa. . . . When Cowell got ashore, the natives were busy putting the Maoris they had killed into the oven, chopping them up to make them cook quicker. It was dusk by the time they all got aboard. Many brought kits of human flesh, for they had killed all they could find in the pa – men, women and children. The next day [at sea] Maranui's wife pushed her child through the window of the cabin to save its being eaten by Rauparaha's mob.

When the brig made Kapiti, the natives took Maranui and his wife ashore. The chief's head was beautifully dressed up with feathers, and they gave him two days to sit with his wife and friends. During this time Rauparaha's mob were busy rigging up a sort of gallows, about 60 feet high. On the beach were several white men, mostly convicts, and among them a man I knew well, Ben Turner. [Turner died some time ago at Newmarket]. At the end of two days they took the chief Maranui, and pulled him up with ropes by the feet to the top of the gallows, then let go the rope and the chief came crashing down on his head. This was repeated three times . . . the veins of the neck were then opened, and the wife of the dead chief Rakakura, holding her hands beneath, drank the blood. When this was done, the body was cut down, cooked and eaten.

Captain Stewart told me this story himself, but laid the blame for the whole affair on Cowell, the interpreter. . . . I said at the time they were both bad alike, and it was no use saying it was the other. Soon after this was told me, I fell in with Ben Turner at the Bay of Islands, and he confirmed the truth of the whole story . . . he thought both had a hand in it.[42]

Despite the public outcry in New South Wales concerning the massacre, Stewart and Cowell went unpunished for lack of evidence. Stewart is believed to have sailed to South America while John Cowell eventually acquired vast landholdings and became a successful hotelier at Waipa. Benjamin Turner left Kapiti Island and became a prosperous tavern keeper and merchant at Kororareka during the 1830s.[43]

The *Herald* memoir provides a version of the *Alligator* incident during which the whaling woman Elizabeth Guard and her two children were captured by Ngāti Ruanui following the wreck of her husband's ship *Harriet* on the Taranaki coast in 1834. The hostages were recovered following a six-month captivity when the New South Wales Government dispatched HMS *Alligator* and the colonial schooner *Isabella* carrying contingents of the 50th Regiment. Although based on information, orally transmitted by Māori and by the *Alligator*'s crew, when the warship visited the Bay, Marmon's account contains several errors but is generally accurate.

The Harriet, Captain Richard Hall, went to Taranaki for flax. She got ashore somehow and was wrecked. The natives from all parts came and took what they could belonging to the vessel . . . a tribe of natives from inland, came down to Taranaki, looking for plunder from the wrecked vessel, and being the strongest, killed the captain and those of the crew that had been left. All the white people were killed except for Mrs Guard and her two children. When they left they took the woman and children to their own kainga.

The government sent a man-o-war with Jack Guard on board to look

The tohunga Papahurahia

Penetana Papahurahia (in white cloth) participating in a haka at Waimea, Hokianga.
The occasion was a hauhunga or ceremonial display of the bones of the dead.
Watercolour by John Webster. Maori Journal, *Mss 116, Auckland Public Library.*

for his wife and children. When they arrived at Taranaki they heard that the women and children were safe. One of the children was with another chief who lived further inland, and had to be sent for which detained them two days more. At last the child was brought [tied to] the back of a slave. A sailor standing there . . . with his knife cut not only the flax, but the throat of the unoffending native. Nothing was said about the murder. It never reached the ears of the captain of the man-o'-war . . . Guard's wife and children were safe and well. A few trifling presents were given to the natives, and the vessel returned to Sydney.[44]

The rescue of Elizabeth's son John was accompanied by much bloodshed and destruction. Two large coastal pā were burned and the Ngāti Ruanui and Taranaki people left destitute. Assembling on the beach to watch the handover of John Guard, many Māori were killed when the *Alligator* opened fire with grapeshot. The incident was investigated by the British House of Commons the following year and Captain Lambert was censured for use of excessive force.[45]

By 1835 the famed tohunga and prophet Papahurahia had moved from the Bay to Hokianga to preach about a new god he called Te Atua Wera (The Red God). Among his converts was the chief Kaitoke of Mangamuka. Becoming an 'inveterate against Christians', in 1837, Kaitoke and some Papahurahia followers killed two Wesleyan converts,

Matiu and Rihimona, who were preaching in his village. Marmon recalled the incident in his *Herald* memoir which was published under the subheading 'How Religious Differences were Adjusted'.

Kaitoke came down from Utukira and told one of the native missionaries Wi Barton that he was not to come to this place [Mangamuka] again. If he did he would shoot him. Kaitoke said he would not change his old religion for anybody and did not want to be bothered with this new religion the Pakeha had brought. He liked a good many things – the blanket, tobacco and other things, but he did not want the new God. . . . The [Maori] missionaries did go up to Utukura and [two] of them [were] shot dead.[46]

There is no evidence that Papahurahia instigated the attack, although there are persistent stories that he gave Kaitoke a musket with red hieroglyphics for the ritual killing.[47] Marmon and his wife joined the pro-Wesleyan force under the chiefs Te Taonui and Te Nene that attacked Papahurahia's supporters in their pā at Utukura. Marmon recalled that when enemy captives were taken, 'my wife saved two of the chief's wives from being killed'.[48]

During the year 1838, 'the first cold-blooded murder of a *pakeha* by Maori on the Hokianga River caused a great sensation in Maori Land'. Marmon, a witness at the trial of the murderer, provided an account of the incident which appears in both the *Herald* and *Star*.[49] In April 1838, Henry Biddle, a settler based at Whirinaki near the heads, had visited Rawene to buy stores and was journeying home in a canoe paddled by Kite, a slave, and a boy, Rete, who was a chief's son. Kite later admitted that he was envious of Biddle's goods and on landing near Hokianga heads, forced the Pakeha's head under water until he drowned. Fearing European reprisals, Patuone and Waka Nene persuaded Kite's owner to hand him over for trial before a tribunal of European residents and chiefs headed by Busby at the Wesleyan chapel at Mangungu.

With the Rev Mr Hobbs acting as chaplain, my father-in-law as sheriff and with little ceremony, [the chief] Pangari stripped himself and shot the native who was immediately buried on the island. One thing I noticed which was not in accordance to our Maori laws, was that the man was shot while in irons.

The *Herald* memoir also contains Marmon's account of the last amphibious raid to the south conducted by Bay of Islands Ngāpuhi. This 1838 predatory expedition of just 60 men in three canoes landed on Great Barrier Island and, that night, seeing a fire on the mainland paddled towards it and landed.

They killed all they could find. It turned out that it was a small fishing party, and they had with them two runaway sailors from a ship in the Thames who were then living with the natives. These two rushed out of the huts when they heard the row, singing out 'Halloo, halloo.' These sailors were killed and eaten, and the 'Halloo, halloo' of these unlucky white men was for a long time a cant word among the natives of the Bay of Islands.

Throughout the 1830s, Marmon continued to support Patuone and his hapū in raids and skirmishes. Charles Davis recalled: 'John Marmon . . . had been in the habit of shouldering his musket, and fighting side by side with Patuone's people against the foes of the tribe, whether at Hokianga, Taranaki or elsewhere.'[50] Among the booty taken on these raids were cured human hands which were fastened to the interior walls of the victor's homes, 'the fingers crooked and so made to hold kits, fishing lines and any odd thing that could be hung on hooks'. Towards the end of 1838 Marmon took part in his last cannibal raid when he accompanied a Rarawa force against a pā at Mangonui to the north of the Bay of Islands.

Towards the close of 1838 occurred my last tribal war in New Zealand. Our tribe . . . had long had a standing feud with a hapu of the Ngapuhis, of which Taupitaki was chief. It had originated through Murewai's grandfather killing, in a fit of passion killed Taupitaki's aunt, who was his wife. For long the feud slumbered, neither party caring to commence hostilities, but when one of our people travelling through Taupitaki's country was killed and eaten, this was regarded as an insult that could not be overlooked.

For war, then, each side prepared, and most unwillingly was I dragged into it both as *tohunga* and warrior. We marched upon Taupitaki, who was encamped within a strong *pah* at Mangonui near the sea coast. . . . At last we decided to storm the *pah*. An attack accordingly was made on three sides at once, and sharp fighting became general. I was leading one of the parties that were relieving the attacking forces, and, as the bullets were flying pretty thickly round about, I wished myself anywhere than where I was. The Ngapuhis made a stubborn defence. A few of them had been with Hongi in his expeditions, and they strove to infuse their own courage into the breasts of their comrades by shouting that the spirit of Hongi was looking on. But it was unavailing.

Gradually they were forced back, and at length an entrance was gained into the *pah*. For an hour there was the indiscriminate slaughter of men, women, and children: for it seemed to our men as if the dying groans of their enemies were the sweetest music. Succeeding this was the customary feast upon our foes. It was the last time I was a cannibal, the last time I could lay claim to the name of 'Cannibal Jack'.

As the number of timber ships and the quantities of imported rum increased, there was less demand for Marmon's locally brewed liquor. By 1838 his main source of cash income had become timber. The great kauri forests grew down to the river's edge at Hokianga and Marmon continued to operate as a sawyer, assisted by men from his own hapū and by his slaves. The kauri trees on his own lands at Rawhia were sawn into planks, stockpiled and sold to visiting timber ships. On his voyage up the river that year, Rev. James Buller recorded the importance of timber and the impact of alcohol on the lives of Hokianga's culture-crossing settlers.

At nearly every bend a rude and lonely hut was standing. A boat, or a canoe, floated in front of it, or was lying on the beach. It was the home of some white man, living in a semi barbarous style, with a Maori woman and surrounded by their half-caste progeny. He was perhaps an escaped convict or a runaway sailor. About 200 of these classes were living on the shores of the river. They worked as axemen, sawyers, etc. for the few traders who were located on their respective establishments. Too generally, the poor fellows were the slaves of drunkenness and the

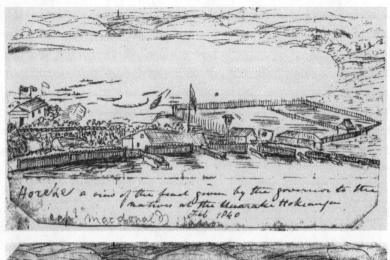

Te Horeke, Hokianga, 13 February 1840
The missionary Richard Taylor entitled this drawing 'A View of the Feast given by
the governor to the natives at the Hauraki'. The feast followed the signing of the
Treaty at Mangungu the previous day.
E-296-q-169-3, Alexander Turnbull Library.

arrival of a ship was usually their time of unbridled indulgence in this
vice.[51]

In February 1840 Captain William Hobson arrived at the Bay on HMS
Herald to present a treaty to a gathering of northern chiefs. Concerned
about the loss of their authority and what remained of their lands, the
chiefs were initially hostile. Marmon's patron Patuone turned the mood
of the assembly, arguing that it was too late to reject the Pākehā and that
Hobson should remain and be a father to both peoples. Some 80 chiefs
at the Bay signed the Treaty and copies were taken to locations around
New Zealand, including Hokianga.

[W]e heard that New Zealand had been created a British colony, and that Captain Hobson, R.N. had received a commission as governor of the new dependency. This was certainly news that filled me with joy and regret – the former because now things would be more settled, so as to induce immigrants to come out; the latter, because our actions would now be curtailed by the arm of law. Those bright days when a man could act according to the freedom of his own sweet will had passed for evermore, and henceforth we would be bound down to act according to the will of others.

By a combination of shrewdness and aggression, Marmon not only survived but thrived in the lawless era preceding the Treaty and the annexation of tribal New Zealand by Britain. Lamenting the passing of 'the good old times' in *Old New Zealand*, Marmon's neighbour, Frederick Maning, succinctly summed up the nature of this turbulent era and, coincidentally, Jacky Marmon: 'Might was to a very great extent right, and . . . bodily strength and courage were almost the sole qualities for which a man was respected or valued. At that time in a country like New Zealand, every man was a fighting man or nothing.'[52]

The natives went into this change merely because they believed it would provide them an unlimited supply of muskets and ammunition. Another Council was held at Hokianga in August of the same year . . . I opposed the creation of the colony might and main both as Maori-tohunga and as European. I saw that it would injure my grog manufacture, as before long a duty would be put on all excisable spirits, as had been done in the early days at Sydney.

When Hobson took the Treaty to the Hokianga more than 2000 Māori and 60 chiefs attended the debates at the Mangungu mission. Hōne Raumati, Marmon's father-in-law, spoke in favour of the Treaty, having signed the document three days earlier at Waitangi. Hobson believed, incorrectly, that the opposition among some chiefs was traceable to the Catholic Bishop Pompallier and, correctly, that it was also traceable to '[a] set of escaped convicts and other low ruffians who have congregated on this river in considerable numbers'.[53] Maning, who translated for the chiefs, bluntly told Hobson that he had advised the chiefs to resist colonisation as it would degrade them. Marmon meanwhile encouraged Māori opposition from behind the scenes. Hobson had been thoroughly briefed by the Wesleyans about Marmon's opposition to the Treaty and they detailed his crimes with relish for he was not only a cannibal Pākehā-Māori but of course Irish and Catholic. Seeing the benefits of a governor, the Hokianga chiefs ignored the fulminations of their Pākehā-Māori and signed the Treaty, but Hobson still wrote in exasperation:

Another person altogether of a lower description [than Maning] known under the name of 'Jacky Marmon', who is married to a native woman, and has resided in this country since 1809, is also an agent of the bishop. He assumed the native character in its worst form – is a cannibal – and has been conspicuous in the native wars and outrages for years past. Against such people I shall have to contend in every quarter.[54]

CHAPTER EIGHT

Sawyer, soldier and recluse, 1840–80

And another white warrior came in with his gun. This was Jacky Marmon, a wild figure, and the chief actor in many a bloody episode of Old New Zealand. He was an ex convict from the chain gangs of Sydney; he had settled among the Maoris in the days when New Zealand was a 'no Man's Land', fought in their wars, and even shared in their cannibal feasts; his fondness for human flesh was notorious among both Maori and Pakeha in the 'thirties' and early 'forties'.[1]

This description of Marmon was the work of the New Zealand War's historian James Cowan, who rode with colonial troops during the Hokianga Dog Tax Rebellion of 1898. Cowan, who was bilingual, collected and published material on many known and previously unknown Pākehā-Māori in his books and newspaper articles. Valuing oral testimony at a time when many New Zealand historians did not, his description of Marmon's appearance at the siege of Ohaeawai Pā during the Northern War was based on the recollections of Māori and Pākehā veterans.[2] Interestingly, there is no mention of a tā moko or face tattoo. Cowan added: 'In his war-paint of red ochre, with bare chest and arms tattooed, his shaggy head decked out with feathers, musket slung across his back, cartouche-box belts buckled around him, a long handled tomahawk in his hand, he looked the perfect picture of savage warrior.'

The 15,000-word conclusion to the *Star* memoir provides a relentlessly detailed account of the background to and the battles of the Northern War. Refreshingly free of Maning's attributions and embellishments, it was published in four instalments during March 1882. Filled with dates, people, ships and events readily verifiable in the historical record, these instalments indicate the depth and quality of Marmon's original maritime and Pākehā-Māori reminiscences. Freed by Maning to speak in his own voice, Jacky confirms a courageous, loyal and fiercely independent character. Although he tends to overstate the significance of his advisory role during the war, Maning dared not undermine Marmon's role and distort descriptions of the people and events of the Northern War without incurring the wrath of European veterans who had known Marmon and were still living in Auckland and Hokianga in 1882. Though he refers to himself on one occasion in this section as a 'white man', rather than a Pākehā-Māori, the extent to which Marmon still identified with his hapū is evident in the way he lived among and fought beside them Māori style.

By 1840, Marmon was one of approximately 150 Pākehā-Māori middlemen living and prospering among the New Zealand tribes. As the settler population increased and the chiefs began dealing directly with the newcomers, many Pākehā-Māori became impoverished and their influence and numbers declined. With the influx of shipping and trading competitors at Hokianga, Marmon's own role as a key mediator and translator was gradually undermined. Additionally, during the 1840s, the price of local land and kauri timber declined sharply and in this depressed market Marmon and his fellow kauri traders suffered poverty and distress. Unable to pay the costs necessary to have his land claim to Rawhia heard in court, Marmon wrote directly to Governor FitzRoy in January 1844:

The Petitioner therefore trusts that your Excellency will not allow him to lose the only property he possesses in the Land of his adoption though poverty brought on by the downfall of the timber trade, our only dependence heretofore in his part of the country, and which enabled us till within the last two years to live tolerably comfortably.[3]

Early sawyer's cottage
With the collapse of the kauri industry many northern Pākehā-Māori traders became
impoverished and disgruntled with British rule.
R. A. A. *Sherrin and J. H. Wallace,* Early History of New Zealand: From Earliest Times to 1840,
Auckland, 1890, p. 643.

Later that year, Marmon improved his financial position by agreeing
to give up some of his additional land holdings to the crown in exchange
for government scrip to the value of £650, some of which he used to buy
land on Auckland's North Shore.[4]

At the Bay of Islands, Ngāpuhi and their Pākehā-Māori also suffered,
losing many of the economic benefits enjoyed before the Treaty,
particularly revenue from shipping duties which now went to the
government. The capital was shifted from Kororareka to Auckland in
1842, the felling of kauri was banned for a time and, under government
control, the number of land sales declined.[5] Hone Heke, the nephew
of Hongi Hika and the leading chief at the Bay, was angered by these
developments which he viewed as the undermining of his chiefly
authority by the crown. Pākehā-Māori frequently meddled in tribal
affairs. Motivated largely by material gain and the threat posed to his
liquor trading by the imposition of British law and order, Marmon was
one of many northern Pākehā-Māori who had encouraged their chiefs
to resist the Treaty in 1840, though he exaggerated the extent of his
own influence.

In 1844 we had a visit from Hone Heke, then the Ariki of the Ngapuhi
tribe. . . . He had not gone in heartily with the scheme of making New
Zealand a British colony, because he thought, and that justly, that it only

meant the slavery and extinction of the Maori race. . . . I said to myself, now here is a chance of getting things once more into our own hands. I therefore persuaded him that the British only made a show of leaving the natives independent, that in reality they were abject slaves.

Visiting Auckland in late 1844 to secure title over his lands at Rawhia, Marmon was presented with an opportunity to make amends for his anti-British machinations. Questioned extensively by government officials about Māori politics in the North, he was also interviewed briefly by Governor FitzRoy, Hobson having died in 1842. 'Having lived so long with the natives, he thought I could be of great service, and if I did so, he would see that government recompensed me for anything I did.' Marmon continued: 'Of course I promised His Excellency to do all I could to help the white people. I told the Governor it would be my duty to do everything in my power, "and I *will* sir," says I.'

I left Auckland, and returned by way of Kaipara to Hokianga. On my way, I heard a capital story from an old chief, who had been visiting Taranaki. How I did laugh when I heard it. He was an old acquaintance, and I had not seen him for many years. A great many Sydney trading vessels were in the habit of visiting Taranaki, exchanging flax for gunpowder. On opening their casks of powder, the natives found that they were not more than three parts full, the empty space stuffed full of paper. The Taranaki chiefs said nothing, but prepared their flax as usual, and the neat little bales weighed the proper weight and look as nicely dressed as possible. When the flax bales were opened in Sydney they were found to contain several stones, which of course, took a great deal off the proper weight. On the return of the vessel from Sydney, the captain who traded with the chiefs showed the stones, and said he could not understand how they got into the bales. 'It's all right,' said the Taranaki chief with the greatest politeness and good humour, 'Quite right. "Utu" or payment for paper you sent us in the powder casks.' How I did laugh when I heard it.

Hone Heke considered the Union Jack flying on Flagstaff Hill above Kororareka a symbol of Māori subservience. When he cut it down for the third time, Governor FitzRoy sent to New South Wales for military assistance. In a co-ordinated attack on 11 March 1845, Heke and his

Hone Heke

Marmon was one of several Pākehā-Māori to have encouraged Heke's opposition to British authority.

R. A. A. *Sherrin and J. H. Wallace,* Early History of New Zealand: From Earliest Times to 1840, *Auckland, 1890, p. 694.*

ally, the elderly Musket War veteran Kawiti, cut down the flag for a fourth and final time. In the ensuing fighting and confusion Kororareka was sacked and burned and the town abandoned by its European residents who sailed to Auckland. Marmon's brief summary of events was based on reports obtained from local Māori and trader Pākehā-Māori eyewitnesses.

I was at home living quietly as usual, when some natives told me there was another row at the Bay of Islands I did not believe it as I knew there was a man-of war there at the time – the Hazard, at Russell. I heard too that Kawiti's tribe had gone over to Heke's party. . . . About three o'clock in the morning Heke with a mob of about 100 men . . . made for the hill where the flagstaff stands. Kawiti and his men came to the other end of Kororareka beach, and waited the signal from Heke. Heke and his tribe cut down the flagstaff, then fired into the signal house, shot the sentry dead. . . . The officer on duty and the soldiers ran away down to the magistrate Captain Beckham. Kawiti then came from Pomare Bay. . . . The captain of the Hazard landed with his marines, and attacked the natives, killed one chief, and wounded several others. Kawiti's men, finding they were getting the worst of it, got away as quickly as they could. . . . Heke came down with the flag, and when he saw the white people flying in all directions he tried all he could to stop them. . . . The white people got aboard the vessels and left [their] houses to the natives.

'My slaves had been putting in uwhi, or winter potatoes . . . and on this day I was to give a sort of feast – it was the custom when the work was done. On my return home I found the Chief [Te Taonui] and about sixty others at my place.'

Marmon subsequently became one of several Hokianga Pākehā-Māori recruited by Patuone's brother, the loyalist chief Tamati Waka Nene, to support the British against the 'rebel' chiefs Heke and Kawiti. Too elderly to lead his warriors in battle, Marmon's old patron, Patuone, played a limited role in the fighting. In March 1845, Marmon marched with a force of 500 Hokianga Māori under the chiefs Nene, Taonui, Moses Tawhai and others to join the British forces at Waimate Mission station in the Bay of Islands.[6]

Just before we got to the Waimate settlement, we found a great stack of potatoes placed on the side of the road, to feed us on our way. We did not stop to cook any, but just picked up a few kits and marched on . . . we saw another stack of potatoes in kits – about 200, I should think – ten bags of flour, a bullock cut in two, and placed on top of the potatoes: besides the food, there was a cask of tobacco. These things had been placed there for the natives by the missionaries. . . . Mr Atkins and several of the residents in Hokianga sent us a present of some tobacco and powder; Mr William Webster made and sent us a present of some cartouch boxes, ready bored and covered; so you see our white friends on the river did not forget us.

Expecting British retribution for their attack on Kororareka, Heke and Kawiti built a strong, new pā, Puketutu, on the shore of Lake Omapere, a small stretch of water in the Bay district. Waka Nene's force built their own pā as a base of operations two miles away near Okaihau. Constant skirmishing between the opposing Māori forces meant Heke and Kawiti were unable to complete their defences before the arrival of British forces. Marmon regretted not being able to participate in the first skirmish as his father-in-law had borrowed his musket. 'It was late when I got My gun, so I did no fighting that day.'

One day, Mr Manning, John Leaf and a number of Hikutu's tribe came over, and soon after their arrival Dr Burrows [a missionary] came into the pa [and] seeing the white men, said, 'No white man has any right to be here – they should be in Auckland.' 'Sir' says I, 'every white man in the country has a right to be here, and with a gun in his hand. You too sir.' . . . Next morning I went down and asked Mr Manning if he would come with me. I could show him how the natives went skirmishing. 'No thank you Jacky,' says he, 'I am going with my friend Hauraki.' Mr Manning then went off with his people from Whirinaki. He had turned up his trousers to the knees, and rubbed his legs and arms with charcoal, so that no one would take him for a Pakeha. Mr Manning, John Leaf (Starboard Jack as he is always called) and myself were the only white men fighting that day.

Led by Colonel William Hulme, a force of 300 British regulars, 120 sailors and marines, and some 40 European volunteers marched from the Bay to Heke's pā at Lake Omapere during April 1845. Serving as an irregular scout, Marmon warned the advancing column of an ambush set by Heke's men.

I saw Colonel Hulme at the head of the soldiers, with Captain Beckham, and on the roadside, a little ahead of them, was a party of the natives belonging to the enemy, sitting down waiting. I saw at once who they were, and sang out to warn [them]. They stopped at once. . . . The enemy, seeing they were detected, went back into Heke's pah.

Tamati Waka Nene
During the Flagstaff War of 1845, Marmon joined Nene's loyalist warriors in their
clashes with Hone Heke and 'rebel' Māori.
R. A. A. Sherrin and J. H. Wallace, Early History of New Zealand: From Earliest Times to 1840,
Auckland, 1890, p. 470.

Marmon also assisted in locating a suitable firing position for one of
the two rocket guns. 'The lieutenant, a gunner from the North Star and
I went to the point. The Lieutenant said the elevation was a very good
one [and] the spot very suitable to fire from.'

The first battle of the Flagstaff War began on 8 May with an 'artillery'
barrage from the two rocket tubes before Colonel Hulme ordered the
attacking force of 216 men forward. Despite suffering heavy casualties
in the confused and fierce fighting that followed, co-ordinated sorties
by Hone Heke from within the pā and Kawiti from without (a tactic the
historian James Belich has described as two matadors dealing with a
bull) eventually pushed back the British force, which lost 52 killed and
wounded.[7] Standing among a group of European observers, Marmon
watched the battle unfold and assisted where he could.

A shot was fired at me, but it struck Mr Russell who was beside me. It fell into his coat pocket; it was a spent ball, so did no damage. I fell in with the doctor belonging to the soldiers. He asked me if I could find anyone to help carry a wounded man to another Doctor a little higher up, he was so busy. I got the man up, then the Quarter-Master asked me to get natives to carry cartridges to the soldiers, but being chased by the enemy they threw the cartridges which were in bags into the water. . . .

It was night when we all returned to the pah. The next day we buried the dead in a hollow near the entrance to Okaihau Bush. . . . We heard that Kawiti had lost his eldest son, his fighting chief, and about thirty men. Heke and his people buried the white men who had fallen near his pah. Heke went himself to the Waimate for Dr. Burrows to come and read the funeral service over the dead soldiers. While Heke went to fetch the parson, some of his men stripped the dead men of their clothes: this so enraged Heke that he took the clothes and had them all burned. . . . The following day the little army of soldiers and sailors returned to the Bay of Islands, Tamati Walker going with them.

Having abandoned Puketutu, Heke returned to Te Ahuahu, one of his old pā. When Heke and his men went off one day in search of provisions, Taonui seized the unguarded position and was quickly reinforced by Waka Nene. Regathering his force of 500 warriors, Heke advanced to retake his fortress, but in a pitched battle reminiscent of the Musket Wars, Taonui and Waka Nene's force of 300 descended from the pā and fought them on the plain below.

On the morning of 13th June, we saw a large party of Heke's men coming along the road . . . [Taonui's] men were soon out and fired on the advancing party; Patuoni (Walker's brother) and I got our guns and joined them.

Marmon's participation in the battle was witnessed by another comrade in arms, John Webster, who wrote his own memoir which he gave to his son George. This was subsequently published in 1908 as *Reminiscences of an Old Settler*.

Next day a recruit joined us as we left Nene's camp, the notorious John Marmon [who] seemed to dodge the bullets for he was forever ducking his head or jumping from side to side as bullets whistled passed us. He took shelter under a small hillock, found a party of wahines there for shelter also, but the humming and spitting of the bullets over our heads was incessant. . . . At Ahu-ahu fight he lay behind a scoria wall and potted one of Heke's men and brought his flintlock into camp.[8]

Described by the historian James Belich as 'the forgotten battle', Te Ahuahu was the decisive battle of the Flagstaff War.[9] Heke lost three senior chiefs, was badly wounded and suffered an outright defeat. It is at this point in the *Star* account that Marmon provides a glimpse of his performance in battle as a Pākehā toa and his assimilation of the Māori law of utu.

After a little while I went up to the flagstaff to try and see what was going on; there I found . . . about 300 of the enemy coming towards Walker's pah . . . we went down on the flat and waited for the enemy on the west side of a field of kumaras. Our tribe was divided into two parties, one on the east side, and one on the west.

The attack on Heke's pā at Okaihau
A. S. *Thomson*, The Story of New Zealand, *London, 1859, p. 110.*

The enemy rushed on those on the east side and shot a chief who was dumb. One of the enemy jumped on to the fence to shoot Tino when I at once shot him dead. [Taonui's] men were still firing on the enemy that had first engaged with them. Some of ours that had run away now rallied; a few more had come up, so that they were stronger, and made a dash on Heke's party. Wi Hobson got ahead in the rush and wounded Heke in the thigh. A native tried to get at the chief Kukuha in the confusion; I killed that fellow also. . . . The enemy were flying in all directions. Rapaha killed one of the enemies big chiefs. I fired on old Wharepapa but missed him. We chased them about two miles . . . I spotted one fellow belonging to the enemy, and meant to kill him the first chance I could get. He was one of the party who drowned [a] wounded soldier in Omapere Lake after the first fight.

Heke and Kawiti later established themselves at Ohaeawai Pā with a force of 100 defenders and four cannon. By late June, a force of 630 British regulars and sailors supported by artillery and Nene's large force of loyalist Māori had assembled outside the position. Marmon made friends with a naval officer, Lieutenant Phillpot, and again served the British army in the role of irregular scout.

Repulse of storming party at Ohaeawai
A. S. Thomson, The Story of New Zealand, London, 1859, p. 116.

The soldiers camped about a mile from the pah, under command of Colonel Despard. I went with [Waka Nene], and we saw a better spot for the encampment than the one they had chosen, sheltered from the fire of the pah. Colonel Despard approved of the site and ordered a change to be made. I pointed out a good place for a stockade, and there they placed the two first cannons.

The battle, directed by Colonel Henry Despard, began with a six-day bombardment but the pā, cleverly designed by Kawiti to completely protect the defenders, withstood the barrage. Harassed by accurate sniping and sudden sorties from the pā against loyalist Māori and the artillery battery, Despard ordered an assault by 250 crack troops. Finding the stockade undamaged, they were suddenly decimated by close-range volleys from the hidden defenders. The survivors staggered back to their own lines leaving 110 dead and wounded behind. Following the battle Heke announced a truce during which Marmon distinguished himself by recovering the bodies of the slain who lay outside the stockade.

I heard that they were going to rush the Heke's pah. The doctor ordered me to stop and assist guarding the magazine, and point out our natives from the enemy if they came out of the pah. . . . The soldiers went down towards the pah, and were soon out of sight. I heard the firing and the bugle sounded the retreat . . . there was great confusion everywhere. The road was crowded with the soldiers returning carrying wounded men . . . Lieutenant Phillpot had climbed on to one of the posts of the pah, and was reaching over to kill one of the enemy when the man fired and killed him. He was the finest and bravest gentleman I ever knew. Another native fired and killed the sailor-boy beside him.

On my way home that night I had to pass Colonel Despard's tent; the trumpeter called out to me to come in and speak to the Colonel. 'Well Marmon,' said he, 'this is a bad job. Do you think the enemy are likely to attack us to-night?' 'No sir,' I said; 'it will take them all the night to talk over how well they fought. I know their ways so well; you need not be alarmed, they will never come out to-night.' The Colonel Dismissed me and I went home.

We could see from where we were that dogs, pigs, ducks and geese were getting at the dead soldiers lying in front of Heke's pah. I asked an officer if I might call out and try to get the dead. I got permission and went up and sang out; a native got on one of the posts and asked who it was. 'Me Jacky,' I replied. He said, 'you can come in if you like.' 'no,' I said, 'you come out.' This chief's name was Hara; he came outside and I asked him if I might get the dead soldiers. 'Yes.' said he, 'but don't bring up any soldiers, and when you take these dead ones bury them at Russell.' I took some native boys to help me and asked for a blanket from the Colonel to put around Lieutenant Phillpot. I carried him on my back from the pah . . . a large pit was dug for the dead.

Colonel Despard was initially dubious about the usefulness of Marmon 'who had been a good deal about the camp, though without any employment'. He later reported, when efforts by the Rev. Henry Williams had failed, 'On the occasion of recovering the bodies of the men killed on 1 July 1845, Marmon made himself very useful, and I always considered his exertions as the principal means by which they were brought back to Camp.'[10] On 10 July, it was found that the defenders had abandoned their position and Despard's troops returned wearily to Waimate. For five months there was peace as FitzRoy unsuccessfully negotiated with Heke and Kawiti.

During the siege of Ruapekapeka (the Bat's Nest) Pā, the last battle of the Northern War, Marmon again served as an irregular scout. With Heke sidelined by his wound and defeat at Te Ahuahu, his ally Kawiti constructed Ruapekapeka, an artillery-proof fortress in rugged bush country in the Bay of Islands district. The attacking force, 1300 British regulars and colonial troops, 850 pro-government Māori and 17 artillery pieces, spent three weeks hacking a road through the bush to reach the pā.[11] Governor FitzRoy had been replaced with George Grey, a former army officer who personally organised the British attack on the stronghold on December 1845. After a two-week bombardment, Kawiti was reinforced by a contingent under Heke.

At this time there were several man-of-war lying in the Bay of Islands. I stayed at home till the last day of 1845. I thought I would go and find out what was going on . . . Three days after I had joined Walker's men [at the Bay], we marched over to Ruapekapeka. There were about 200 of us. On the road I fell in with Baron De Thierry and Mr John Webster. They were taking letters for Governor Grey who was at the front. I too had a letter to deliver to Governor Grey from Sir Everard Home, captain of the 'North Star'. After I had delivered my letter to the Governor, he sent me to Col Despard, who asked me what I was going to do? 'shoot as many of them as I can, sir,' The colonel asked me if I would join the Volunteers? . . . There was no reason why I should join with any body. I just wished to be my own master, going and coming when I pleased.

The artillerymen, who were now firing 32 pounders from the big stockade, knocked down the flagstaff inside the pah, and a woman was blown to pieces. At sunset the firing ceased. Soon afterwards a whole lot of the enemy came into the pah, and began dancing about, shouting in derision, and firing off their muskets, with all kinds of antics, to show their contempt for us. The next day was Sunday, and as soon as it was light [Hōne Raumati] sent my slave to see if there was anyone in the pah. The slave crept along among the fern until he got right to the pah. He came back and said there was only one man inside. . . . This news was soon known in the camp, and directly a whole crowd of soldiers and sailors ran off to the pah.

The pā had been abandoned by the defenders, though fierce fighting took place at the rear of the position and in nearby bush. After making peace with Waka Nene and other loyalist chiefs a week after the battle, Grey took no further action against Heke and Kawiti.

Returning to the Hokianga, Marmon found the price of kauri had slumped again as the demand for spars had fallen with the advance of steam shipping. Persistently frustrated by colonial bureaucrats, Jacky never received remuneration for his war service, could not obtain title to his lands at Rawhia and unlike many colonial veterans was not granted a pension. Suffering financial difficulties, but ever adaptable, Marmon attempted to reinvent himself as a harbour pilot. In a letter to a friend in 1848, John Webster wrote, 'Did I ever tell you that Mr Mac got a paper signed by Jacky Marmon sent in to government begging to be appointed pilot for the river. This is some time ago. Is he not a horrid fellow.'[12] By the late 1840s, old Hokianga was changing. Māori population, customs and power were in decline and, remembered by the authorities and respectable settlers as a fugitive convict, renegade and cannibal, Marmon's application was, predictably, unsuccessful.

'Ruapekapeka'

Watercolour 206 x 328 mm. John Williams, A-079-030, Alexander Turnbull Library.

In 1848 my wife died. I did not marry again. In 1850 I went up to Sydney to see about a piece of land, where the gasworks now stand, that had belonged to my father. He had bought it in the early days. I found that I could not do much about the land, so I put it into a lawyer's hands; he was to attend to it for me. I felt very lonely, all my old companions were either dead, or gone away; one sister only was left of my family, and she seemed quite a stranger, did not know me, and only remembered me by name; she was a child when I left home the last time. When I came back to Hokianga to see about raising some money to pay the lawyer, I found that the bushmen had been killing my cattle, and I was in a fix. I had no money, the lawyer died soon after, and I have never been able to get money enough to assert my rights, for without money one cannot go to law.

In the decades following the Northern War, Pākehā-Māori through-out New Zealand were reabsorbed by the new settler society. As the inclusive, bicultural society at Hokianga faded, Frederick Maning abandoned his Pākehā-Māori existence and was appointed a Native Land Court judge by Governor Grey in 1865. From a figure who was well known in government and military circles during Heke's War, Marmon faded into obscurity. Fellow traders and comrades in arms like Maning and Webster became part of the self-appointed colonial aristocracy at Hokianga and became increasingly distant. An uncomfortable reminder of their own lapses into 'savagery' in old New Zealand, they later ridiculed and slandered Marmon whose own reminiscences are devoid of malice.

Historical records provide further brief glimpses of Marmon between the end of the Northern War and his death in 1880. His only recorded child, Mere, the daughter of Hauāuru, his second Hokianga wife, married Jim the Boy and had her own child named Mary. In 1858, this granddaughter was in the charge of Bishop Pompallier in Auckland at the school of the French Sisters.[13] In a letter to the editor of the *Southern Cross* in April 1863, Marmon complained that 15 of his cattle had been shot by 'a certain petty chief'. When brought before the tribunal of senior chiefs who had been appointed Native Magistrates, the offender had simply defied the court.[14]

In 1865, following a 36-year campaign of letter writing and personal representations to successive officials, Governors and Land Claims Commissioners, Marmon was finally given title to his 523 acres at Rawhia.[15] This landholding was one of the largest blocks on the Hokianga, but the land proved unsuitable for long-term cattle rearing. There was a brisk demand for kauri gum and timber during the Vogel Boom of the 1870s and though he remained lucid and active, Marmon's economic activities and contact with Europeans decreased as his age and the number of new settlers increased.[16]

Marmon lived mainly at Rawhia during the 1860s. James Buller noted in November 1869, 'Jackie Marmon's house is on the [other?] side. He is a character. His children living as Maoris with the Maoris, the weather-beaten old man dwells alone. I saw him this afternoon at Mr Maning's.'[17] Marmon sometimes lived with his granddaughter and Māori relatives during the 1870s, according to the historian Eric Ramsden, 'at Whangape Harbour, and having outlived his wives, he was regarded as a recluse'.[18] Jacky sometimes appeared at the old Rangiahau Hotel on the upper harbour where a chair was reserved for him in the corner of the bar. Such was his reputation that no local dared sit there.[19] He had little time for the new settlers and having led such an eventful life, simply wished to enjoy a quiet, uncomplicated existence.

Marmon was not the only Pākehā-Māori to become fully assimilated

Barnet Burns
Most of Marmon's contemporaries including this Ngāti Kohungunu Pākehā-Māori
recrossed cultures to live again in European society.
PUBL-0074, Alexander Turnbull Library.

but was unusual in not recrossing cultures with the passing of old New Zealand. Despite his attendance at Catholic services, Marmon's longevity and ongoing Māori connections made him the subject of gossip and judgements which entrenched his notoriety at Hokianga where the old stories about his convict, renegade, tohunga and cannibal past continued to haunt him. Invited by Alice Bennett to dictate his memoirs in the 1870s, he managed a remarkably detailed and precise account of his life and times. Nothing he said, however, would ever end the controversy surrounding him.

The Hokianga historians Cecil and Celia Manson collected a variety of stories about Marmon from local Pākehā families during the 1950s. One visitor to the Bennett house recalled in later years how Marmon, who liked to have Alice read back his dictation, scolded Alice for sanitising one of his more graphic descriptions.[20] The Mansons also recorded:

Edward Markham   **Bishop Pompellier**   **Thomas McDonnell**

THIS AND FACING PAGE: Marmon's exploits are described in the letters, journals and
reports of visitors, missionaries and British officials at the Bay of Islands and Hokianga.
*Markham: F-19133-1/2, Alexander Turnbull Library (detail); all others R. A. A. Sherrin and
J. H. Wallace,* Early History of New Zealand: From Earliest Times to 1840, *Auckland, 1890.*

Mr Hammond [citing his grandfather] told us, he [Marmon] lived alone
for a time near Whangape Harbour. His loved Maori wife was dead, and
his two daughters were married and had gone away. So he buried himself away in an old whare deep among the manuka, where he cultivated
a small patch of potatoes. Sometimes he would be seen by travellers,
trudging home to his hidden shack, carrying a string of eels or fish, his
beard showing white against the old blue shirt he always wore. In place
of trousers he wore a blanket or shawl.[21]

The old lady of 91, whom we had previously visited, had also spoken
to us of Jacky Marmon. One day, she said, when she was a small girl
living in her home at Rawene, John Webster, who was in the house at
the same time, came into the drawing-room and said to her: 'Go into the
kitchen, quickly. Jacky Marmon is there. You may never see him again.'

Sitting in the kitchen was a small, ruddy-faced man, nursing his famous home-made top hat; he claimed that inside it were his 'papers'.[22]

Marmon was always remembered by Māori with affection and the
greatest respect, for he had known, advised and fought beside many of
the great northern chiefs. Among his Māori kinsfolk he was regarded
and treated as one of their own. Unwilling to abandon his Pākehā-

William Hobson   **Rev. Butler**   **James Busby**

Māori identity, he was never accepted by the Hokianga settlers who referred to him as Cannibal Jack or Tiaki the white tohunga. A relic of a bygone era, Marmon in his final years became an object of curiosity and the bogeyman with whom Hokianga parents threatened their errant children.[23] Embittered by the government's failure to pay him a pension for his military service, Marmon concluded his *Star* reminiscences, ruefully acknowledging his truculence and status as an outsider.

It is now 1877, and I am a very old man, and suppose I shall die here. I think the Government might have given me a small pension, for during the war I did many things which, had they been done by others, would have been both praised and rewarded; but then I had no friends with influence, nor anyone to speak for me. Had the brave Lieut. Philpott (whose body I brought out of Heke's pah at Ohaeawai) lived, I feel sure I should have been rewarded. In him, I lost my best and only friend: somehow, that brave sailor officer understood me, and was very kind to me during the short time I knew him. I can't quite make it out, but I never did make friends; too much pepper in my composition I suppose.

My story is finished; from first to last, it is made up of recollections of the early days in New Zealand. If it interests you, my end is served, and I shall rest in peace upon the memories of Cannibal New Zealand.

Having completed his reminiscences, Marmon lived a further three years with his Māori relatives at Whangape and Hokianga before his death at Rawhia on 3 September 1880. The mystery and controversy surrounding his life followed him to the grave. Long regarded by his Hokianga kinsmen as Māori, Jacky was honoured with a tangihanga, reported one descendant, 'appropriate for a man who married the daughter of one of our chiefs'.[24] Jacky's interment, on Rawhia hill above the Waihou and his own house, included a group of drunken settlers of mainly Irish descent who had known Jacky and wanted to ensure a Christian burial.[25] It is possible, therefore, that a priest conducted a second service for the Catholic Māori and Pākehā. A party of Marmon's relatives interred his coffin sideways, into an existing niche just below the crest and survey peg, before filling in and concealing the entrance.[26] While in keeping with Māori customary practice, Jacky's distinctive entombment was to become the source of many extraordinary stories.

The specific location of Marmon's grave remains a carefully guarded secret. His Māori guardians recently permitted the felling of mature trees in a commercial pine plantation on Rawhia hill. Concerned, however, that their ancestor's resting place remain undisturbed, they refused permission for the pines nearest the grave to be felled and here they stand as sentinels.[27]

The Mansons concluded that, with 'all kinds of wild stories . . . whispered about him – that he had the evil eye, that he still had the cannibal habits' it is not surprising that superstitious settlers at Hokianga believed Marmon to be genuinely possessed of supernatural powers, a malevolent figure whose gaze must never be met directly.[28] One local, Mrs McBreen, was said to have danced on his coffin, so intense was her fear and loathing.[29] Another account states that when Marmon's coffin was exposed by 'terrific rains just after the funeral . . . they said the earth refused to hold him and threw him out of the grave'.[30] Conflicting reports state that he was subsequently buried vertically, standing up or, alternatively, head down, to confine his supernatural powers.[31] A further report states that an unidentified priest crossed the river to Rawhia, disinterred Marmon and re-interred him on consecrated ground at the Purakau Catholic mission to confine his restless spirit.[32]

CONCLUSION

John (Jacky) Marmon has many claims to distinction and was no lesser a star than Pākehā-Māori such as Maning, Barrett or Tapsell who were the bicultural founding fathers of their own districts. Among Pākehā-Māori however, Marmon was remarkable for the depth of his assimilations and ongoing rejection of European ways of life. For many Māori families at Hokianga, he remains an important and highly regarded ancestor. A rarity among Pākehā-Māori, Jacky was one of a handful of pre-Treaty Europeans who made a full psychological and spiritual transformation from Pākehā to Māori. He is the only pre-Treaty white 'savage' known to have survived the Musket Wars and to have remained living among his Māori kinsfolk into the late nineteenth century.

Marmon's early presence among Māori exposed them to some of the values, attitudes and behaviours of Europeans. In the process, he helped cushion the onset of cultural change by explaining the nature or motivations of Europeans. Crucially, these explanations were given by someone trusted by Māori and with no vested interest in facilitating European settlement to the detriment of Māori.[1]

The first and most notorious Pākehā-Māori to settle at Hokianga, Marmon lived a life full of deeds and adventures, surpassed by few of his kind. Although an adventurous spirit, he was never a natural risk taker. Valuing the security and traditions of village life, Jacky understandably preferred the cut and thrust of the barter trade to the mayhem of intertribal war. As a trader he had a dramatic impact on his own hapū, the Hikutu on the Kerikeri River and the Popoto and Ngāti Hao clans at Hokianga where he introduced guns, swearing, tobacco and alcohol, the last fuelling violence and debauchery among his people.

As a trader Pākehā-Māori, Jacky also introduced many objects and items that his Māori kinsfolk found useful in their daily lives, including metal cauldrons, knives, scissors, needles, clothing, blankets, tools and agricultural implements. Marmon also raised the first crops of wheat and barley and the first herd of beef cattle at Hokianga. However, his most vital contribution as a trader Pākehā-Māori was the guns he provided to his hapū.

The Rev. Henry Williams roundly condemned the gun-trading activities of Pākehā-Māori as 'devils's work', but Jacky's gun trading ensured the survival of his hapū and also opened up the flax trade on the Kerikeri and the flax and provisions trade at Hokianga. Consequently, his Māori patrons were able to increase their political and military power by turning their traditional semi-subsistence agricultural economies into thriving semi-commercial ones. By fully arming their hapū with guns, Marmon and his Pākehā-Māori contemporaries ultimately contributed to a new intertribal balance of power, based on mutual terror, that saw intertribal musket warfare peter out during the late 1830s.

Marmon's mediating role and successive strategic marriages to local women of rank were important in limiting misunderstandings and violence between his hapū and the European settlers, and in shaping nineteenth-century and modern race relations at Hokianga. In raising 'quite a colony of children' both on the Kerikeri and at Hokianga Marmon and his peers helped blur the lines between the races by a process of genetic and cultural interaction that occurs to this day. During his researches at Hokianga during the 1960s, Smithyman found 'kin of three surnames' claiming 'descent from him'.[2]

Among Māori, Jacky found a value system that he could live with and strictly adhered to Māori protocols. This loyalty to his Māori kinsfolk and their value systems meant that he invariably joined their raids and sieges. As a tohunga Pākehā and Pākehā toa, on campaign, Marmon was expected by the chiefs to be like them, courageous, uncompromising and merciless. While never enjoying the prospect of combat, Jacky excelled as a warrior on Māori battlefields where his achievements were acknowledged and rewarded by the chiefs. Never a great leader of men, he did, however, lead contingents of Ngāpuhi reinforcements during desperate intertribal battles and, during their aftermath, behaved as viciously as any of the 'savage' Pākehā-Māori.

Crossing and recrossing many geographical and cultural boundaries and changing roles many times during his lifetime, Marmon has been consistently depicted by colonial, post-colonial and modern writers as a minor bit player in Hokianga's colourful past. Yet by the 1830s he became a well-known New Zealand as well as Hokianga identity. Before voyaging to New Zealand, many visiting missionaries, colonial officials and travellers/observers were already well informed about Marmon's exploits by references to him in letters, journals and official reports and through George Craik's popular book *The New Zealanders*, published in London in 1830.

As the first Pākehā-Māori on the Kerikeri River and at Hokianga, Marmon bridged the gap between the cultures by mediating trading relations and interpreting for both. Able to straddle two worlds, he performed a vital role in clearing a way for European newcomers and many early commercial exchanges. Jacky served as a political and spiritual advisor, hired gun and interpreter for Kawhitiwai, Hongi Hika and many of the great Hokianga chiefs including Muriwai, Patuone and Tamati Waka Nene. In these roles he did have some influence on his patrons during the 1810s and 1820s, but this declined as European settlement increased and it was always overrated by missionaries, colonial officials and more respectable settlers. Marmon also knew, advised and interpreted for many of the first shipbuilders, missionaries, settlers and colonial officials at the Bay of Islands and at Hokianga, including Captains Clarke and Dillon, Samuel Marsden, Bishop Pompallier, Baron de Thierry, James Busby, Colonel Despard and Governor FitzRoy.

One of Marmon's most important legacies was the memoir he dictated to Mrs Bennett as a cantankerous old man. These recollections are more than a 65-year record of his life and adventures. They open a window on Māori life in pre-Treaty New Zealand, revealing an indigenous society in a state of flux as it attempted to cope with the impacts of European technology, ideas and settlement. The memoir gives substance to the Māori people Jacky knew, and to the locations he visited or inhabited.

Having lived as a Māori for so long, Marmon became indifferent to European ways of living and did not abandon his family and adoptive people to recross cultures. By contrast, Frederick Maning ultimately rejected his Māori children and kinsfolk and refused all contact with Māori in general. Also, unlike Maning, Jacky maintained a good relationship with his Māori family, naming and describing his Māori wives in his reminiscences, and was able to express the depth of his love for his young wife Hawea. Marmon consequently remained living with his last Māori wife, children and relatives who cared for him in old age.

Marmon's intimate knowledge of the Bay of Islands and Hokianga tribes is reflected in his own descriptions of noted chiefs, his Māori wives, tribal beliefs and customs of peace and war. His eyewitness descriptions of numerous events, major and minor, at the Bay and Hokianga are rivalled by few contemporary accounts. Plagiarised by late nineteenth- and early twentieth-century ethnologists, Marmon's *Herald* and *Star* 'autobiographies' are valued as rare 'inside' accounts by modern anthropologists, historians and literary scholars and continue to contribute to a better understanding of Māori culture by Pākehā readers.

The spurious asides and after-thoughts that Frederick Maning inserted into the *Star* account represent Marmon erroneously as a good-natured but powerless 'football of fate' who was prone to exaggeration and, more accurately, as a calculating manipulator of Māori. Jacky's own narrative certainly confirms a shrewd and acquisitive character. Alone among Māori, he was initially obliged to think well ahead, and consider all possibilities, particularly the likely responses of his chiefs. Highly adaptable and mentally quick, Marmon was by necessity perceptive of, and receptive to, the moods and motivations of these men.

Shaped and hardened by his seafaring, convict and Pākehā-Māori experiences, Marmon was a tough, uncouth and belligerent man, who resented overbearing European authority figures and the laws and rules they attempted to introduce into pre-Treaty Hokianga. Fiercely individualistic, he strove to preserve and assert his mana, contesting every challenge and trespass on his rights by both Māori and Pākehā. When drunk he became dangerously unpredictable and in this state during the 1830s was prone to bullying Wesleyan missionaries and given to the violence that so terrified Eliza White and killed his Pākehā-Māori neighbour Bill Styles. Nevertheless, Marmon was far from being the devil incarnate that his detractors would have us believe.

Pākehā-Māori were often cast in early reports as hang-dog, mean-spirited, lower-status men; fugitives slinking between the cultures, too often criminal and reclusive. Marmon revelled in his unique status and identity as a Pākehā-Māori and enjoyed interacting with a range of stimulating and eccentric European characters. There is no evidence that he behaved dishonourably in his dealings with Māori or the new European settlers and officials at Hokianga who found him totally dependable. Nor is there evidence that he was ever intimidated by them, for he did not begin to live reclusively until the late 1860s. The significance of his public service as military scout, translator and advisor and his reputation for competence and reliability was always undermined by stories about his convict and cannibal past and by his self-confessed violent temper and acerbity. Consequently, Jacky gained few long-term friends among the new settlers while the more pretentious Hokianga 'old settlers' began to treat him as a pariah.

Historians, too, have not treated Marmon kindly and continue to emphasise his quick temper, violence and cannibalism, their images shaped by the writings of nineteenth-century men and women who had been the targets his wrath.[3] Even the merchant John Webster, the least vitriolic of his critics, believed that Marmon 'was always an evil doer, both a murderer I believe, and a cannibal'.[4] As we have seen, a few contemporary journals were complimentary. Edward Markham acknowledged the Pākehā-Māori's fluency, excellent building skills and extensive knowledge of Māori customs. Rev. Stack recorded the depth of the chief Patuone's regard for this Pākehā-Māori and Colonel Despard noted Jacky's achievement in recovering the bodies of the British dead lying outside Ohaeawai Pā.

Jacky Marmon was such an ungovernable, turbulent and controversial figure that even before his death his reputation among Māori and Pākehā was characterised by a mishmash of false reports, rumours, accusations and attributions. So potent were these that they persist in modern-day Bay of Islands and Hokianga where Māori and Pākehā still use Marmon's name and specific terms in the same sentence, particularly: 'white cannibal', 'Pākehā-Māori' and 'bogeyman'.

Marmon's adaptations and adventures as described in the *Herald* and/or *Star* memoirs seem extraordinary, but colourful lives and changing identities and roles were not unusual among Pākehā-Māori. In *The Dictionary of New Zealand Biography Vol. 1*, Jacky's biographer, Roger Wigglesworth, has appropriately fixed Marmon's diverse roles in Hokianga and New Zealand frontier history as 'Sailor, convict, Pakeha-Maori, interpreter, shopkeeper, sawyer, carpenter, soldier'.[5]

It was customary in nineteenth-century New Zealand to mark the gravesite of deceased Pākehā, Pākehā-Māori and Māori with a wooden board or pole, inscribed with words or carved with patterns or both. Often wrought from kauri or rimu, some endured to the mid-twentieth century when Kendrick Smithyman made a photographic record. Searching for Marmon's grave on Rawhia hill, Smithyman recorded the event and hatched a compelling image for his subject in the poem 'At Jacky Marmon's Grave'.

> If the grave is found, have someone
> make him a wooden marker. This country has
> peculiar grave markers. Add one.
> Cut it to a totem, or what will do duty for a totem. A horse
> headed
> weta – that will do fine. . .
> When I went to look for his grave I heard
> only a cryptic breeze among the pines on the crest
> and the telling silence of the Waihou's
> low tide summer torpor.[6]

REFERENCES

Acknowledgements

1. Jack Lee, *An Unholy Trinity*, Russell, 1997.
2. Roger Wigglesworth, 'The Myth and the Reality: A Study of the Adaptation of John Marmon', Massey University, 1974. See also his 'Marmon, John, 1798–1800?–1880. Sailor, convict, Pakeha-Maori, interpreter, shopkeeper, sawyer, carpenter, soldier', *The Dictionary of New Zealand Biography [DBNZ]*, Vol. 1, Wellington, 1990: 270–71.

Introduction

1. J. B. Condliffe and Willis Airey, *A Short History of New Zealand*, 1957: 34. See also John Parker (ed.), *Frontier of Dreams*, Auckland, 2005: 88.
2. Ormond Wilson, *From Hongi Hika to Hone Heke*, Dunedin, 1985: 80.
3. James Belich, *Making Peoples*, Auckland, 1996: 172. Laurie Barber, *New Zealand: A Short History*, 1989: 36.
4. Anne Salmond, *Between Worlds*, Auckland, 1997: 304–05, 369.
5. Wilson, 1985: 82.
6. Kendrick Smithyman, 'At Marmon's Grave' in 'Uncollected Northland Poems', Jack Ross (ed.), *Brief*, 26 January 2003: 19–49. Also see (online): http://www.nzepc.auckland.ac.nz/authors/smithyma/northland.asp
7. Wigglesworth, 1974: 75. See also Smithyman, 'Making History: John White and S. Percy Smith at Work' in *Journal of the Polynesian Society*, vol. 88, no. 4, 1979: 48.
8. R. A. A. Sherrin and J. H. Wallace, *Early History of New Zealand: From Earliest Times to 1840* (Sherrin); *From 1840 to 1845* (Wallace), Thomson W. Leys (ed.), Auckland, 1890; Robert McNab, *The Old Whaling Days*, Christchurch, 1913; T. Lindsay Buick, *New Zealand's First War*, Wellington, 1926; James Cowan, *The New Zealand Wars*, 2 vols, Wellington, 1923.
9. Lee, 1997: viii; Wigglesworth, 1974: 73–80.
10. Wigglesworth, 1974: 75–80.
11. Frederick Maning, *Old New Zealand*, Auckland and London, 1863: 5, 154, 212.

12. See Trevor Bentley, 'Images of Pakeha-Maori', PhD Thesis, University of Waikato, 2007: 92.
13. Richard Taylor, *Te Ika a Maui*, London, 1870; H. Carleton, *The Life of Henry Williams*, Auckland, 1874.
14. *Auckland Star*, 26 November 1881.
15. Lee, 1997: ix.
16. Wigglesworth, 1974: 80.
17. George Bruce, *The Life of a Greenwich Pensioner, By Himself*, ANL, Ms 3608. For Rutherford's reminiscences see George Craik, *The New Zealanders*, London, 1830.
18. Smithyman, 1979: 375, 406, 409, 411, 413.
19. Sherrin and Wallace, 1890: 156, 200.
20. *Auckland Star*, 26 November, 24 December, 31 December 1881.
21. Edward Jerningham Wakefield, *Adventure in New Zealand*, 2 vols, London, 1845; George Angas, *Savage Life and Scenes in Australia and New Zealand*, 2 vols, Adelaide, 1847; Ernst Dieffenbach, *Travels in New Zealand*, 2 vols, London, 1843; Arthur Thomson, *The Story of New Zealand*, 2 vols, London, 1859.
22. Charles Marshall, 'Forty Years in the Waikato', in John St John, *Pakeha Rambles Through Maori Lands*, Christchurch, 1873; Angela Caughy, *The Interpreter: The Biography of Richard 'Dicky' Barrett*, Auckland, 1998. See also Maurice Shadbolt, *Monday's Warriors*, Wellington, 1990.

Chapter One: Sailor, 1805–17

1. Lee, 1997: 3; Wigglesworth, 1974: 7.
2. *The New Zealand and Australian Encyclopaedia, Vol. 2*, World Reference Library, 1964: 881.
3. Ibid., *Vol. 1*: 226.
4. P. G. Canham, 'New England Whalers in New Zealand Waters 1800–1850', Masters Thesis, University of Auckland, 1959: 5–11.
5. Louisa W. Pittman, 'Appeasing Neptune: The Functions of Nautical Tradition', available online at: http://www.cofe.edu/chrestomathy/vol5/pittman.pdf
6. *New Zealand Herald*, 9 October 1880.
7. Sherrin and Wallace, 1890: 156, 200, 305.
8. Robert McNab, *Murihiku and the Southern Islands*, Invercargill, 1907: 98.
9. Tim Severen, *In Search of Moby Dick*, London, 2000: 236.
10. Herman Melville, *Moby Dick: or, The Whale*, 1988, available online at: http://www.cofe.edu/chrestomathy/vol5/pittman.pdf

11. Ibid.
12. Maning, 1863: 136–46.
13. Robert McNab, *Historical Records of New Zealand*, 2 vols, Wellington, 1908–14: 336.
14. *Auckland Star*, 26 November 1881.
15. J. S. Cumpston, *Shipping Arrivals and Departures, Sydney, 1788–1825*, Canberra, 1964: 64.
16. Wigglesworth, 1974: 10.
17. Sherrin and Wallace, 1890: 136.
18. Salmond, 1997: 369.
19. *New Zealand Herald*, 9 October 1880.
20. *Auckland Star*, 31 December 1881.
21. *New Zealand Herald*, 9 October 1880.
22. Ibid.
23. Alexander Berry, 'Account of the Destruction of the Ship "Boyd"', ATL qms – 0163.
24. 'Early Shipping in New Zealand Waters', available online at: http://www.myancestorsstory.com/shiplist-
25. Pittman, available online at: http://www.cofe.edu/chrestomathy/vol5/pittman.pdf
26. *New Zealand Herald*, 9 October 1880.
27. Ibid.
28. Robert McNab, *From Tasman to Marsden*, Dunedin, 1914: 194.
29. W. T. Parham, 'Tapsell, Phillip 1777?–1873. Mariner, whaler, trader', *DNZB, Vol. 1*, Wellington 1990: 425–26.
30. Ibid; *Auckland Star*, 31 December 1881.
31. Ibid.
32. Buick, 1926: 174.
33. Trevor Bentley, *Pakeha Maori*, Auckland, 1999.

Chapter Two: Gun-trader, 1817–20

1. Thomson, *Vol. 1*, 1859: 301.
2. Wigglesworth, 1974: 82.
3. Ibid: 3.
4. Augustus Earle, *Narrative of a Residence in New Zealand*, London, 1832, Wellington, 1963: 96, 97.
5. Gavin White, 'Firearms in Africa: An Introduction', *Journal of African History*, vol. 12, no. 2, 1971: 182.
6. M. L. Brown, *Firearms in Colonial America 1492–1792*, Washington, 1980: 217, 293.
7. Earle, 1963: 92, 93.

8. Bentley, 1999: 76–99.
9. Dumont D'Urville, *The New Zealanders: A Story of Astral Lands*, Wellington, 1992: 286–88.
10. *Auckland Star*, 24 December 1881.
11. Trevor Bentley, 'Tribal Guns, Tribal Gunners', MA Thesis in History, Waikato University, 1997: 20–22.
12. L. M. Rogers (ed.). *The Early Journals of Henry Williams, 1826–40*, Christchurch, 1961: 217.
13. G. White, 1971: 174–75.
14. R. J. Barton (comp.), *Earliest New Zealand: The Journals and Correspondence of the Rev. John Butler*, Masterton, 1927: 173.
15. Maning, 1863; Marshall, Part 1 in St John, 1873.
16. Thomson, 1859: 291
17. *New Zealand Herald*, 9 October 1880.
18. Canham, 1959: 5–11.
19. *New Zealand Herald*, 18 November 1880.
20. Judith Binney, *The Legacy of Guilt*, Auckland, 1968: 241.
21. John Nicholas, *Narrative of a Voyage to New Zealand, Vol. 1*, London, 1817: 128–29.
22. McNab, *Vol. 1*, 1808: 378.
23. J. R. Elder (ed.), *The Letters and Journals of Samuel Marsden, 1765–1838*, Dunedin, 1932: 266.
24. Ibid.
25. S. Percy Smith, *Maori Wars of the Nineteenth Century*, Christchurch, 1910: 106.
26. R. S. Oppenheim, *Maori Death Customs*, Wellington, 1973: 13.
27. Maning, 1863: 219.
28. Nicholas, *Vol. 1*, 1817: 28.
29. Maning, 1863: 184.
30. Barton, 1927: 84.
31. Craik, 1830: 87.
32. Thomson, *Vol. 1*, 1859: 86–87.
33. *New Zealand Herald*, 9 October 1880.

Chapter Three: Tohunga Pākehā, 1820

1. Wigglesworth, 1974: 3. See also Lee, 1987: ii, iii.
2. Joel Polack, *New Zealand: Being a Narrative of Travels and Adventures, Vol. 1*, London, 1838: 73.
3. Maning, 1863: 154.
4. Ormond Wilson, 'Papahurahia, First Maori Prophet', *Journal of the Polynesian Society*, vol. LXXXIV, 1965: 473–83.

5. E. H. McCormick (ed.), *Markham, Edward, New Zealand, or Recollections of It*, Wellington, 1963: 38, 39.
6. Barton, 1927: 137.
7. *Auckland Star*, 11 March 1882.
8. Thomas Hocken (ed.), 'A Biographical Sketch', in Maning, 1922: vii–xvi.
9. Alan Mulgan, *Great Days in New Zealand Writing*, Wellington, 1962: 214.
10. Salmond, 1997: 516–17. See also Elder, 1932: 66.
11. Ibid: 516–17, 397.
12. S. Percy Smith, 'The Tohunga-Maori: A Sketch', *Proceedings of the Royal Society of New Zealand*, vol. 32, 1899: 254.
13. Wilson, 1985: 171.
14. Bentley, 1999: 111.
15. Wilson, 1965: 473–83.
16. Elsdon Best, *Maori Religion and Mythology, Vol. 2*, Wellington, 2005: 23. See also Dumont D'Urville, *Voyage Pittoresque Autour du Monde, Vol. 2*, Paris, 1835: 328.
17. James Cowan, *The Adventures of Kimble Bent*, Wellington, 1911: 88.
18. Smith, 1899: 270.
19. Elder, 1932: 287.
20. Edward Shortland, *Traditions and Superstitions of the New Zealanders*, London, 1854: 162.
21. Maning, 1863: 162.
22. T. W. Gudgeon, 'The Tohunga Maori', *Journal of the Polynesian Society*, vol. 23, no. 2, 1967: 19, 22
23. Cowan, 1911: 105, 106.
24. Smith, 1899: 267.
25. Ibid: 265–70.
26. *Auckland Star*, 28 January 1882.
27. Williams, in Rogers, 1961: 318–19, 156–57; Elder, 1932: 473, 467, 472.
28. Ruth Ross, 'The Autochthonous New Zealand Soil', in *The Feel of the Truth*, Peter Munz (ed.), Wellington: 1969: 56.
29. Smith, 1899: 265–70.
30. Ibid: 270.
31. Bridget Haggerty, 'God between Us and All Harm', available online at: http://www.irishcultureandcustoms.com
32. Maning, 1863: 208.
33. Cowan, 1911: 327.
34. Ibid: 21.

35. Ibid: 327.

36. Binney, 1968: 225.

37. Canham, 1959: 9–13.

38. *New Zealand Herald*, 9 October 1880.

Chapter Four: War tohunga, 1821

1. Trevor Bentley, 'The Musket Wars', in *The Oxford Companion to New Zealand Military History*, Ian McGibbon (ed.), Auckland, 2000: 340–44.

2. George Graham, *Auckland: A Guide to the City and Province*, Auckland, 1925. See also C. O. Davis, *The Life and Times of Patuone*, Auckland, 1876.

3. Elder, 1932: 355–57.

4. A. Sharp, *Duperrey's Visit to New Zealand in 1824*, Wellington, 1971: 65.

5. Smith, 1910: 182.

6. Barton, 1927: 173.

7. Earle, 1963: 65. See also Polack, *Vol. 2*, 1838: 239.

8. Richard Davis, *Missionary Register*, 1833: 283.

9. J. Montifiore, *British Parliamentary Papers*, 1837: 40.

10. Samuel Butler, in Barton, 1927: 172.

11. Elder, 1932: 355.

12. Butler, cited in Barton, 1927: 98.

13. Holloway, 1962: 68.

14. Elsdon Best, *The Pa Maori*, (1927) Wellington, 1995: 288.

15. K. Holloway, *Maungarei*, Auckland, 1962: 73.

16. Sharp, 1971: 65.

17. Richard Cruise, *Journal of a Ten Month Residence in New Zealand*, London: 1823: 283.

18. Cruise, 1823: 282. See also Polack, *Vol. 2*, 1838: 82.

19. Sharp, 1971: 152.

20. C. O. Davis, *The Life and Times of Kawiti*, Auckland, 1855: 7.

21. Elder, 1932: 356.

22. Ibid: 279.

23. B. Brown, *The Age of Firearms*, Illinois, 1976: 108–09.

24. Thomson, *Vol. 1*, 1859: 128.

25. Sharp, 1971: 65.

26. Elder, 1932: 358.

27. *Sydney Herald*, 7 May 1837.

28. Bentley, 1997: 113.

29. Tamihana Te Rauparaha, *Life and Times of Te Rauparaha*,

Martinborough, 1980: 44–45. See also J. Grace, *Tuwharetoa*, Auckland, 1959: 289.

30. T. W. Gudgeon, 'Maori Wars', *Journal of the Polynesian Society*, vol. 61, no. 1, 1967: 41.
31. Richard Taylor, *Te Ika a Maui*, Wellington, 1974: 110.
32. Smith, 1910: 189.
33. John White, *Ancient History of the Maori*, Wellington, 1980: 165.
34. Dieffenbach, 1843: 187.
35. Smith, 1910: 189.
36. Elder, 1932: 364.
37. Ballara, *Taua: 'Musket Wars', 'Land Wars' or 'Tikanga'?: Warfare in Māori Society in the Early Nineteenth Century*, Auckland, 2003: 225, See also B. Byrne, *The Unknown Kaipara*, Auckland, 2002: 345.
38. Smith, 1910: 190
39. Leslie G. Kelly, *Tainui*, Christchurch, 2002: 351.

Chapter Five: Eyewitness and convict, 1821–23

1. Ballara, 2003: 225–26. See also Smith, 1910: 195.
2. Angela Ballara, 'Hongi Hika, 1772–1828', *DNZB*, Vol. 1, 1990: 202.
3. Smith, 1910: 194.
4. Bentley, 1997: 66–87.
5. Cowan, 1911: 327.
6. Ibid.
7. *New Zealand Herald*, 6 November 1880.
8. Ibid.
9. *New Zealand Herald*, 18 November 1880.
10. J. Shepherd, Journal, cited in Angela Ballara, 'Warfare and Government in Ngapuhi Tribal Society', MA Thesis, University of Auckland, 1973: 75.
11. McNab, 1907: 165.
12. Markham, 1963: 84.
13. *New Zealand Herald*, 11 December 1880.
14. John Webster, *Reminiscences of an Old Settler in Australia and New Zealand*, Christchurch, 1908: 273.
15. Smithyman, 2003: 19–49.
16. Barton, 1927: 299.
17. *New Zealand Herald*, 9 October 1880.
18. *Sydney Gazette*, 1 May 1823, in Wigglesworth, 1974: 301.
19. *New Zealand Herald*, 9 October 1880.
20. Wigglesworth, 1974: 129. See also *New Zealand Herald*, 9 October 1880.

21. Wigglesworth, 1990: 270.
22. *New Zealand Herald*, 9 October 1880.
23. Barton, 1927: 312.
24. D'Urville, 1992: 286–88.

Chapter Six: Pākehā-Māori, 1823–30

1. *Northern Luminary*, 4 September 1880.
2. *New Zealand Herald*, 16 October 1880.
3. Markham, 1963: 39. See also Wigglesworth, 1974: 41.
4. Wigglesworth, 1990: 271.
5. *New Zealand Herald*, 16 October 1880.
6. Ibid.
7. *Auckland Star*, 18 February 1882.
8. *New Zealand Herald*, 16 October 1880.
9. *Auckland Star*, 18 February 1882.
10. Polack, *Vol. 2*, 1838: 74.
11. Lee, 1997: 1.
12. Peter Gibbons, 'Some Thoughts on the Pre-1840 Pakeha-Maori', Term Paper in History, Massey University, 1969: 11. See also Wigglesworth, 1990.
13. Smithyman, 2003: 19–49.
14. Bentley, 1999: 184.
15. Webster, 1908: 155.
16. Polack, *Vol. 2*, 1838: 239.
17. John Hobbs in J. M. R. Owens, 'The Wesleyan Mission to New Zealand, 1819–1840', PhD Thesis, Victoria University, 1969: 287–88.
18. Ballara, 1973: 284.
19. Ballara, *Vol. 1*, 1990: 304.
20. Smith, 1910: 333–34.
21. Smithyman, 1979: 375–415.
22. G. Clarke, Journal, 7 September 1825, cited in Ballara, 1973: 117.
23. James Kemp cited in Byrne, 2002: 25.
24. Ibid.
25. James Drummond (ed.), *John Rutherford: The White Chief*, Wellington, 1908: 29.
26. Maning, 1863: 46–47.
27. George Clarke, letter, 26 March 1825, cited in Byrne, 2002: 24.
28. Smith, 1910: 333–34, 343.
29. Drummond, 1908: 151.
30. Dorothy Cloher, *Hongi Hika*, Auckland, 2003: 186.
31. *New Zealand Herald*, 16 October 1880.

32. Smith, 1910: 344.
33. *New Zealand Herald*, 16 October 1880.
34. *New Zealand Herald*, 6 November 1880.
35. Williams, in Rogers, 1961: 37.
36. Webster, 1908: 273.
37. *New Zealand Herald*, 6 November 1880.
38. Rev. J. Stack, Journal, 27 March 1828, in Owens, 1969: 326.
39. *New Zealand Herald*, 6 November 1880.
40. Owens, 1969: 353.
41. *New Zealand Herald*, 6 November 1880.
42. Elder, 1932: 443.
43. Ibid.
44. *New Zealand Herald*, 16 October 1880.
45. Turton, 1882: 222.

Chapter Seven: Landowner, hotelier and renegade, 1830–40

1. Dom Vaggioli, *History of New Zealand and its Inhabitants*, (1896), Dunedin, 2000: 45.
2. Williams, in Rogers, 1961: 219.
3. Harrison Wright, *New Zealand, 1769–1840*, Cambridge, Massachusetts, 1959: 84.
4. Wigglesworth, 1974: 53. See also Lee, 1997: 18–21.
5. McCormick, 1963: 45–48.
6. Cecil and Celia Manson, *The Tides of Hokianga*, Wellington, 1956: 69.
7. Markham, 1963: 39.
8. Interview with Peter Maddren, hotelier, Horeke Hotel, Hokianga, 17 May 2007.
9. *New Zealand Herald*, 27 November 1880.
10. Eric Ramsden, *Busby of Waitangi*, Wellington, 1942: 36.
11. Wigglesworth, 1974: 53. See also Lee, 1977: 18–21.
12. Lee, 1997: 41.
13. *New Zealand Herald*, 27 November 1880.
14. St John, 1873: 167.
15. Basil Howard, *Rakiura*, Dunedin, 1940: 363. See also Edward Jerningham Wakefield, *Adventure in New Zealand, Vol. 1*, 1868: 278.
16. Hocken in Maning, 1922: vii–xvi.
17. Markham, 1963: 17.
18. Ibid: 39.
19. Wigglesworth, 1974: 36.
20. Manson, 1956: 69.
21. Markham, 1963: 40.

22. Buller, 'Notes on a Journey', cited in Wigglesworth, 1974: 72.
23. Markham, 1963: 39.
24. Wigglesworth, 1974: 45
25. Ramsden, 1942: 64.
26. Wigglesworth, 1974: 46.
27. Ibid.
28. Ibid: 45.
29. Stack, Journal, 27 March 1828, in Wigglesworth, 1974: 97.
30. C. O. Davis, 1876: 37.
31. *New Zealand Herald*, 27 November 1880.
32. Wilson, 1985: 21
33. *New Zealand Herald*, 11 December 1880.
34. Polack, *Vol. 2*, 1838: 431.
35. Ibid.
36. *New Zealand Herald*, 18 November 1880.
37. Ibid.
38. C. O. Davis, 1876: 33.
39. Wigglesworth, 1990: 270.
40. Vaggioli, 2000: 84.
41. Wigglesworth, 1974: 93.
42. *New Zealand Herald*, 18 November 1880.
43. Bentley, 1999: 313.
44. *New Zealand Herald*, 27 November 1880.
45. 'The Sailor's Account', in McNab, 1913, Appendix C: 425.
46. *New Zealand Herald*, 11 December 1880.
47. Judith Binney, 'Penetana Papahurahia ?–1875 Nga Puhi tohunga, war leader, prophet', *DNZB, Vol. 1*, 1990: 329–31.
48. *New Zealand Herald*, 27 November 1880.
49. Ibid.
50. C. O. Davis, 1876: 37.
51. J. Buller, *Forty Years in New Zealand*, London, 1878: 27.
52. Maning, 1876: 35.
53. Wigglesworth, 1974: 41.
54. Ibid.

Chapter Eight: Sawyer, soldier and recluse, 1840–80

1. Cowan, *Vol. 1*, 1923: 41.
2. Bentley, 2007: 208.
3. Wigglesworth, 1974: 90.
4. Freda Kawharu, 'Heke Pokai, Hone Wiremu ?–1850, Nga Puhi leader, war leader', *DNZB, Vol. 1*, 1990: 185.

5. *Auckland Star*, 4 March 1882.

6. *Auckland Star*, 11 March 1882.

7. James Belich, *The New Zealand Wars*, Auckland, 1988: 43.

8. J. Webster, 'Notes on Jacky Marmon', M5.84/33, Hocken Library, cited in Wigglesworth, 1974: 61.

9. Belich, 1988: 45.

10. Despard, cited in Wigglesworth, 1974: 65.

11. Belich, 1988: 59.

12. J. Webster to G. F. Russell, letter, 22 October 1848, in Wigglesworth, 1974: 91.

13. Old Land Claims, 158b/316, cited in Wigglesworth, 1974: 69.

14. *Southern Cross*, cited in A. H. Reed, *The Story of Northland*, Wellington, 1956: 127.

15. Old Land Claim Files, 158d/316, in Wigglesworth, 1974: 56.

16. Wigglesworth, 1974: 100.

17. Buller, 'Notes on a Journey', cited in Wigglesworth, 1974: 72.

18. Ramsden, 1942: 36 ftn. 1.

19. Manson, 1956: 69.

20. Ibid: 72.

21. Ibid.

22. Ibid: 73.

23. Wigglesworth, 1990: 270.

24. Interview, Queenie Puru, Mangungu mission, Hokianga, 7 May 2009.

25. Manson, 1956: 69.

26. Interview, Queenie Puru, 7 May 2009.

27. Interview, Queenie Puru, Mangungu mission, Hokianga, 14 May 2009.

28. Manson, 1956: 72.

29. Bentley, 1999: 186.

30. Manson, 1956: 69.

31. Ibid; Bentley, 1999: 186.

32. Manson, 1956: 68.

Conclusion

1. H. E. Maude, *Of Islands and Men*, Melbourne, 1968: 162.

2. Smithyman, 2003: 19–49.

3. George Rusden, *History of New Zealand*, *Vol. 1*, London, 1883: 120. See also Belich, 1996: 132.

4. John Webster, Ms 84/23 Ho, cited in Wigglesworth, 1974: 86.

5. Wigglesworth, *Vol. 1*, 1990: 270–71.

6. Smithyman, 2003: 19–49.

BIBLIOGRAPHY

New Zealand books and articles before 1900

Angas, George, *Savage Life and Scenes in Australia and New Zealand*, 2 vols, Adelaide, 1847.

Bourke, E. M., *A Little History of New Zealand*, Melbourne, 1881.

Buller, James, *Forty Years in New Zealand*, London, 1878.

Carleton, H., *The Life of Henry Williams*, 2 vols, Auckland, 1874–77.

Craik, G., *The New Zealanders*, London, 1830.

Cruise, Richard, *Journal of a Ten Month Residence in New Zealand*, London, 1823.

D'Urville, Dumont, *Voyage Pittoresque Autour du Monde, Vol. 2*, Paris, 1835.

Davis, C. O., *The Life and Times of Kawiti*, Auckland, 1855.

——, *The Life and Times of Patuone*, Auckland, 1876.

Davis, Richard, *Missionary Register*, 1833.

Dieffenbach, Ernst, *Travels in New Zealand*, 2 vols, London, 1843.

Earle, Augustus, *Narrative of a Residence in New Zealand*, (1832), Wellington 1963.

Maning, Frederick, *History of the War in the North*, Auckland, 1862.

——, *Old New Zealand*, (Auckland and London, 1863), Auckland, 1922.

Moss, Frederick, *School History of New Zealand*, Auckland, 1889.

Nicholas, John, *Narrative of a Voyage to New Zealand*, 2 vols, London, 1817.

Polack, Joel, *New Zealand: Being a Narrative of Travels and Adventures*, 2 vols (1838), Christchurch, 1974.

Reeves, William Pember, *The Long White Cloud: Ao Tea Roa*, (1898), Christchurch, 1973.

Robley, H. G., *Moko: The Art and History of Maori Tattooing*, London, 1894.

Rusden, George, *History of New Zealand*, 3 vols, London, 1883.

St John, John, *Pakeha Rambles Through Maori Lands*, Christchurch, 1873.

Sherrin, R. A. A. and Wallace, J. H., *Early History of New Zealand: From Earliest Times to 1840* (Sherrin); *From 1840 to 1845* (Wallace), Thomson W. Leys (ed.), Auckland, 1890.

Shortland, Edward, *Traditions and Superstitions of the New Zealanders*, London, 1854.

Smith, S. Percy, 'The Tohunga-Maori: A Sketch', *Proceedings of the Royal Society of New Zealand*, vol. 32, 1899.

Taylor, Richard, *Te Ika a Maui*, (1st ed., 1855, 2nd ed., 1870, 3rd ed., 1874), Wellington, 1974.

Thomson, Arthur, *The Story of New Zealand*, 2 vols, (London, 1859), Christchurch, 1974.

Vaggioli, Dom, *History of New Zealand and its Inhabitants*, (1896), Dunedin, 2000.

Wakefield, Edward Jerningham, *Adventure in New Zealand*, 2 vols, London, 1845.

——, *Adventure in New Zealand*, Vol. 1, Wellington, 1868.

Williams, W. L., 'The Story of John Rutherford', *Transactions of the New Zealand Institute*, vol. 23, 1890.

Yate, William, *An Account of New Zealand*, London, 1835.

Books and articles after 1900

Anderson, Johannes, *Maori Life in Aotearoa*, Christchurch, 2000.

Ballara, Angela, *Taua: 'Musket Wars', 'Land Wars' or 'Tikanga'? Warfare in Maori Society in the Early Nineteenth Century*, Auckland, 2003.

——, 'Hongi Hika, 1772–1828', *Dictionary of New Zealand Biography, Vol. 1*, 1990.

Barber, Laurie, *New Zealand: A Short History*, Auckland, 1989.

Barton. R. J. (comp.), *Earliest New Zealand: The Journals and Correspondence of the Rev. John Butler*, Masterton, 1927.

Bateman New Zealand Encyclopaedia, 5th edition, Lynne Richardson (ed.), Auckland, 2000.

Belich, James, *Making Peoples*, Auckland, 1996.

——, *The New Zealand Wars*, Auckland, 1986, 1988.

Bentley, Trevor, *Captured By Maori*, Auckland, 2004.

——, *Pakeha Maori*, Auckland, 1999.

——, 'The Musket Wars', *The Oxford Companion to New Zealand Military History*, Ian McGibbon (ed.), Auckland, 2000.

——, 'Muskets, Munitions and Marauders: The Rise, Operations and Decline of the Maori Musket Armies', *New Zealand Legacy*, vol. 9, no. 1, 1997.

——, 'White Tribesmen, Transients and Traders: Foreign Fighting Men in Pre 1840 Maori Expeditions of War', *New Zealand Legacy*, vol. 10, no. 1, 1988.

Best, Elsdon, *Maori Religion and Mythology, Vol. 2*, Wellington, 2005.

——, *The Pa Maori*, (1927), Wellington, 1995.

Binney, Judith, *The Legacy of Guilt: A Life of Thomas Kendall*, Auckland, 1968.

——, 'Penetana Papahurahia ?–1875 Nga Puhi tohunga, war leader, prophet', *Dictionary of New Zealand Biography, Vol. 1*, 1990.

Brown, B., *The Age of Firearms*, Illinois, 1976.

Brown, M. L., *Firearms in Colonial America 1492–1792*, Washington, 1980.

Browne, C. R., *Maori Witchery*, London, 1929.

Buick, T. Lindsay, *New Zealand's First War*, Wellington, 1926.

——, *The Treaty of Waitangi*, Wellington, 1914.

Butler, Samuel, *Earliest New Zealand*, R. J. Barton (comp.) Masterton, 1927.

Byrne, B., *The Unknown Kaipara*, Auckland, 2002.

Caughy, Angela, *The Interpreter: The Biography of Richard 'Dicky' Barrett*, Auckland, 1998.

Cloher, Dorothy, *Hongi Hika*, Auckland, 2003.

Condliffe, J. B. and Airey, Willis, *A Short History of New Zealand*, Auckland, 1957.

Cowan, James, *The Adventures of Kimble Bent*, Wellington, 1911.

——, *The New Zealand Wars*, 2 vols, Wellington, 1923.

Crosby, R. O., *The Musket Wars*, Auckland, 1999.

Cumpston, J. S., *Shipping Arrivals and Departures, Sydney, 1788–1825*, Canberra, 1964.

D'Urville, Dumont, *The New Zealanders: A Story of Astral Lands*, C. Legge (trans.), Wellington, 1992.

Drummond, James (ed.), *John Rutherford: The White Chief*, Wellington, 1908.

Earle, Augustus, *Narrative of a Residence in New Zealand*, Wellington, 1963.

Elder, J. R., *Marsden's Lieutenants*, Dunedin, 1934.

——, (ed.), *The Letters and Journals of Samuel Marsden, 1765–1838*, Dunedin, 1932.

Grace, J., *Tuwharetoa*, Auckland, 1959.

Graham, George, *Auckland: A Guide to the City and Province*, Auckland, 1925.

Gudgeon, T. W., 'Maori Wars', *Journal of the Polynesian Society*, vol. 61, no. 1, 1967.

——, 'The Tohunga Maori', *Journal of the Polynesian Society*, vol. 16, no. 2, 1967.

Hocken, T. M. (ed.), 'A Biographical Sketch', F. E. Maning, *Old New Zealand*, Auckland, 1922.

Holloway, K., *Maungarei*, Auckland, 1962.

Howard, Basil, *Rakiura*, Dunedin, 1940.

Kawharu, Freda, 'Heke Pokai, Hone Wiremu ?–1850, Nga Puhi leader, war leader'. *Dictionary of New Zealand Biography, Vol. 1*, 1990.

Kelly, Leslie G., *Tainui*, Christchurch, 2002.

Lee, Jack, *An Unholy Trinity*, Russell, 1997.

——, *Hokianga*, Hong Kong, 1987.

——, *'I Have Named it the Bay of Islands…'*, Auckland, 1983.

McCormick, E. H. (ed.), *Markham, Edward, New Zealand, or Recollections of It*, Wellington, 1963.

McNab, Robert, *From Tasman to Marsden*, Dunedin, 1914.

——, *Historical Records of New Zealand*, 2 vols, Wellington, 1908–14.

——, *Murihiku and the Southern Islands*, Invercargill, 1907.

——, *The Old Whaling Days*, Christchurch, 1913.

Manson, Celia and Cecil, *The Tides of Hokianga*, Wellington, 1956.

Maude, H. E., *Of Islands and Men*, Melbourne, 1968.

Melville, Herman, *Moby Dick: or, The Whale*, (1851), Chicago, 1988.

Morrell, W. P., *A History of New Zealand Life*, Wellington, 1957.

Morton, Harry, *The Whale's Wake*, Dunedin, 1962.

Mulgan, Alan, *Great Days in New Zealand Writing*, Wellington, 1962.

Nicholson, John, *White Chief: The Colourful Life and Times of Judge F. E. Maning of the Hokianga*, Auckland, 2006.

Oppenheim, R. S., *Maori Death Customs*, Wellington, 1973.

Parham, W. T., 'Tapsell, Phillip. 1777?–1873. Mariner, whaler, trader', *Dictionary of New Zealand Biography, Vol. 1*, Wellington, 1990.

Parker, John (ed.), *Frontier of Dreams*, Auckland, 2005.

Ramsden, Eric, *Busby of Waitangi*, Wellington, 1942.

——, *Marsden and the Missions*, Dunedin, 1936.

Reed, A. H., *The Story of Northland*, Wellington, 1956.

Rogers, L. M. (ed.), *The Early Journals of Henry Williams, 1826–40*, Christchurch, 1961.

Ross, Ruth, *Te Tiriti o Waitangi*, Wellington, 1958.

——, 'The Autochthonous New Zealand Soil', *The Feel of the Truth*, Peter Munz (ed.), Wellington, 1969.

Salmond, Anne, *Between Worlds*, Auckland, 1997.

Severen, Tim, *In Search of Moby Dick*, London, 2000.

Shadbolt, Maurice, *Monday's Warriors*, Wellington, 1990.

Sharp, A., *Duperrey's Visit to New Zealand in 1824*, Wellington, 1971.

Sinclair, Keith, *A History of New Zealand*, Auckland, 1980.

Smith, S. Percy, *Maori Wars of the Nineteenth Century*, Christchurch, 1910.

Smithyman, Kendrick, 'Uncollected Northland Poems', Jack Ross (ed.), *Brief*, vol. 26, 26 January 2003.

——, 'Making History: John White and S. Percy Smith at Work', *Journal of the Polynesian Society*, vol. 88, no. 4, 1979.

Tapp, E. J., *New Zealand: A Dependency of New South Wales*, Melbourne, 1958.

Te Rauparaha, Tamihana, *Life and Times of Te Rauparaha*, Martinborough, 1980.

The New Zealand and Australian Encyclopaedia, 2 vols, World Reference Library, 1964.

Vadya, A. P., *Maori Warfare*, Wellington, 1960.

Webster, John, *Reminiscences of an Old Settler in Australia and New Zealand*, Christchurch, 1908.

White, G., 'Firearms in Africa: An Introduction', *Journal of African History*, vol. 12, no. 2, 1971.

White, John, *Ancient History of the Maori*, Wellington, 1980.

——, 'Making History: John White and S. Percy Smith at Work', *Journal of the Polynesian Society*, vol. 88, no. 4, 1979.

Wigglesworth, Roger, 'Marmon, John, 1798–1800?–1880. Sailor, convict, Pakeha-Maori, interpreter, shopkeeper, sawyer, carpenter, soldier', *Dictionary of New Zealand Biography, Vol. 1*, Wellington, 1990.

Wilson, Ormond. *From Hongi Hika to Hone Heke*, Dunedin, 1985.

——, 'Papahurahia, First Maori Prophet', *Journal of the Polynesian Society*, vol. LXXXIV, 1965.

Wright, Harrison. *New Zealand, 1769–1840*. Cambridge, Massachusetts, 1959.

Published and unpublished collections of manuscripts, and official publications

Berry, A., 'Account of the Destruction of the Ship "Boyd"', ATL qms – 0163.

Black, G. J., 'Cannibal John', *Northlander Extracts*, 5–19 October 1922, ATL qPAM 1922 BLA 174.

Bladen, M., *Historical Records of New South Wales*, vols I–VII.

Bruce, George, *The Life of a Greenwich Pensioner, By Himself*. ATL MS-0336; ANL, Ms 3608.

Buller, J., 'Notes on a Journey to Hokianga', ATL MS-0361.

Busby, J., 'Despatches of the British Resident', Despatch No. 17, 17 June 1833. ATL qMs-0345.

Carrick, R. O., *Historical Records of New Zealand Prior to 1840*, Dunedin, 1940.

Historical Records of Australia, The Library Committee of the Commonwealth Parliament, January 1809–June 1813.

McNab, R. (ed.), *Historical Records of New Zealand*, 2 vols, Wellington, 1908.

Parliamentary Papers, Great Britain (Papers relating to New Zealand) 1836–40.

Parliamentary Papers, Great Britain (Papers relating to New Zealand) 1844–1870.

Turner, N., 'Journal, 15–18 May 1837', ATL.

Turton, H. Hanson, *Maori Deeds of Old Private Land Purchases in New Zealand, From the Year 1815 to 1840, with Pre-emptive and Other Claims,* Wellington, 1882.

Newspapers

Marmon, John, 'Scenes from the Life of John Marmon', *New Zealand Herald,* 9 October–11 December 1880.
——, 'The Life and Adventures of John Marmon, the Hokianga Pakeha Maori; or, Seventy Five Years in New Zealand', *Auckland Star, Saturday Supplement,* 21 November 1881–25 March 1882.
——, 'The Life and Adventures of John Marmon, the Hokianga Pakeha Maori; or, Seventy Five Years in New Zealand', *Otago Witness,* 26 November 1881–15 April 1882.
Northern Luminary, 4 September 1880.
Sydney Gazette, 1 May 1823.
Sydney Herald, 7 May 1837.

Theses and research essays

Ballara, Angela, 'Warfare and Government in Ngapuhi Tribal Society', MA Thesis in History, University of Auckland, 1973.
Bentley, Trevor, 'Images of Pakeha-Maori: A Study of the Representation of Pakeha-Maori by Historians of New Zealand from Arthur Thomson (1859) to James Belich (1996)', PhD Thesis in History, University of Waikato, 2007.
——, 'Tribal Guns, Tribal Gunners: A Study of Acculturation by Maori of European Military Technology during the Intertribal Musket Wars 1818–1839', MA Thesis in History, University of Waikato, 1997.
Canham, P. G., 'New England Whalers in New Zealand Waters 1800–1850', MA Thesis in History, University of Auckland, 1959.
Gibbons, Peter, 'Some Thoughts on the Pre-1840 Pakeha-Maori', Term Paper in History, Massey University, 1969.
Kerbel, Ivan, 'Notorious: A History of Kororareka and the New Zealand Frontier, c. 1800–1850', MLitt in History, University of Auckland, 1998.
Owens, J. M. R., 'The Wesleyan Mission to New Zealand, 1819–1840', PhD Thesis, Victoria University, 1969.
Schaniel, William, 'The Maori and the Economic Frontier: An Economic History of the Maori in New Zealand, 1769–1840', PhD Dissertation, Knoxville, University of Tennessee, 1985.
Wigglesworth, Roger, 'The Myth and the Reality: A Study of the Adaptation of John Marmon (1800?–1880) with Comments on his Three Newspaper Autobiographies', Research Essay in History, Massey University, 1974.

Internet references

Early Shipping in New Zealand Waters: http://www.myancestorsstory.com/shiplist-

Haggerty, Bridget, 'God between Us and All Harm': http://www.irishcultureandcustoms.com

Pittman, Louisa W., 'Appeasing Neptune: The Functions of Nautical Tradition', http://www.cofe.edu/chrestomathy/vol5/pittman.pdf

Smithyman, Kendrick: http://www.nzepc.auckland.ac.nz/authors/smithyma/northland.asp

Whaling in New Zealand Waters 1791–1863: http://teara.govt.nz/1966/vv/...Early Whaling operations/en-

INDEX